TEEN
LEGAL
RIGHTS

— REVISED EDITION —

TEEN LEGAL RIGHTS

KATHLEEN A. HEMPELMAN

Greenwood Press

Westport, Connecticut • London

Library of Congress Cataloging-in-Publication Data

Hempelman, Kathleen A.
    Teen legal rights / Kathleen A. Hempelman.—Rev. ed.
       p.   cm.
    Includes bibliographical references and index.
    ISBN 0–313–30968–X (alk. paper)
       1. Minors—United States.   2. Teenagers—Legal status, laws, etc.—
    United States.   3. Children's rights—United States.   I. Title.
    KF479.H46   2000
    346.7301'35—dc21   99–056809

British Library Cataloguing in Publication Data is available.

Library of Congress Catalog Card Number: 99–056809
ISBN: 0–313–30968–X

First published in 2000

Greenwood Press, 88 Post Road West, Westport, CT 06881
An imprint of Greenwood Publishing Group, Inc.
www.greenwood.com

Printed in the United States of America

∞

The paper used in this book complies with the
Permanent Paper Standard issued by the National
Information Standards Organization (Z39.48–1984).

10 9 8 7 6 5 4 3 2 1

For Geraldine B. Hempelman

Contents

Introduction to the Revised Edition: Teen Legal Rights Today

The purpose of *Teen Legal Rights: Revised Edition* is again to educate teens, parents, teachers, and counselors about the legal rights of young people and to explain the many aspects of American law that teens want to know more about. Like its 1994 predecessor, *Teen Legal Rights: A Guide for the '90s*, the revision is in question-and-answer format.

As a practical matter, minors in America had no legal rights when the twentieth century dawned. They were regarded as little more than "property." Children in the upper and middle classes were usually healthy and safe. But if a child's parents were poor, the child might be a wage-earner, grossly overworked and grossly underpaid, by the age of eight. If a youngster's parents were cruel and abusive (whether poor or not), the child undoubtedly suffered both emotionally and physically and suffered in private. In the early 1900s, countless immigrant children worked in mills and mines. Orphanages and care homes warehoused abandoned, abused, and needy youths, and often these institutions treated their charges with great cruelty.

As America began to discuss and document these injustices, and as the rights of both workers and women expanded, young people came to be perceived as more than a property interest. By 1910 this perception gave rise to the idea that children should be protected and that governments should play a role in child protection efforts. As a result, Americans began to regard even the poorest child differently (except that White America continued to consider children of color to be young barbarians). Settlement houses appeared in most U.S. cities. However, the idea of "children's rights" did not yet exist. It would not take hold until the 1950s and would not truly flourish until after 1970.

Today, America's young people are protected as never before. Some believe they are a privileged class. Their legal rights are fully established, and indeed, many an American law practice thrives on matters pertaining to youth. Even so, the rights of young people will always exist in relation to, and usually in a tug-of-war with, the idea of the primacy of the family. What this means in modern America is that as families continue to change—as single-parent families and two-worker families continue to replace the traditional family, as nontraditional lifestyles find their place in the sun, and as minors become independent in new ways—their rights will change as well.

Teen Legal Rights: Revised Edition again addresses young persons' rights at home, at school, on the job, in civil and criminal courts, and in their private relationships. It also discusses the rights of racial and ethnic minorities, the rights of minors online, gay and lesbian rights, and minors' rights and restrictions in the area of birth control. The reader will find that the tables, bibliographical material, and glossary in this edition are more comprehensive, and accordingly, more informative.

Although the rights and responsibilities discussed in *Teen Legal Rights: Revised Edition* apply to "minors"—the legal term for young people under age 18—the terms "teen" and "teenager" are also used in a general sense to apply to minors. The terms "child" and "children" are used when the issue relates to the relationship of parent and child.

— 1 —

Behind the Wheel

OBTAINING A DRIVER'S LICENSE

At what age can a young person obtain a driver's license?
Usually at age 16. Most states require teens to drive on a learner's permit before they can take the test for a regular driver's license. With a learner's permit, a young person can operate a vehicle only if a licensed adult driver is also in the front seat. Once the permit holder has driven on a learner's permit for a specified number of weeks or months, he or she can apply for a regular license.

Some states require young people to pass a driver's education course before applying for a driver's license. Whether or not a driving course is required, a teen who passes a driving course is usually able to obtain car insurance at lower rates.

See Table 1 for a summary of state licensing laws for driving.

Is driving without a license always illegal?
As a practical matter, yes. Both adults and minors must have a current driver's license to drive a vehicle, and the license must be in the driver's possession while driving. However, in Mississippi and a few other states, a license or permit isn't required to operate farm equipment.

Can a parent prevent a minor child from obtaining a driver's license or learner's permit?

Table 1
Driver's License Laws, 1999

State or Jurisdiction	Age for Regular License	Age for Learner's Permit	Age for Restrictive License	Duration/Yrs.; Expiration	Rules for New Licenses	Cost
Alabama	16	15 d	14 f	4; issue date		$20.00
Alaska	16 h	14 b,d,h	14 b,h	5; birthday		$15.00
Arizona	16	15 yrs. 7 mos.; b	16 b	until 60th birthday		$10.00-$25.00
Arkansas	16	14-16 b,d,h	14 b,h	4; birthday	R	$14.00
California	18	15 c,g,u	16 c	5; birthday	P1/P2	$15.00
Colorado	21	15-1/2 b,h,d	15 yrs. 3 mos.;	5; birthday	P1/P2	$15.00
Connecticut	16 c,d,p	16 c,d,p,r	b,g,h	4; birthday		$28.75-$43.75
Delaware	16	15 yrs. 10 mos.; c,d,i	16 b,c	5; birthday		$12.50
Florida	16	15 b,h,k,o,t		4 or 6; birthday	R/P2	$20.00
Georgia	16	15 h,p	16 b,k,p	4; birthday	P2	$20.00
Hawaii	18	15 d	15 b	2 after age 72;		$ 6.00-2 yr.
				4 if 15 to 17 yrs.;		$ 6.00-4 yr.
				6 if 18 to 71 yrs.; birthday		$18.00-6 yr.
Idaho	17	15 c,d,e,s	15 c,k	4; birthday	R	$20.50
Illinois	18	15 b,g,s	16 b,c	4, 5; birthday	R	$10.00
Indiana	16-1/2	16 b,d,g,h;	16 yrs. 1 mo.;	4; 3 after age 75	P2	$ 6.00
		15 g,k	b,c	last day birth month		
Iowa	17	16 c,d,k	14 c,d	4 if 18 to 69 yrs.;		$ 8.00-2 yr.
				2 for others; birthday		$16.00-4 yr.
Kansas	16	15 c,i	14 j	4 if under 21 to over 65;	R/P2	$ 8.00-$18.00
				6 if 21 to 65; birthday		
Kentucky	16	b,d,h,k	16 b,k	4; last day birth month	R/P2	$ 8.00
Louisiana	15 n	15 b,k	16 b,k	4; birthday	P1	$18.00
Maine	18	15 c,s,d	15 c	6; birthday	P1/P2	$30.00
Maryland	18 m	15 yrs. 9 mos.; b,d,h	16 b,c,k	5; birthday		$30.00
Massachusetts	18	16 b,c,d,h,k	16-1/2 yrs.; b,c,d,h,k	birthday	R	$33.75

2

Table 1 (*continued*)

State						
Michigan	18	16 c,d,h,k	14 yrs. 9 mos.; b,c,h	4; birthday	P2	$13.00
Minnesota	18	d	16 c	4; birthday		$18.50-$37.50
Mississippi	16	d	15 q	4 if under 18 yrs.; birthday		$20.00
Missouri	16	15-1/2 i	5 l,g	3; issue date		$ 5.00-1 yr. / $ 7.50
Montana	16		16 b,c	8 if age 21 to 67; 4 for others; birthday	P1	$32.00-8 yrs. / $16.00-4 yrs.
Nebraska	17	15 d,h	14	5; birthday		$18.75
Nevada	16 b,c	15-1/2 b,d	14 b	4; birthday	P2	$15.50-$20.50
New Hampshire	18	k,u	16 b,c	4; birthday	P2	$32.00
New Jersey	17		16	4; month of issue	P2	$16.00 / $18.00-Photo
New Mexico	16	15 b,c,d,i	14 g,l	4; birthday	R/P2	$16.00
New York	17 c	16 d,e,v	16 b,k	5; birthday	P2	$28.00
North Carolina	16	15 b,c,k	16	5; birthday	R/P2	$12.50
North Dakota	16	d	14 c	4; birthday	P/2	$10.00
Ohio	18	15-1/2 c,h,k,t	14 f	4; birthday		$10.75
Oklahoma	16	15 b,g	14 f	4; issue date	P2	$19.00
Oregon	16	15 d,h	14	4; birthday	P1	$26.25
Pennsylvania	16	16 b,d,e,k	16 b,k	4; last day birth month	R/P2	$29.00
Rhode Island	16	d	16 c,k	5; birthday	P2	$30.00
South Carolina	16	15 c,i,k	16 i,k	5; birthday		2.50
South Dakota	16	14 i	14 k,x	5; birthday	R/P2	$ 8.00
Tennessee	16	15 c,d,h	14	5; birthday	P2	$19.50
Texas	16 c	15		4/5/6; birthday	P1	$16.00-$24.00
Utah	16 c	15 yrs. 9 mos.; i	15 c,e	5; birthday	P1	$15.00-$20.00

Table 1 (*continued*)

State or Jurisdiction	Age for Regular License	Age for Learner's Permit	Age for Restrictive License	Duration/ Expiration	Rules for New Licenses	Cost
Vermont	18	15 d,l,u	16 e	2 or 4; birthday	P1	$12.00-$20.00
Virginia	18	15 b,h	16 b,c	5; Last day birth month		
Washington	18	15 d,g	16 c	4; birthday	P2	$14.00
West Virginia	18	15 b,d,h	16	5; birthday	P2	$13.00
Wisconsin	18	15-1/2; d,g,j,l	16 c,u	8; birthday	P2	$18.00-$64.00
Wyoming	16	15 b,e	16 b,e,k	4; birthday	R/P2	$20.00
Washington, D.C.	16	b,d,e	16 b	4; birthday		$20.00

a. Full driving privileges at the age set forth in the "Regular" column. A license restricted or qualified in some manner may be obtained at the age set forth in the "Restricted" column.

b. Guardian or parental consent is required.

c. Approved driver education training course is required.

d. Learner's permit is required.

e. Driver with a learner's permit must be accompanied by a locally licensed operator age 18 or older.

f. Restricted to mopeds.

g. Must be enrolled in a driver education training course.

h. Driver with a learner's permit must be accompanied by a locally licensed operator age 21 or older.

i. Driver with a learner's permit must be accompanied by a licensed parent or guardian.

j. Driver with a learner's permit must be accompanied by a licensed operator age 19 or older.

k. Hours of operation restricted.

l. Must be accompanied by an approved instructor.

m. All new drivers must complete a 3-hour alcohol awareness program.

n. All first-time licensees must complete a state approved pre-licensing course.

o. Must complete traffic law and substance abuse education course.

p. If under age 18, must complete a 5-hour drug and alcohol training course.

q. Minor resides with physical-impaired parent or guardian who cannot obtain a license and depends on the minor for transportation.

r. Learner's permit is required for motorcycles and some commercial motor vehicles.

4

s. Driver with a learner's permit must be accompanied by a licensed operator at least age 20 who has at least two years of driving experience.

t. Learner's permit required and must be held for six months or until 18th birthday.

u. Driver with a learner's permit must be accompanied by a locally licensed operator age 25 or older.

v. Must complete a 5-hour course in driver training.

x. Restriction is automatically void when the holder reaches his or her 16th birthday.

New Driver's Licenses:

Legend

R = Restricted

P2 = Probational

P = Provisional

Cost:

a. Listed are regular passenger car license costs. If the renewal cost differs from the cost of the original license, the cost of the original license is shown.

b. If the applicant is 70 years old or over, the cost is $3.00.

c. Includes insurance and administration fees.

Source: AAA, Digest of Motor Laws, Sixty-Fifth Edition, 1999.

Yes. In most states a parent must sign the minor's license or permit application. If the parent refuses, the minor can't obtain a driver's license, and therefore can't legally drive.

If someone other than a parent, such as a legal guardian or foster parent, is in charge of the minor's care and upbringing, he or she is the one who must sign (and may refuse to sign) the application. For more about guardians see Chapter Three, "At Home," and for more about foster parents see Chapter Ten, "Your Right to Be Healthy and Safe from Abuse."

If state law requires parental consent for a young person to obtain a driver's license, at what age is consent no longer needed?

Usually age 18, which is the age of majority in most states. For more about the age of majority see Chapter Three, "At Home."

Can a parent revoke a minor's license or learner's permit?

It depends on the state's driving laws, but whether or not a state allows this, it is clearly within the authority of parents to forbid a minor to drive.

RESPONSIBILITY FOR ACCIDENTS

What should a teen do if involved in a traffic accident?

The first rule is *stay at the scene*. In most states it is at least a misdemeanor to leave the scene of an accident before the police arrive and all the required paperwork is completed.

The second rule is *keep a clear head*. As soon as possible, take the following measures:

1. Write down the license plate number and a description of all other cars involved in the accident.

2. Check to see whether anyone in any car has sustained an injury.

3. Check to see the extent of property damage to all cars and any other property.

4. Call the police and also a parent, or ask another person to do so, particularly if an injury or property damage has occurred.

5. Exchange names, addresses, and telephone numbers with all other drivers, and obtain the names of their auto insurance companies and auto policy numbers.

6. Ask any witnesses to the accident, including passengers, for their addresses and telephone numbers.

7. Check the licenses of other drivers to determine whether they are carrying their own licenses and whether the licenses are subject to any restrictions.

The third rule is *cooperate with the police officer*. Answer his or her questions accurately and courteously. The police officer will undoubtedly ask to see driver's licenses or other identification from all drivers. For more about police questioning see Chapter Twelve, "Teens and Crime."

If a minor injures someone or damages property through his or her own fault while driving, who is financially responsible?

Usually the minor's parents. In every state, one of the conditions for obtaining a driver's license or learner's permit is that the applicant agree to be financially responsible for injuries or property damage he or she causes as a result of negligent or reckless driving. If a parent is required to sign a teenage child's application for a license or permit, most states hold *both* parents responsible for injuries or property damage caused by the minor's negligent or reckless driving, even if only one parent signed.

Parents can be held liable for injuries or property damage caused by a minor child while driving for either personal enjoyment or a family purpose such as running an errand. They also can be held liable for permitting a minor child to drive without a driver's license or learner's permit.

Does this mean a teenage driver can't be held liable for injuries or property damage caused by his or her acts behind the wheel?

No. Almost anyone, including minors, can be taken to court for negligently or recklessly causing injuries or property damage. However, minors usually are "judgment proof," which means they normally don't have the money to satisfy a court-ordered judgment for damages. This is why state driving laws hold parents financially responsible for injuries or property damage caused by the careless acts of their minor children. For more about court actions to recover money see Chapter Seventeen, "Taking Matters to Court."

If a teen's parents are divorced, who is held liable for injuries caused by the teen while driving?

Usually both of the parents, regardless of who has been awarded custody. If a minor's parents divorce *before* the minor is granted a license, in many states parental liability depends on which parent has custody on the date of the application. In joint custody situations, both parents continue to be liable. For more about custody in divorce matters see Chapter Seven, "If Your Parents Divorce."

Can parents avoid being held liable for a minor child's careless acts while driving?

Sometimes. In many states if a minor has a decent income and owns property, the parents can file a statement with the state department of motor vehicles attesting to the minor's separate financial responsibility. Once they do, they can't be held liable for injuries or property damage caused by the minor's negligence or recklessness while driving, except when their actions contribute to the cause of the accident.

In certain states, parents can't be held responsible for a minor child's negligence or recklessness if the minor buys a car with his or her own money and also holds title to it.

If a young person lends the family car to a friend, can the young person's parents be held responsible for injuries or property damage caused by the driver?

Yes. Similarly, if a young person is driving a friend's car with permission, the young person is usually covered under the car owner's policy.

AUTO INSURANCE

How does auto insurance work?

When a person has auto insurance, an insurance company has agreed to pay for property damage and medical care in connection with the ownership and operation of a particular vehicle. The company's agreement to pay under the terms of its insurance policy is conditioned on the payment of a "premium," which is simply the cost of the insurance coverage.

An insurance company will only pay for medical care or property damage up to its policy limits. These limits are shown on the "declarations" page of the insurance policy, which describes the type and amount of coverage.

Insurance companies will usually pay for their own insured's medical care up front, regardless of who caused the accident. But if the other driver was at fault, the insurer may "subrogate," or attempt to recover its costs from the other driver or his or her insurer.

If an insured is at fault for an accident, or if his or her insurance company decides to settle out of court in a disputed case, the insurance company will pay for the other party's property damage up to its policy limits. Also, the insurance company will pay for its own insured's property damage.

Sometimes insurance will also cover towing costs, and it may also provide reimbursement for the cost to rent a car while the damaged car is in for repairs.

When it comes to families, the auto insurance buyer—the "policyholder"—usually is an adult driver of the family car. A spouse and any children under age 21 can be insured under the same policy.

What is a "deductible"?

A deductible is the amount an insured pays for vehicle repairs out-of-pocket. After the deductible is satisfied, the insurance company then pays, but only up to its policy limits. Usually, the higher the deductible, the lower the insurance premium. If someone other than the insured was at fault, the insured may ultimately be reimbursed his or her deductible.

What "risks" does auto insurance cover?

Quite a variety. The types of coverage included in a standard auto insurance policy are:

1. "Collision" coverage, which pays for damage to the insured car when an insured driver isn't at fault.
2. "Comprehensive" coverage, which pays for damage to the insured car resulting from fire, theft, vandalism, hail, falling objects, windshield breaks, and collisions with animals.
3. "Medical payments" coverage, which pays for medical expenses that an insured driver and any passengers incur in a traffic accident. It also covers injuries suffered by an insured person while riding in another car or walking.

4. "Bodily injury liability" coverage, which pays for claims against an insured resulting from injuries to passengers, pedestrians, and persons in other vehicles, up to the policy limits. Bodily injury liability insurance also pays for legal expenses incurred to defend the insured in a lawsuit. If an injury is serious or fatal, liability claims for bodily injury can add up to many thousands of dollars.

5. "Property damage liability" coverage, which pays for claims against an insured when the insured car causes damage to someone else's property. Usually the damaged property is another driver's car, but it also might be damage to a building, telephone pole, or lamppost.

6. "Uninsured motorist" coverage, which pays medical costs of an insured's bodily injuries and car damage when another person is at fault but that person either doesn't have liability coverage or flees the scene. Uninsured motorist coverage often pays for auto damage and bodily injuries in "hit-and-run" situations.

Is a minor required to have auto insurance?

In most states, all drivers must have a minimum amount of auto *liability* insurance. Proof of auto liability insurance in the legally required amount is the standard way for a person to establish financial responsibility. In many states it is the *only* way.

Can minors buy their own auto insurance?

Usually they are unable to. Insurance companies have calculated that teen drivers are very poor insurance risks. They can't profit by insuring teen drivers separately unless exorbitant premiums are charged, because teens as a group have a high accident rate and many insurance claims. (Teenage women are a safer risk than teenage men, but only by a slight margin.)

But as stated earlier, insurance companies permit teen drivers to be covered under their parents' policy. The additional premium to cover a minor under an adult policy is high, but at least it is affordable. This is the way most teen drivers are insured and, again, the way their financial responsibility is established.

If a claim is made on an insurance policy following an accident, will the premium increase?

Usually the premium will increase if the insured was at fault in the accident and the amount paid out by the insurance company totaled at least $400.

Multiple moving violations can also cause the cost of insurance to increase—particularly the cost to cover teens.

Is there anything a teen can do to reduce the premium charged for his or her part of the car insurance?

Yes. Many insurance companies reduce the premium for teen drivers if the teen doesn't smoke. Some companies also reduce the premium if the teen maintains good grades.

If a minor's parents are divorced, which parent's policy is he or she covered under?

Usually the custodial parent's policy, although if the minor is permitted to drive both parents' cars, each must cover the minor.

What is "no-fault" insurance?

It is a type of auto insurance in which each party looks to his or her own insurer for payment, regardless of who caused the accident. Under state no-fault insurance laws, negligence doesn't have to be established before an insurance company agrees to pay. The insured receives prompt payment from his or her insurer and no subrogation follows.

Usually no-fault insurance only applies to injuries and not to property damage. The trade-off for the insurance companies in states with no-fault insurance is that the insured's right to go to court for additional damages is restricted.

How does no-fault insurance differ from traditional car insurance?

Basically in the manner in which the innocent party collects. With regular auto insurance, an accident victim makes a claim against the other driver's insurance company. Before that insurer will pay, the accident victim must establish that the other driver was negligent or reckless. This may be difficult if the cause of the accident is tough to determine.

If the other driver was at fault, the amount payable to the accident victim must be calculated. The figure depends on such factors as the victim's medical expenses, property damage, lost wages, and pain and suffering. Sometimes added are the lawyer's fees for proving who was at fault.

For more about lawsuits, including how to calculate damages in personal injury cases, see Chapter Seventeen, "Taking Matters to Court."

TRAFFIC OFFENSES

If a person commits a minor traffic offense, is he or she placed under arrest?

No. The person is simply cited for violating a traffic law.

If a minor commits a traffic offense, does the case go to juvenile court?

Not usually. In most states, all minor traffic offenses go to the state's adult traffic court. But juvenile courts have the power to suspend a minor's driver's license if the minor commits a delinquent act involving a car. For more about juvenile courts see Chapter Twelve, "Teens and Crime."

What kinds of punishment can a teenage driver receive for a traffic offense?

It depends on the nature and severity of the offense and also the state in which the offense was committed. In any traffic court, fines can be swiftly imposed and licenses can be suspended or revoked.

Can a minor's license be revoked because of too many traffic tickets?

Yes. In every state both teen and adult drivers can lose their licenses if they are "habitual violators." This happens most often when the offense is DUI.

What is the punishment for DUI (driving under the influence)?

It varies from state to state, but for a first offense the license of the drunk driver is usually suspended or revoked. Sometimes the offender will receive a restricted license allowing him or her to drive to work but nowhere else. Weekend detention is often given. Repeat offenders are always punished more severely.

If an individual has been drinking or using drugs, that individual should have a "designated driver" take the wheel. This rule of thumb applies to adults as well as teens.

See Chapter Eleven, "Alcohol and Drugs," for more about the legal aspects of drinking and driving.

Does a police officer need a search warrant to search a car?

It depends on the situation. Generally a search warrant is required for a police search. However, if a person is arrested for an offense involving a car, both the car and the arrested person can be searched. This is called a "search incident to an arrest." No warrant is required, but the police must limit their search to areas within the arrested person's reach just prior to the arrest and to items in plain view (such as items in the back seat).

In addition, the police can search a car if they have "probable cause" to believe that evidence of a crime is in the car, which may vanish if not seized right away. And, if the car is "impounded" by the police to preserve evidence, police personnel can inventory its contents, but may only search the trunk and glove box after obtaining a warrant.

For more about police searches and search warrants see Chapter Twelve, "Teens and Crime."

Can a minor be arrested for having a weapon in the car?

A minor needs written permission from a parent to possess a weapon or ammunition. If a minor can't produce this upon request, a police officer can place the minor under arrest for possessing a weapon, regardless of the time or place.

Firearms may not be sold to minors.

If you are in possession of a gun or other weapon at the time of a car stop, don't try to hide the gun or even touch it. Immediately put both hands on the steering wheel. The police officer will see the weapon if it is in plain view. If the officer asks whether you have a gun or other weapon in the car, tell the truth.

Is hitchhiking illegal?

It depends on state or local law. Some states and cities prohibit hitchhiking altogether, some don't regulate it at all, and others permit it only when the hitchhiker is standing at a certain location near the roadway. For example, some states prohibit hitchhiking on freeways, urban roadways, bridges, and highway on-ramps and off-ramps, but permit it on other roads and streets.

Can a minor ride on a motorcycle without wearing a helmet?
Again, it depends on the state or local law. In some states a minor must wear a helmet while on a motorcycle, whether operating it or riding as a passenger.

Do any laws regulate the use of cellular phones in vehicles?
For most states, the only applicable laws are those regulating the operation of a vehicle. So if you are driving carelessly because you are arguing on a cellular phone, a police officer can pull you over and ticket you.

The American Automobile Association offers the following advice regarding cellular phones:

1. Before you get behind the wheel, familiarize yourself with the location and function of the phone's buttons.
2. Pull off the road if the call is an emotional or complex one, or if it requires notetaking.
3. Consider asking a passenger to make the call for you.
4. Monitor traffic conditions before answering or placing your calls.
5. For emergencies, tell the operator whether you are reporting a medical or police emergency and whether there appear to be injuries.
6. Secure the phone in its cradle so it won't become a flying object in a crash.

Most states have an "emergency" number for cellular phone users. In addition, emergency number (800) 525–5555 will direct your phone call to the state police.

CURFEWS

What is a curfew?
It is a state or local law that prohibits individuals from being on the street between specific hours after dark. Curfews usually apply to young people, but they have also been applied to adults. In the past they have been used illegally against racial and ethnic minorities.

Under curfew laws, being on the street includes riding or sitting in a car. But a minor usually isn't in violation of a curfew law, whether on the street or in a car, if he or she is with an adult.

When are curfews illegal?

When the state or local curfew law is too vague or too broad. As explained in Chapter Twelve, a law must be written clearly and specifically, so that citizens have fair notice of exactly what actions the law prohibits. Many courts have ruled that curfew laws that simply prohibit "loitering" or "vagrancy" are unenforceable because they forbid perfectly legal acts such as having a smoke outside a restaurant.

In a 1971 case from the state of Washington, a city ordinance that simply declared "loitering" and "wandering" illegal was declared unconstitutional after a high school senior was pulled over at 4:30 A.M. by the police. The young man was returning from a party and wanted to take a drive along the beach near downtown Seattle. The statute was declared unconstitutional because its wording made his perfectly innocent behavior illegal.

On the other hand, many state courts, and even the Supreme Court, have let stand well-drafted curfew laws as a way to reduce juvenile crime at night. The justification for these laws is the vulnerability of minors, their relative lack of maturity when it comes to decision making, and the importance of parental discipline.

What happens if a minor violates a curfew?

The police have a number of options. If the minor has a legitimate reason for being out, the police officer might send the minor home with a stern warning. In other cases the minor might either be taken home, cited for a minor traffic violation, or transported to the police station and "booked" for committing another more serious act.

The best way to find out if a city or state has a curfew is to ask a police officer, call the police station and inquire, or go to the public library and read up on local curfew laws. A reference librarian can provide assistance in finding the law.

OWNING AND RENTING A CAR

Can a teen buy a car?

Nothing in the law prevents a minor from buying a car or other expensive item. But some car dealers refuse to sell to minors for one basic reason. As discussed in Chapter Sixteen, "Entering into Contracts," minors are permitted to walk away from or "disaffirm" most contracts, provided they do so soon after the sale. This rule of law, which strikes many as out-of-date and even unfair, is supposed to protect minors from unscrupulous salespeople.

This means, for example, that if a minor buys a car but then decides the purchase was a bad idea, the dealer can't refuse to take the car back even if the minor paid full price. (However, the dealer can reduce the refund to reflect any damage or wear and tear to the car while in the minor's possession.) Basically, the law places the risk of financial loss on the dealer and not the minor.

In some states, minors can only disaffirm contracts until age 16.

If a teen does buy a car, it must be titled, registered, and licensed, and the teen driver must have auto insurance.

Can a teen take out a car loan?

That would be difficult. In order for a teen to obtain a car loan, he or she would have to be earning enough money to make monthly loan payments without a lot of effort. Most teens don't earn this much. Besides, most lenders have a basic policy of rejecting all loan applications from minors.

Can a teen rent a car?

Whether a minor can rent a car always depends on whether the car rental agency is willing to rent cars to minors. Few will rent to persons under age 25.

FOR FURTHER READING

Berardelli, Phil. *Safe Young Drivers: A Guide for Parents and Teens*. McLean, VA: EPM Publications, Inc., 1996.

Brown, David. *Beat Your Ticket: Go to Court and Win*. Berkeley: Nolo Press, 1999.

Grosshandler, Janet. *Coping with Drinking and Driving*. New York: Rosen Publishing Group, Inc., 1997.

Grosshandler, Janet. *Drugs and Driving*. New York: Rosen Publishing Group, Inc., 1997.

Haas, Carol. *Your Driving and the Law: A Crash Course in Traffic Tickets and Courts, Auto Accidents and Insurance, and Vehicle-Related Lawsuits.* Bountiful, UT: Horizon Publishing Co., 1991.

OTHER INFORMATION SOURCES

Organizations

American Automobile Association Foundation for Traffic Safety
1440 New York Avenue NW, Ste. 201
Washington, DC 20005
(202) 638–5944
E-mail: aaafts@aaafts.org
Home page: www.aaafts.org

Mothers Against Drunk Driving (MADD)
Box 541688
Dallas, TX 75354
(800) GET-MADD
E-mail: info@madd.org
Home page: www.madd.org

National Motorists Association
402 West Second Street
Waunakee, WI 53597
(608) 849–8697
E-mail: nma@motorists.org
Home page: www.motorists.com

Students Against Driving Drunk, Inc. (SADD)
(also, Students Against Destructive Decisions, Inc.)
Box 800
Marlborough, MA 01752
(508) 481–3568
Home page: www.saddonline.com

Online Sources

Curfew.Org
Home page: www.curfew.org

Insurance Information Institute
Home page: www.iii.org

—2—

At School

ATTENDANCE AND GRADES

Does everyone in the United States have a right to an education?

Every young person in the United States has a right to a free public education, and every young person in the United States has an obligation to attend school. State laws guarantee this. Minors in most states must attend school between the ages of 7 and 16, and in some they are required to attend longer. A student can only quit school if the applicable state law no longer requires attendance.

In many states a student who misses too much school can be brought under court supervision so that his or her attendance can be monitored by a probation officer. Parents can be prosecuted for "education neglect" for failing to keep a child in school.

See Table 2 for age requirements for school attendance in the 50 states and the District of Columbia.

Are teens allowed to remain in high school longer than it normally takes to finish?

Yes, although most states have a maximum age limit. It varies from state to state, but most set it at age 21.

Can a student's grades be lowered for poor attendance?

This practice has been tested in courts across the country, with varying results. Some have ruled it isn't improper to grade "truants" or "tardies"

Table 2

Age Requirements for School Attendance, by State

State or Jurisdiction	Age	State or Jurisdiction	Age
Alabama	7 to 16	Nebraska	7 to 16
Alaska	7 to 16	Nevada	7 to 17
Arizona	6 to 16	New Hampshire	6 to 16
Arkansas	5 to 17	New Jersey	6 to 16
California	6 to 18	New Mexico	5 to 16
Colorado	7 to 16	New York	6 to 16
Connecticut	7 to 16	North Carolina	7 to 16
Delaware	5 to 16	North Dakota	7 to 16
Florida	6 to 16	Ohio	6 to 18
Georgia	7 to 16	Oklahoma	5 to 18
Hawaii	6 to 18	Oregon	7 to 18
Idaho	7 to 16	Pennsylvania	8 to 17
Illinois	7 to 16	Rhode Island	6 to 16
Iowa	6 to 16	South Carolina	5 to 16
Indiana	7 to 16	South Dakota	6 to 16
Kansas	7 to 16	Tennessee	7 to 17
Kentucky	6 to 16	Texas	6 to 17
Louisiana	7 to 17	Utah	6 to 18
Maine	7 to 17	Vermont	7 to 16
Maryland	5 to 16	Virginia	5 to 18
Massachusetts	6 to 16	Washington	8 to 18
Michigan	6 to 16	West Virginia	6 to 16
Minnesota	7 to 16	Wisconsin	6 to 18
Mississippi	6 to 16	Wyoming	7 to 16
Missouri	7 to 16	District of Columbia	7 to 17
Montana	7 to 16		

Source: The Alan Guttmacher Institute, "Teenagers Right to Consent to Reproductive Health Care," *Issues in Brief*, 1997.

more harshly because learning to be responsible is consistent with the overall goals of a school curriculum. Others say that lowering grades for poor attendance misses the point of what grades are really for.

In one case a Kentucky high school was forbidden to lower a student's grades for absences due to a suspension. Since the student was denied credit for work he missed during his suspension, additional grade reductions for his absences were said to be "overkill."

If a school has a policy of lowering grades for truancy, the school should tell the students at the beginning of the year how many absences will result in reduced grades and whether the rule applies to both excused and unexcused absences. If grades can also be lowered for misconduct, students should be told what kinds of behavior might actually result in lowered grades.

Can a student flunk out of public high school?

"Flunking out" is a phrase usually associated with college, but it does have an equivalent in the high school setting.

If a student doesn't attend school for a specified number of days in a school year, he or she can be expelled and will usually lose school credit for that year. Furthermore, if a student doesn't fulfill the requirements of a particular course of study, he or she won't be able to graduate. The student can repeat courses until reaching the maximum age for attending high school, but has to leave upon reaching that age if he or she doesn't graduate first. After that the student can obtain a graduate equivalency degree, or GED, but generally would be unable to receive a high school diploma in the absence of a special state law or program.

Are married students required to stay in school? Can married students be kept out of school?

In answer to the first question, married students usually are "emancipated" from the obligation of having to attend high school, even if they are otherwise too young to quit. As to the second question, the Constitution requires that all students be permitted to attend classes and participate in their high school graduation ceremonies regardless of marital status.

For more about emancipation see Chapter Five, "On Your Own," and for more about teen marriages see Chapter Nine, "Marrying and Having Children."

Can a pregnant teen be prevented from attending high school? Can students with children be prevented from attending high school?

The answer to both questions is no. In times past, pregnant students either dropped out of high school or were told to leave, and of course, many never went back. But these days, pregnancy and parenting can't keep a student from completing high school. Most school districts have special programs for teen mothers, either on or off campus. A school counselor can provide information on this point.

Can students who have HIV/AIDS (human immunodeficiency virus/acquired immunodeficiency syndrome) be prevented from attending high school?

In the 1980s, some school boards tried to bar students with HIV/AIDS from attending classes, but courts ordered the students enrolled once health officials certified that they weren't likely to infect others.

HIV is the virus that causes AIDS. It can be transmitted during sexual intercourse. Although HIV/AIDS is life-threatening, research shows that it can't be transmitted through casual contact. Students with HIV/AIDS are permitted to attend school unless they have open cuts, display dangerous behavior such as biting, or can't control their bodily discharges.

FREEDOM OF EXPRESSION

> Congress shall make no law . . . abridging the freedom of speech, or of the press.
>
> —First Amendment, U.S. Constitution

Do students have free speech rights at school?

Yes. The constitutional guarantee of free expression extends to public high school students. However, these rights can be limited in certain situations, as this section explains.

The right of students to express their opinions freely is guided by an important United States Supreme Court case, *Tinker v. Des Moines Independent School District*. This 1969 case made it clear that students in public high schools don't forfeit their constitutional right of free expression when they step onto school property.

In *Tinker*, the Supreme Court upheld the right of students at an Iowa high school to wear black armbands to protest America's involvement in Vietnam. Because the armbands were a means of communicating an idea and not just an item of dress—because the armbands were a form of "symbolic speech"—wearing them raised a First Amendment issue.

The Supreme Court established in *Tinker* that in order to limit student expression, school authorities must prove that the expression either "materially and substantially" disrupts school work and school discipline or collides with the rights of others. The school must base its decision to limit speech on concrete facts showing that the expression would probably cause "substantial and material" disruption at school. Its decision must be motivated by more than the desire to avoid the discomfort that often accompanies an unpopular viewpoint.

According to the Supreme Court, the student armbands in *Tinker* didn't create any problems that substantially interfered with either school activities or the rights of the other students. Because the school rule couldn't be justified as a valid restriction on First Amendment rights, the Supreme Court declared it unconstitutional.

The basic analysis set out in *Tinker* applies to this day to cases involving the free speech rights of students.

What types of student expression does the First Amendment regulate?

Virtually every kind of communication, both verbal and nonverbal, including speeches, essays, leafleting, armbands and buttons, books in the library, school newspapers, underground newspapers, walk-outs, and sit-ins.

In the area of free expression, what does "material and substantial" disruption really mean?

Consider the following situations. Students could probably distribute handouts between classes unless doing so would seriously interfere with hall traffic. On the other hand, students could be prohibited from distributing such materials during class time. School officials could refuse to let students use the school's photocopiers to duplicate handouts if the students planned to use them instead of going to class. But the school would probably be required to let students use the copiers after school, whether or not school officials agree with the content of the handouts. Students would be able to post written materials such as newspaper articles and meeting announcements on school bulletin boards whether or not the subject matter is controversial, provided the posted material isn't vulgar by standards that the community generally adheres to.

Can a student be punished for openly criticizing a teacher or school policy?

Only if the criticism or manner of expression either materially and substantially interferes with school activities or offends the rights of others. In a 1973 case, a court upheld a high school's decision to confiscate signs that students planned to distribute to protest a certain teacher's dismissal. The court agreed that the school had a realistic basis for believing that the protest would interfere with school work and school discipline.

Although the school claimed victory in this situation, students have won many First Amendment cases. In 1972, an Illinois court upheld the actions of high school students who published and distributed an underground newspaper criticizing certain school officials. The newspaper, styled on the *National Lampoon*, urged the student body to discard reading materials relating to school policy that were intended for their parents. The students prevailed because the school couldn't prove that the newspaper caused material and substantial disruption or offended the rights of others.

Can a student insult a teacher and still be protected under the First Amendment?

No. Furthermore, the student can be punished.

Does the First Amendment protect students who libel or slander school officials?

The First Amendment doesn't protect anyone who libels or slanders.

Libel is a written, published statement that the writer either knows or should know is untrue. *Slander*, on the other hand, is a spoken statement that the speaker either knows or should know is untrue. Libel and slander are types of "defamatory" statements, and statements such as these are said to "defame" people. Defamatory statements are never protected by the First Amendment, and persons who defame others can be sued for damages caused by their defamatory acts.

School authorities always have the power to censor libelous material written by students and can stop its distribution, whether or not the material was prepared at school. In addition, school officials can punish students who make slanderous statements.

Can school officials prohibit obscene language on school grounds?

Yes. School officials have extensive authority to determine what kind of language is obscene, to discipline students for using it, and to make clear that such forms of expression do not represent the school. Schools are said to have an interest in teaching students the boundaries of socially appropriate behavior, including their manner of speech.

This rule doesn't apply just to "four-letter" words, and in fact, the language that schools often prohibit wouldn't strike every high school student as vulgar or obscene. Consider the following speech, which a student gave before a high school assembly:

I know a man who is firm—he's firm in his pants, he's firm in his shirt, his character is firm—but most . . . of all, his belief in you, the students of Bethel, is firm.

Jeff is a man who takes his point and pounds it in. If necessary, he'll take an issue and nail it to the wall. He doesn't attack things in spurts—he drives hard, pushing and pushing until finally—he succeeds.

So vote for Jeff for A.S.B. vice-president—he'll never come between you and the best our high school can be.

The speaker was given a two-day suspension for this speech, and the Supreme Court ultimately sided with the school. If this ruling seems harsh, it is important to know that the situation in the case was unique. The speaker's audience consisted mostly of 14-year-olds. Upon hearing the speech some students hooted and yelled, and others were bewildered and embarrassed. According to the Supreme Court, because the speech disrupted classes and confused many of the students, the school didn't violate the First Amendment when it disciplined the speaker. However, it said the speech might have been protected if the student had delivered it in a different setting and to older students.

Schools may always prohibit the distribution of materials that are generally considered obscene and may legally confiscate obscene materials.

If a student can't use four-letter words on school grounds, would teachers and administrators be held to the same standard?

They should be—and in fact, most schools explicitly forbid the use of vulgar language by everyone on campus. But these days a teacher probably wouldn't lose his or her job if a single profanity slipped out during a class discussion, and a student probably wouldn't be expelled.

DISTRIBUTING MATERIALS ON SCHOOL GROUNDS

Can school authorities legally enforce a rule prohibiting students from distributing written materials on school property before, during, and after school?

No. School officials can only enforce such a rule if they can show that distributing written materials at school would *always* interfere with school activities or the rights of others. That would be a tough case to win.

Can school authorities legally enforce a rule permitting students to distribute written materials before and after classes but not during school hours?

Only if the school is able to prove that leafleting during school hours is *always* likely to disrupt school work or school discipline materially. School officials would have to prove, for example, that the student leafleters would always block the halls, disrupt classes, cause damage to school property, or interfere with the legal rights of others. That might be another tough case.

Can a school legally enforce a rule prohibiting students from bringing "controversial" or "distasteful" materials on school property, regardless of the subject matter?

No, for an important constitutional reason. Because blanket rules like these fail to let students know what kinds of materials *in fact* are prohibited and what kinds of materials *in fact* are acceptable, the Constitution says they are "overbroad" and therefore "void for vagueness." If rules such as these could legally be enforced, a school could prohibit materials that the most oversensitive teacher or administrator might happen to have a problem with. The limits on the constitutional right of free speech don't reach this far.

If certain students distribute materials in an orderly manner but others react disruptively, can the school step in? *Should* **the school step in?**

These questions raise an important issue because the disruption isn't being caused by students who want to exercise their free speech rights, but by the reactions of others.

In such situations the school must strike a balance between the rights of the pamphleteers and the students who bear the effects of the disruption. It would be permitted to regulate the "time, place, and manner" of the students' leafleting activities to make certain that their right to distribute the materials isn't diminished. It may have to provide for their extra protection. It could only stop the leafleting if serious problems occur, or if the activity tends to aggravate an already touchy situation.

Can a school forbid leafleting on a particular issue altogether?

No. This would be an unconstitutional restraint on the First Amendment rights of *all* students.

In one important case, a school policy prohibited the use of school facilities for all political activities, including activities relating to presidential politics. When a number of students were punished for distributing materials supporting Senator George McGovern's 1972 bid for the presidency, some of their parents took the issue to court.

The parents won. The state supreme court refused to uphold the school's restrictive policy, stating that it violated the First Amendment rights of the entire student body.

If a school policy requires prior approval of materials to be distributed, how would a student go about obtaining it?

Ask a teacher for a copy of the school's approval procedures. These guidelines should always be in writing and should be precise. If they aren't clear enough or don't address important issues, the student should ask a school official for a more detailed explanation.

The approval procedures should require the school to decide on the student's materials right away. They shouldn't permit school officials to "sit" on a request for approval until the best time for the student to exercise his or her First Amendment rights has come and gone.

Approval procedures can be illegal when they are unclear or in any way tend to discourage students from exercising their constitutional rights.

If a school refuses to approve student material for distribution, what can be done?

The student should request a written copy of the school's decision, to test the reason for its refusal against the *Tinker* case. Students always have a right to know why the school believes the rejected materials will seriously interfere with school activities or offend the rights of others.

If the student disagrees with the decision, he or she should consider appealing. Appeals are discussed later in this chapter.

STUDENT NEWSPAPERS

Can school officials censor student material in school newspapers?

They can in certain cases. In a 1988 case the Supreme Court modified *Tinker* by upholding the position of school officials who censored stories in a school-sponsored student newspaper. The school vetoed stories written by journalism students on teen pregnancy and the effects of divorce on children. Under *Tinker* the articles probably would have been protected. However, the Supreme Court ruled that they could be censored because they conflicted with the school's overall educational goals.

Because of this decision, known as *Hazelwood School District v. Kuhlmeier*, schools across the country now are able to censor articles in school-sponsored student publications. They have the power to censor "poorly written, prejudiced or vulgar articles" and articles that are "not suited for immature audiences." They may censor material on teen sex and articles advocating the use of drugs or violence and other conduct inconsistent with the "shared values of a civilized social order." They may, according to the Supreme Court, even censor material that associates the school with "anything other than neutrality on political issues."

However, *Hazelwood* doesn't apply if the school-sponsored publication has consistently made a point of publishing student opinions—if the publication has been a "public forum" for student expression in the past. Nor does it apply if student editors have the last word on the content of the newspaper.

In light of *Hazelwood*, school officials in Nevada recently were able to prevent a Planned Parenthood advertisement from running in a school-sponsored newspaper, even though the school had previously accepted ads from casinos, bars, churches, political candidates, and the U.S. Army. The censorship was upheld because the school's decision was shown to be in keeping with sound academic concerns and because the newspaper hadn't been a public forum for student expression in the past.

California, Massachusetts, New Jersey, Colorado, and other states have passed laws giving students greater liberties in the areas of free speech and freedom of the press. These laws permit students—they actually *invite* students—to exercise greater rights than *Hazelwood* would allow.

What law applies if the newspaper is school-sponsored but not part of the journalism curriculum?

The courts are divided on this issue.

May schools prohibit students from distributing underground newspapers at school or require approval before passing them out?

In some cases, yes. Because underground newspapers aren't school-sponsored, they aren't subject to *Hazelwood*'s restrictions. This means, in turn, that they retain greater First Amendment protections. School officials may forbid underground publications, but only if they have specific reasons for believing the contents will materially and substantially disrupt school activities, offend the rights of others, or aggravate a situation that is already tense. Courts are more likely to uphold a disciplinary action taken after the expression occurred.

Do *Hazelwood*'s limits apply to forms of expression other than school newspapers?

They weren't intended to, but the reasoning of the decision has been used to restrict other forms of expression. A high school student was disqualified from running for student council president in 1989 after he gave a campaign speech criticizing a school official and also the school administration. Here is his speech:

The administration plays tricks with your mind and they hope you won't notice. For example, why does Mr. Davidson stutter while he is on the intercom? He doesn't have a speech impediment. If you want to break the iron grip of this school, vote for me for president. I can try to bring back student rights that you have missed and maybe get things that you have always wanted. All you have to do is vote for me.

The court said the election campaign wasn't a public forum, so the school had greater control over the speeches. Then it stated that encouraging students to express their views "without attacking individuals and hurting their feelings" could be considered part of the school's academic goals. For these reasons, and because the candidate admitted that his remarks were intended to get extra votes, his disqualification didn't violate the First Amendment.

CLOTHES AS A FORM OF EXPRESSION

Can public school officials prohibit students from wearing insignias, protest buttons, colors, T-shirts bearing special images, and other symbols of an idea?

It depends on the image and also the situation. *Tinker* made it clear that forms of "symbolic speech" can't be banned merely because someone, such as a parent or teacher, thinks they are offensive. A symbol of expression only can be banned if school officials can predict that it will materially and substantially interfere with school, or if it is vulgar.

These days it's difficult to imagine how a protest button could cause problems at school. But wearing a protest button is a form of expression and therefore subject to the provisions of *Tinker*. Some courts have observed that if one student reacts disruptively to another's protest button, the school shouldn't impose an overall ban on buttons—the disruptive student should simply be disciplined. On the other hand, if students who wear buttons harass students who don't, school officials can probably prohibit them altogether.

Clothes are a separate issue. Dress codes that prohibit students from wearing clothes displaying biker and gang symbols and colors, beer ads, suggestive images, and vulgar language have been upheld by the courts upon proof that the clothing causes discipline problems. Schools have also been able to prohibit students from wearing T-shirts of particular sports teams, especially when students wear them to signify membership in a gang. It's now quite clear that schools can forbid T-shirts bearing such messages as "Drugs Suck!" and "See Dick Drink, See Dick Drive, See Dick Die, Don't be a Dick"—even if, as one court observed, "the message is laudable." In light of the *Tinker* case, these rules wouldn't violate the First Amendment.

Courts have also upheld school rules requiring students to wear underwear and regulating the length of slacks and skirts. Also, a school could legally require a student to cover up a tattoo. For more about laws relating to personal attire see Chapter Six, "Your Personal Appearance."

Can public schools forbid students to wear particularly fancy or expensive clothing?

In fact, yes. Some schools prohibit students from wearing gold jewelry, fur coats, and certain brand names. These modern-day rules are meant to discourage theft and locker break-ins.

Can public schools legally forbid women students to wear pants or slacks on campus?

It's not likely. Such a rule would probably be unreasonable and arbitrary because it couldn't be proved to promote safety, order, or discipline. But a school could legally enforce a rule prohibiting "too tight" pants.

Can public schools require students to wear uniforms?

Uniforms have become a hot issue in recent years. A rule requiring students to wear uniforms could be enforced if they are shown to promote safety and discipline and are cost-effective. So far, this hasn't been overwhelmingly difficult for schools to establish.

SCHOOL LIBRARIES AND SCHOOL BOOKS

Can public school authorities legally ban books from school libraries because of the ideas in them?

No. In 1982, the Supreme Court took up the issue of book-banning in *Board of Education v. Pico*. In *Pico*, a school board attempted to remove certain books from a high school library that it claimed were "anti-American, anti-Christian, anti-Semitic and just plain filthy." Among the books it wanted to remove were *Soul on Ice* by Eldridge Cleaver, *Slaughter House Five* by Kurt Vonnegut, and *Black Boy* by Richard Wright— all modern American classics.

The Supreme Court ruled against the school board on First Amendment grounds. "The special characteristics of the school library," it said, "make that environment especially appropriate for the recognition of the First Amendment."

Can a public school forbid younger students to check out a particular library book at school because school officials think the book is too "adult"?

The answer to this question is unclear. Under *Pico*, probably not; although under the *Hazelwood* case, discussed earlier, this probably could happen.

The American Library Association's Bill of Rights prohibits libraries from discriminating on the basis of age when lending books. This document doesn't have the force of law, but it does assert an important First Amendment position.

Can school boards constitutionally restrict the types of reading material that teachers may use in class?

Yes. Although school boards can't have books removed from school libraries because of the ideas in them, they can prohibit the use of teaching materials that are considered vulgar or obscene by community standards.

In 1989 a federal appeals court in Florida upheld a high school's decision to remove a collection of essays from a school reading list because certain parents thought some of the essays were vulgar. The selections objected to were *Lysistrata* by the ancient Greek Aristophanes and "The Miller's Tale" from Chaucer's *Canterbury Tales*. Both selections contain references to sex.

After the school board sided with the parents, other parents took the matter to court, claiming violations of the First Amendment. The judge said he had trouble understanding how Aristophanes and Chaucer could cause eleventh and twelfth graders in modern America any harm. Even so, he let stand the school board's decision because, he said, striking the books from the reading list was related to legitimate curriculum concerns of the school board.

These two cases point to an odd distinction in the law and one that is troublesome to many. Removing books from the shelves of a school library because someone disapproves of the ideas in them is a First Amendment violation. On the other hand, public schools may exercise almost total control over their curricula. Courts have permitted schools to prohibit even mildly offensive reading material from their lesson plans.

FREE EXPRESSION AND MODERN TECHNOLOGIES

Are public schools legally required to train students on computers?

No, unless the state or the local school district mandates computer instruction.

Under the First Amendment, can teachers legally control access to certain types of computer images and information?

Yes, but this raises a thorny legal issue. Schools can prevent students from accessing information that is obscene or inappropriate by community standards—or try to. Even so, teachers, librarians, and lawyers are asking, "Wouldn't blocking be overbroad and therefore unconstitutional?" On the other hand, they also ask, "If teachers don't supervise access to obscene expression online, won't they provoke a public outcry? And won't they violate professional standards and school policies relating to the First Amendment?"

Schools can legally use software filters to block access to selected online material. Often blocked are sites depicting or describing violence and profanity, nudity, sexual acts, racism and racist acts, satanism and cults, and drugs and drug cultures. But sometimes information that is harmless, and often valuable, is blocked unintentionally. For example, restricting minors' access to the "alt.sex" newsgroups would also block access to "alt.sex.safe" and "alt.sex.abstinence." The information in these newsgroups, although sexually explicit, might be very valuable to high school students.[1]

If a court decides that obscene material online violates local obscenity laws, who is the guilty party?

This is another tough issue. Obtaining and viewing obscenity online requires that it be accessed (with a modem and telephone line) by someone other than its creator. But in most states, to be guilty of "purveying" obscene materials, an individual must have knowingly distributed them. Many argue that if the creator isn't the one distributing or purveying the materials, he or she can't really be guilty.

Another question is, who's laws apply? That is, if material or images are placed online in Los Angeles, California, but are accessed or downloaded in Moab, Utah, should the community standards of Los Angeles or Moab apply in determining whether the material is obscene?

These issues have not been resolved. But in any event, educators and school librarians tend to be most concerned with access to sexually explicit and sadistic materials online—and less concerned with the strictly legal definition of obscenity or its particular locale.

Most school districts have specific written policies relating to online computer use. A teacher or school counselor should be able to guide any student through these policies.

Can a school legally prohibit cellular phones and pagers on campus, even if the parents want their children to carry them?
Yes.

FREEDOM OF ASSEMBLY

> Congress shall make no law . . . abridging the right of the people peaceably to assemble.
> —First Amendment, U.S. Constitution

Can a public school prevent students from forming a club at school that promotes an unpopular point of view?
Courts in some states have ruled that school facilities can be used only for activities relating directly to the curriculum. In these states, classrooms and meeting halls can be used only by organizations such as honor societies and foreign language clubs. In others, any club can meet unless its activities cause material and substantial disruption or deprive other students of their legal rights.

The law in this area is not entirely clear. A Pennsylvania high school was able to prevent a student group, the Student Coalition for Peace, from using school facilities for an antinuclear presentation. The school board's stated goal was to "keep the podium of politics off school grounds." But a Michigan court stated that "absent a threat to the orderly operation of the school, to deny recognition to a student group because it advocates 'controversial' ideas is unconstitutional."

Unless the Supreme Court takes up this issue, the "freedom" in "freedom of assembly," at least with respect to club meetings on school grounds, will continue to vary from state to state.

Can public school officials legally stop sit-ins, walk-outs, and protest marches on school property?

It depends on the situation. Demonstrations raise free speech issues and also free assembly issues, and this makes them subject to the guidelines in the *Tinker* case discussed earlier in this chapter.

Demonstrations and walk-outs can indeed disrupt school work and school discipline, and when they do, school authorities can and should intervene and may legally suspend students for participating. However, some courts have said that students should be given less punishment for participating in nonviolent demonstrations, or shouldn't be punished at all, given the importance of free speech in our society.

Sit-ins aren't necessarily illegal because they occur inside school, but any demonstration has a better chance of coming within the First Amendment's right to assemble peaceably if it occurs outdoors and before or after school. School officials have the right to stop protests that block halls or make students miss class and may discipline students who damage property or cause injuries. Students can be arrested if a situation becomes so serious that property is damaged or laws are broken. But a school violates the Constitution if it enforces a rule banning demonstrations altogether.

Have students been able to organize gay or lesbian rights clubs in public high school?

Some high schools permit them, and federal law appears to limit the power of schools to prevent them. Under the Equal Access Act of 1984, a federal law, if a public high school receiving federal assistance permits any student group to meet after hours on matters outside the regular curriculum, it can't forbid any other group from forming because of its religious, political, or philosophical beliefs. What this means is that if a school permits any non-curriculum-related groups to organize, it probably can't forbid a gay or lesbian rights club from forming. For more information on gay and lesbian rights see Chapter Fourteen, "Gay and Lesbian Teens."

RELIGION AND SCHOOL PRAYER

> Congress shall make no law . . . respecting an establishment of religion, or prohibiting free exercise thereof.
> —First Amendment, U.S. Constitution

Can public schools prevent students from praying during school hours?

Nobody can prevent anybody from praying.

Can schools set aside a time for students to pray or observe a moment of religious silence?

No. Under the Establishment Clause of the First Amendment (shown above), public schools can't take actions that appear to advance or promote religion. For this reason, giving students a special time during the day to pray or observe a moment of prayerful silence is unconstitutional. On the other hand, public schools may allow students a moment of silent meditation, and many do.

School prayers and Bible readings in school also are prohibited under the Establishment Clause, even if participation is voluntary.

Is it illegal for an instructor to teach about religion in a public school?

No. It is only illegal for an instructor to *promote* prayer or religion. Discussing prayer and religion in the framework of a school subject such as social studies is acceptable and, in the opinion of many, quite appropriate.

Can a school permit religion instructors to hold class in a public high school building after hours?

No, even if the school is willing to give *all* religions a chance to hold class in the building.

Can schools release students from school during the day for religion classes?

In fact, yes. Public schools may "accommodate" religion by letting students leave school for religious instruction. According to the courts, these "release-time" programs don't advance religion illegally even though they do help students to practice their faith.

Schools may also release students from sex education classes for religious reasons, but only if there are other ways (such as a health class) to satisfy the overall class requirements.

Why don't rules limiting religion in public schools violate the First Amendment right to the free exercise of religion?

Because in public schools the rule against government involvement in religion overrides the right of young people to exercise the religion of their choice. (The First Amendment, including the Free Exercise Clause, is shown above.) To permit a student or teacher to practice his or her religion openly in public school would infringe on the personal rights of others.

The tension between these two rights has arisen when teachers have tried to promote their religious beliefs in class. For example, a public school teacher in Pennsylvania was dismissed for opening class with the Lord's Prayer and a Bible story. The teacher took the issue to court, arguing that he was dismissed because he had exercised his rights under the Free Exercise Clause. The court upheld the teacher's dismissal, saying his right to practice his religion didn't entitle him to promote his personal beliefs in class.

If evolution is taught in a public high school, shouldn't "creation science" also be taught?

The Supreme Court has ruled "no" on this issue. It recently ruled that a Louisiana law requiring "equal time" for evolution and creation science is unconstitutional. The Court noted that evolution has been a fully accepted *scientific* theory for decades. For a public school to allow equal time for creation science would be an instance of promoting a religious theory—and a violation of the Free Exercise Clause.

Even so, in 1999, the Kansas Board of Education voted to remove most references to evolution from the state's science curriculum and to eliminate the subject from high school competency tests. This move quickly sparked anti-evolution brushfires in Oklahoma, Kentucky, and New Mexico.

May student religious groups use public school facilities for meetings?

Yes, under certain conditions. In the past, student religious groups weren't allowed to meet in public schools—the school would be giving the appearance of advancing religion. But under the federal Equal Access

Act of 1984, if a public school permits any student group to meet after hours on matters outside the regular curriculum, it can't forbid any other group from forming for religious, political, or philosophical reasons. This means that if a school permits any non-curriculum-related groups to use its meeting rooms, it can't forbid a religious group from doing the same. The meetings must be voluntary, initiated by students, held during non-school hours, and not sponsored or controlled by school personnel.

Would a prayer at a public school graduation ceremony be illegal?

Yes. The Supreme Court surprised many in 1992 by ruling that a high school violated the Establishment Clause when it arranged for a minister to give a short prayer at a high school graduation. In court, the school argued that the students hadn't been forced to participate in a religious event because they could have skipped the ceremony. It also argued that it had sincerely attempted to come up with a nonsectarian prayer.

The Supreme Court rejected these arguments, saying that because each graduate was undoubtedly going to attend graduation, each was also required to participate in the prayer. The school therefore promoted religion in violation of the Establishment Clause.

The Supreme Court reconsidered this issue in early 2000. Its ruling may modify the position it took in 1992.

Are prayers at public school athletic events also forbidden?

The Supreme Court hasn't dealt with this issue, but the high school graduation case discussed earlier probably applies to prayers at athletic events as well.

Can students stay out of public school on religious holidays without risking punishment?

Yes, at least with respect to important holidays of major religions.

Can a student be punished for refusing to salute the American flag or recite the Pledge of Allegiance at school?

No, because refusing to salute the flag or recite the Pledge of Allegiance are forms of symbolic speech. Punishment by school officials would be a First Amendment violation, whether the reason for the refusal was political or religious. Anyone can also refuse to stand during the Pledge of Allegiance or the "Star Spangled Banner."

DISCIPLINE AND DUE PROCESS

> No State shall . . . deprive any person of life, liberty, or property, without due process of law.
> —Fourteenth Amendment, U.S. Constitution

Do students have an absolute right to be advised of their school's disciplinary rules?

Yes. Most school districts require that their schools' disciplinary rules be written out and distributed to each student at the beginning of the school year. This makes sense because students naturally have a better chance of knowing when they've broken a school rule if they have had an opportunity to read it. But whether or not a public school has written rules, school officials can't punish a student for breaking a school rule if the student had no reason to know it existed.

Does a school have to advise students of the punishment for violating a particular rule?

It depends on the offense. When it comes to serious violations, schools need to spell out in advance the types of punishment a student can receive. For less serious violations, schools don't have to specify the range of possible punishments.

Is a student entitled to a school hearing before being punished?

It again depends on the seriousness of the offense. If a student faces suspension or other serious form of discipline, he or she is always entitled to "due process of law." This is an important concept—every adult and adolescent should know what it means.

What is "due process of law"?

Due process of law or simply "due process" is the overall method by which a society decides whether someone's legal rights should be taken away. It means that a public body can't punish someone or take away his or her rights without following specific procedures to determine whether the "taking" would be fair. The procedures almost always involve a hearing to give the "accused" a right to deny or defend his or her actions and hear the "accuser's" version of what happened. The clearest example of due process is a trial to determine whether a person has committed a crime and whether a particular form of punishment should be imposed.

What does due process mean in the high school setting?

It means that a student can't be seriously punished without being afforded at least an informal hearing to determine the offense and the surrounding circumstances. The amount of due process depends on the seriousness of the offense, and therefore the seriousness of the possible punishment.

The Supreme Court established in *Goss v. Lopez* that students as well as adults have due process rights. In this landmark case, a number of students were suspended after demonstrating at their public high school in Ohio. Their student records were unclear as to why the school took action against them, and none was given a due process hearing to either deny or explain his or her participation.

The Supreme Court ruled that the Due Process Clause of the Fourteenth Amendment required the school to advise each student in advance that he or she was being suspended. Also, it ruled that the school should have advised each student of the facts supporting his or her suspension and should have provided each at least an informal hearing, with adequate prior notice to either deny or defend the charges.

When does due process apply to students?

It applies whenever a student is accused of an act that could result in suspension, expulsion, a lowered grade, or other serious disciplinary measure. Due process doesn't mean the student will be found innocent. It simply means that procedures are in place and are used to ensure that the school treats its students fairly.

Sometimes states or school districts afford students more due process than is guaranteed under the Constitution. When this happens, the school must follow the state or school district's broader procedures.

What is the difference between suspension and expulsion?

Although school districts or individual schools establish their own time frames for suspensions and expulsions, a short-term suspension usually lasts up to ten days. A long-term suspension usually lasts longer and may extend as long as two semesters.

In an expulsion the student normally is dismissed from school permanently. Students can be expelled for being violent at school, damaging or stealing either school property or the property of another student, or having drugs or weapons on campus.

How does due process apply to expulsions?

Formal due process procedures are required for an expulsion. A student who faces the prospect of being expelled should receive adequate advance notice of the charges and adequate notice of the time, place, and nature of the hearing. The student is entitled to a fair hearing before an impartial person and may be represented at the hearing by an adult, and in some states by an attorney.

The student or adult representative should be entitled to introduce evidence, cross-examine the school's witnesses, and receive a written record of the school's decision. The decision always should describe the evidence it relied on in deciding to expel.

These procedures apply to all serious offenses. They should also apply if the school has proposed a long-term suspension.

What due process guarantees apply to short-term suspensions?

Short-term suspensions require less due process than expulsions and long-term suspensions. A student who faces a short-term suspension has a right to oral notice of the offense, an explanation of the evidence the decision maker plans to rely on, and a chance to disprove the charges. Advance notice of the school's intent to impose a short-term suspension can be shorter than for situations that could result in expulsion or long-term suspension. Cross-examination of witnesses usually isn't allowed, and the student normally can't be represented by a lawyer.

In one extreme (and incredulous) situation, an Ohio third grader actually received a two-day suspension for writing and placing an allegedly threatening message inside a fortune cookie. The youth was a fan of martial arts videos. The fortune read, "You will die an honorable death." Not only was the student represented by counsel at his suspension hearing; the American Civil Liberties Union in Ohio took the case. Ultimately the decision was revoked. Many believe that the suspension was an overreaction by school officials in light of serious student violence occurring at a Littleton, Colorado, high school in April 1999.

If a student is expelled from high school, is he or she out "forever"?

Not usually. Most school districts have an "alternate education program" for expelled students, which may simply mean that the student is sent to another school. Courts rarely uphold the expulsion of a student who is too young to legally quit school.

Do students have due process rights whenever they get in trouble at school?

No. Due process is for serious school violations that may have serious consequences—for violations that could deprive a student of a valuable right and be a blot on his or her record. But as stated, a school board may permit a student to be heard on a disciplinary matter that federal or state law doesn't consider serious enough for due process. School authorities should always advise students of the types of offenses meriting due process, in addition to those that could result in a suspension or expulsion.

How can a student find out about the types of offenses meriting due process? How can a student find out about the school's due process procedures?

Most high schools give each student a handbook explaining the school district's disciplinary rules and its due process procedures. If no such handbook exists, the student should ask a teacher or school administrator for more information on the subject.

Can a student be suspended or otherwise disciplined for an off-campus activity?

Only if the student's actions pose a serious danger to other students, or the student's acts have a direct bearing on the well-being of the school. For example, a serious criminal charge, including a drug-related offense, can be the basis for a suspension. Because a suspension means that the student might be deprived of a valuable right, punishment for an off-campus activity can only occur after the student has been afforded a full due process hearing.

If a student is found guilty of a school offense, can the school impose any punishment it wants?

No. Courts will overturn a form of punishment that is too severe—punishment that is "arbitrary, capricious or oppressive." But schools do have extensive power when it comes to meting out punishment.

If a student is arrested, can he or she be suspended or expelled from school before trial?

Not for that reason alone. As Chapter Twelve explains, an arrest is simply a police action based on an officer's reasoned belief that a person has committed a crime or is in the process of committing one. But an act resulting in a student's arrest can also be a school violation, and when this happens, the school can hold its own due process hearing on the offense.

Here an important concept applies. The amount of evidence needed to discipline a student for a school offense may be less than the amount needed to convict the student for the same offense in juvenile court. As a matter of constitutional law, to convict and sentence a person for committing a crime, the state must prove its charges "beyond a reasonable doubt." But as in a noncriminal or "civil" case, the school only needs to prove it is "more likely than not" that the student violated a certain school rule to impose discipline. Its "burden of proof" is less weighty because the school is only disciplining the student for breaking an internal rule, not a public law.

If the school meets its burden of proof at the school hearing, it can punish the student before his or her courtroom trial. Also, the court may take the school's decision into account in reaching its own decision.

The student should be represented by a lawyer at both the disciplinary hearing and the trial.

Students can't be punished at school for the criminal acts of their parents, relatives, or friends.

If a student gets in serious trouble at school, is he or she entitled to receive the *Miranda* warnings from a school official?

No. Only the police give the *Miranda* warnings. They recite these famous lines to persons who have been placed under arrest. As explained in Chapter Twelve, the *Miranda* warnings advise "arrestees" that they have a right to remain silent, that anything they say to the police may be held against them, and that they are entitled to the services of an attorney.

School officials aren't required to give the *Miranda* warnings because they don't have the legal power to arrest. For more about arrests and *Miranda* see Chapter Twelve, "Teens and Crime."

Can a student's grades be lowered because of particularly bad conduct?

Not in most schools, although in many, grades can be lowered for too many missed classes.

Without a due process hearing, can a student be forbidden to participate in extracurricular activities as punishment for a school offense?

No. The right to participate in extracurricular activities is valuable enough to merit a due process hearing.

Can a student appeal a disciplinary decision?

Yes, provided the offense merited due process. For example, a school's decision to suspend or expel a student can always be appealed.

How do appeals work?

A student's appeal (or an appeal by the student's parents) usually goes directly to the principal. It must be in writing. The principal must conduct an appeal hearing within a short time (usually within five school days) and is required to rule on the appeal shortly after the hearing. The decision can then be appealed to the school superintendent, who must also provide a hearing and make a decision in a prescribed number of days.

If the "appellant" is dissatisfied with the decision of the superintendent, an appeal can be taken to the school board. An appeals hearing before the school board is always more formal.

If the appellant receives an "adverse" decision at every stage of the hearing process, the entire matter can be taken to federal or state court.

Any student who receives an adverse decision from the school principal should request written procedures for appealing. At every stage of the appeal process, the school's decision should be in writing.

CORPORAL PUNISHMENT

What is corporal punishment? Do school officials have a legal right to inflict corporal punishment on students?

Corporal punishment is any type of punishment directed toward a person's body. Striking a student is the most obvious example. The federal Constitution doesn't forbid corporal punishment in public schools, although it is often prohibited by state law or a school rule. Without a provision ruling it out, a school district may approve its use. The laws of some states actually authorize corporal punishment.

Students usually aren't entitled to a due process hearing before corporal punishment is inflicted. The Supreme Court has stated that a school suspension is more serious than corporal punishment, which is why a student is entitled to due process before being suspended but not before receiving bodily punishment.

Even so, a student's constitutional due process rights were violated in a case in which his injuries resulted in ten days' hospitalization, and in another in which a student was injured after a teacher tied him to a desk. In both cases the school intruded on the student's personal privacy to the extent of committing a "taking" without due process of law.

Schools should make every attempt to rule out corporal punishment as a way to deal with problems. Clearly, teachers should first exhaust all other means of disciplining a student. If corporal punishment is used, it should be witnessed by a second school official. In addition, parents should receive a written explanation of the nature of the punishment and why it was used.

Force can be used to break up fights on school grounds and to prevent property damage, but only in appropriate amounts.

SCHOOL SEARCHES

The right of the people to be secure in their persons, houses, papers, and effects, against unreasonable searches and seizures, shall not be violated, and no Warrants shall issue, but upon probable cause, supported by Oath or affirmation, and particularly describing the place to be searched, and the persons or things to be seized.

—Fourth Amendment, U.S. Constitution

May public school authorities legally search a student's clothing, backpack, gym bag, or purse?

In most circumstances, yes, although such searches *do* intrude on students' privacy. To search a student legally, two requirements must be met. First, there must be reasonable grounds for suspecting the search will turn up evidence that the student broke the law or a school rule. Second, the search can't be too broad in its scope and can't intrude on the student's privacy more than is needed to carry out the purpose of the search.

This is a constitutional test, established in 1985 in the Supreme Court case of *New Jersey v. T.L.O.* The basis of the test is "reasonable suspicion." If the search isn't based on reasonable suspicion, it violates the Search and Seizure Clause of the Fourth Amendment.

In the *T.L.O.* case a woman student's purse was searched after she was caught smoking in a restroom. As the principal was removing a pack of cigarettes from her purse, he saw a package of rolling papers. He searched further and found some marijuana, a pipe, some empty plastic bags, a number of dollar bills, a list of students who apparently owed the student money, and two letters suggesting that she might be selling drugs.

The Supreme Court ruled that because the school had "reasonable suspicion," the student's privacy rights hadn't been violated. This made the search legal. It said that although students do have privacy rights, these rights must be balanced against the need of their schools to maintain a safe place for learning. According to the Supreme Court, this balance is achieved by applying the "reasonable suspicion test" to school searches.

What does "reasonable suspicion" really mean?

Reasonable suspicion exists when the school's suspicion is based on the circumstances surrounding the offense, the adequacy of the evidence, the source of the information, and the student's age, gender, and school records. In all cases the school's suspicion must be based on more than a hunch.

Consider the following example. A student's locker was searched for alcohol after a fellow student tipped off a school official. The search turned up evidence of drug use, but no alcohol. The state appeals court determined that the evidence was obtained upon reasonable suspicion even though the school officials weren't searching for drugs. Since the search was legal, the school could discipline the student for having drug paraphernalia on school grounds.

Can school officials legally search lockers and desks?

Yes. Students are said to share control over their lockers and desks with school officials, so their privacy rights with respect to them are lower. Even so, reasonable suspicion is usually needed for a locker or desk search. In some states, lockers and desks may be searched at any time and for any reason on the theory that the student's rights are waived. Students in these states have no privacy rights in desks and lockers whatsoever.

Can school officials conduct strip searches?

Yes, unless state law or a school rule specifically forbids it. A strip search conducted on school property is a very serious matter. As a rule, the more intrusive the search, the more individual suspicion is needed to justify it. A school official may only need reasonable suspicion to ask a student to empty his or her pockets, but the same official would find it almost impossible to justify a body search without full "probable cause" to suspect that the student has evidence on his or her person that a law or school rule has been broken.

Body searches should be left to the police. For more about probable cause see Chapter Twelve, "Teens and Crime."

Are mass searches of students legal?

No, because under the reasonable suspicion test, the school's suspicion must always relate to a particular individual. In one case, school authorities did not have individual suspicion and therefore made unreasonable searches violating the Search and Seizure Clause when they inspected each student's luggage as a condition of going on a field trip. In another case, strip searches of each member of a class to discover who stole three dollars were also illegal.

Can a school require the entire student body or an entire class to take blood or urine tests to check for drug use?

No. Making students submit to urine or blood tests without individual suspicion puts all of their privacy rights in jeopardy. In a 1985 case a New Jersey high school made each student submit to a urine test for 26 different drugs. When the matter went to court on a Fourth Amendment argument, the judge ruled that the school had conducted "searches" without reasonable suspicion, which meant the tests were illegal. In 1999 the Supreme Court let stand an appeals court decision striking down a policy requiring suspended high school students to take a urine test before being reinstated, regardless of whether the suspension was for drug or alcohol use.

Can an individual student be required to take a urine test if the school suspects he or she has been using drugs?

Yes, provided the student is allowed to give the urine sample in the privacy of a bathroom stall.

Drug testing programs for high school athletes are also legal. On this issue, the post-1970s rights of young people are eroding. In *Vernonia School District v. Acton*, the local school district adopted a policy to randomly drug-test ten percent of its student athletes. The athletes' parents were required to sign a consent for the testing, and a student athlete couldn't play until his or her signed consent was returned. One seventh-grader's parents refused to sign. They filed a lawsuit against the school district, claiming that the urine tests were suspicionless searches and therefore unconstitutional.

The case made its way to the Supreme Court—and the parents lost. Upholding the searches, the Court stated that the school's interest in orderliness and safety could legally be balanced against the students' privacy rights. This ruling dealt a blow to the reasonable suspicion requirement outlined in the *T.L.O.* case because the "suspicion requirement" has ceased to mean suspicion of a particular individual.

Can school officials use improperly obtained evidence against a student in a school disciplinary hearing?

In many states, yes. The *T.L.O.* case didn't go so far as to rule out the use of improperly obtained evidence.

Most high school districts have explicit rules in their student handbooks about desk and locker searches, but not always. But whether or not published rules exist, a student should never keep anything in a locker or desk that he or she doesn't want someone else to see.

See Chapter Twelve for information about the use of evidence obtained in an illegal search.

WEAPONS

What happens if a student brings a gun or other weapon to school?

Carrying a weapon is always against school policy. The consequences of bringing a weapon onto school property can range from short-term suspension to automatic and permanent expulsion from the school district.

Schools can require students to pass through a metal detector before entering the school building and may legally "stop and frisk" a student who appears to be concealing a weapon. For more about stop-and-frisk searches see Chapter Twelve, "Teens and Crime."

In school weapons cases, as in all serious disciplinary matters at school, the student is entitled to a due process hearing before being suspended, expelled, or otherwise punished.

STUDENTS AND THE POLICE

Can the police question students on school property?

Police have the right to question students anywhere, and school officials don't have the power to prevent it. But schools usually can require the police to give advance notice to a principal or teacher of their intent to question a student or interrupt class.

In fact, school authorities usually cooperate with police officers when it comes to student questioning. Students can be arrested on school grounds and taken from school for questioning. The police arrest must be based on probable cause to believe that a crime has been committed and that the "arrestee" is the one who committed it.

If the police begin questioning a student, what should the student do?

No one is required to answer police questions. If a student is the target of police questioning, the best thing to do is remain silent, except to give a name and address. The student's parents should be called—the student should request permission to call a parent right away. If the student is placed under arrest, he or she has a constitutional right to contact a lawyer, but should say nothing to either the police or any school official until both a parent and a lawyer arrive.

School officials shouldn't discourage a student from calling a parent or lawyer and should never encourage a student to answer questions. Not only would doing so put the school in a bad light; it might also make the student's confession inadmissible in court. School officials should leave such matters to the police and the student's attorney.

What if the student thinks he or she can answer police questions competently?

The student should still remain silent. Young people often think they can clear up problems on their own by answering questions or trying to explain what happened. They usually are wrong. Their most carefully phrased explanations often damage their case rather than help it. Never forget that the *Miranda* warnings, discussed in Chapter Twelve, remind every criminal suspect, including teens, that "anything you say may be used against you."

Can the police personally search a student on school property?

They can, but they need more than reasonable suspicion to do so. To conduct a personal search, a police officer must have probable cause to believe that a crime has been committed or is being committed, and that the student committed or is committing it. The same rule applies to police searches of lockers and desks. (Some courts have ruled that if the police are simply assisting school officials in a search, they don't need full probable cause.) If the police turn up evidence of a criminal act, it can be used in court.

For more about probable cause see Chapter Twelve, "Teens and Crime."

Can student property that school officials find in a search be used in a criminal investigation?

School officials are always free to turn over evidence of a crime. In some states, even evidence uncovered in an illegal school search can be used in a later criminal investigation.

SPORTS

> No state shall deny to any person within its jurisdiction the equal protection of the laws.
> —Fourteenth Amendment, U.S. Constitution

Are all-male and all-female high school athletic teams ever illegal?

Yes. If the school doesn't have a separate-sex team for a sport that doesn't involve bodily contact, schools can't prohibit women students from participating, or from at least trying out. Track, ski, golf, and tennis are examples of such sports.

Does this mean that separate-sex teams for noncontact sports can be legal?

Yes, although in some states if a school has both a women's and a men's team for a particular noncontact sport, a woman may try out for both. A local high school athletic association is an excellent source of information for gender-related sports issues.

Can women students play contact sports such as football or basketball on the same team as the men?

The answer to this question currently is unclear. Courts in a number of states have ruled that when it comes to contact sports, if no separate-sex team exists and the women can effectively compete against men, they can't be prohibited from playing unless doing so places their health and safety at risk. But if all the men who try out for a contact sport are better than all the women, the women who don't make the team haven't been discriminated against on the basis of gender.

A New York court recently faced the question of whether a woman student could try out for junior varsity football. It ruled that the school district failed to prove that prohibiting mixed competition serves any important objective. Although the school claimed the policy was needed to protect the health and safety of women students, its argument failed because no woman athlete was given the chance to prove that she was as fit as, or more fit than, the weakest man on the team.

If the women shouldn't be competing in mixed play because of health or safety risks, a separate-sex team must be formed. The women's team must be equal to the men's team in terms of funding, available facilities, and coaching staff.

Can a woman be required to play on a women's team involving a contact sport if she is as good as the men?

Yes, on the theory that separate-sex teams increase total participation in high school sports, especially the participation of women.

Can a man be prevented from playing on a women's sports team?
Yes. Rules preventing discrimination in high school sports work in favor of students who want more physical challenge, not less.

TESTING

Is tracking legal?

Tracking—placing students in different classes, usually on the basis of test scores—has been challenged in the courts as unfair to racial and ethnic minorities. The challenges claim that the tests are culturally biased, which means that when they are drafted by members of a particular group, students from that group too often are the highest scorers. If it is proved that the tests are biased and therefore discriminate against minorities, the tracking system discriminates illegally.

A California court recently ruled that too many black students were placed in special education classes after the results of an IQ test were used to place them. On the basis of its finding, the court said the school's tracking system was discriminatory, and therefore illegal.

Courts in a number of states have ruled that after forced school desegregation is ordered, schools can't group minorities in lower tracks until the disadvantages of their earlier discriminatory education have been corrected. Some courts have ruled that a minority student can't be put into a special class without first receiving a due process hearing.

Is competency testing discriminatory?

It can be. Minimum competency tests, or MCTs, are used by many schools to decide whether a student should pass to a higher grade or be awarded a diploma. Competency tests can be discriminatory if they are introduced into a school when, because earlier public schooling was inadequate, minority students can't make passing grades. When this has happened, students have been permitted to advance to the next grade without taking the test.

States with MCTs often build in a series of required skills tests in earlier grades and make schools provide remedial help to students who don't pass. On the basis of these early tests, schools are able to develop improvement plans for students who are behind, focusing on areas where a particular student needs special help.

What happens if a student is denied a high school diploma because he or she can't pass the school's competency tests?

If the tests aren't discriminatory, the student would have to study for a graduate equivalency degree or GED. For more about GED tests, see the discussion at the beginning of this chapter.

OTHER DISCRIMINATION ISSUES

Are all-male or all-female classes still permitted in public high schools?

Changes in this area are happening fast. Clearly, classes that used to be offered just to men can no longer be off-limits to women—except for gym. This means that women students can't be denied the right to take a class in auto mechanics, and men students can't be prohibited from enrolling in a course in secretarial skills or home economics. Student clubs that limit their membership to one gender are also illegal.

But high schools have recently begun experimenting with all-women math and science classes. Although some women students do better in these subjects when the class is "no guys allowed," the jury is still out on this controversy.

Are single-sex high schools illegal?

No, provided the women's school has programs and facilities at least as good as the men's schools, and vice versa.

Do schools have an obligation to prevent students from being sexually harassed at school?

Yes. School officials have a duty to prevent sexual harassment of a particular student if they know about the problem, or should know about it.

Do illegal aliens have a right to attend public high school in America?

Yes. They have just as much right to attend public high school as native-born young people. To attend school, an illegal alien just needs to live within the school's geographic boundaries.

Are schools required to offer classes in a student's native language if the student can't understand English?

No. Bilingual education—classes taught in one's own language while the same classes are taught in English—isn't a legal right. However, public schools must at least provide English language classes for non-English-speaking students to bring down language barriers. These are called ESL classes—"English as a Second Language."

States with high numbers of non-English-speaking students (California, Arizona, and Florida) have extensive school programs to eliminate language barriers.

Are handicapped students entitled to special benefits at school?

Yes, if they need them. Under important federal laws, including the Individuals with Disabilities Education Act or IDEA, public schools must provide for students who, because of a disability, can't learn their lessons through regular teaching methods. Each handicapped student must have a "free appropriate public education" in light of his or her special needs. States must establish programs to identify handicapped students and use nondiscriminatory tests to determine their achievement levels. If schools discriminate, they risk losing financial assistance from the federal government.

Can handicapped students always take classes with nonhandicapped students?

Handicapped students must be integrated with nonhandicapped students as much as possible, at the same time that their special needs are being provided for. This is called "mainstreaming."

To mainstream a student, a teacher may need special learning materials, speech services either in or out of the classroom, or an aide to take care of the student's unique physical needs. Challenged students include those with hearing problems, speech problems, and emotional disturbances, for example. If such a situation exists, a special education plan is developed for the student.

What happens if a handicapped student doesn't adapt to mainstreaming?

He or she usually is transferred from some or all regular classes. Sometimes the student attends "special ed" classes or classes in a "resource room." But the student is still entitled to a "free and appropriate education"—at a special school or perhaps at home.

Can a special education student be suspended or expelled for particularly bad behavior?

The student can only be suspended. A school can temporarily suspend a special student who is a danger to others, but only for ten days. During that time it must decide to change the student's curriculum or take another course of action in the student's best interests.

Are students with human immunodeficiency virus/acquired immunodeficiency syndrome (HIV/AIDS) considered handicapped under these special laws?

Courts in a number of states have ruled that HIV/AIDS students must be regarded as handicapped under the federal laws noted previously. In these states, HIV/AIDS students can't be discriminated against at school because of their condition. Students with hepatitis B also are protected.

STUDENT RECORDS

Can parents see their children's high school records? Can high school students see their own records?

The answer to the first question is yes. Under federal law, parents must be able to review their children's school records and transcripts. As to the second question, students may see their records when they reach age 18, although schools may elect to allow underage students to view them.

Public schools can't give out student records without parental consent, and state laws often provide added privacy protections. Federal law does, however, make certain exceptions. Information in student records can be legally used to compile transcripts, yearbooks, and student directories, and can be made available for academic research. These privacy laws also apply to private schools, particularly if the school receives federal funds.

Can a student do anything about damaging information in his or her student file?

Sometimes. Negative information in a student file shouldn't necessarily be removed or changed. Schools have a duty to record information about students and provide information to colleges and technical schools when students apply to them for admission.

But school records shouldn't be gossip columns. To ensure that a school keeps fair and accurate records, a good rule of thumb would be for parents to inspect their children's records once a year. If information in a student file is incorrect, misleading, petty, or vicious, the parent should ask the school to remove or correct it. If the school decides not to take action on the request, the parents are entitled to a due process hearing. If the school wins, the parents can appeal the decision through the appeal process described earlier.

Can outsiders such as the police see student records?

Law enforcement officials can't view a young person's academic file simply on request, although student records can be demanded or "subpoenaed" by a court. In addition, parents have the power to authorize persons such as relatives, lawyers, guardians, and psychologists to review their children's records.

PRIVATE SCHOOLS, CHARTER SCHOOLS, AND HOME SCHOOLING

Are private schools subject to state education laws?

To a great extent, yes. State laws regarding high school attendance, student health, and teacher certification apply to private as well as public schools.

Do students in private schools have the same kind of constitutional rights as public high school students?

No. Due process under the federal Constitution only protects students in public schools—only when "state action" is involved. Operating a private school is not a type of state action, so due process isn't a constitutional right. However, state constitutions, state laws, and private school policies sometimes grant due process rights to students in private schools.

Can a private school discriminate on the basis of race or gender?

A private school may not deny admission on the basis of race, gender, or nationality. If it does, it loses its tax-exempt status, which means it forfeits important tax advantages of operating as a nonprofit organization under the federal tax laws.

Can a private school discriminate on the basis of a handicap?

Again, if a private school receives federal funds for a particular program (and many do), it may not discriminate on the basis of a handicap.

What is a charter school?

A charter school is a public school without all the strings attached. These schools operate free of certain state or local rules and regulations, although they must still meet specific performance standards. They create and manage their own budgets and often design innovative curricula. Many charter schools are geared to special fields of study such as math and science, music and other arts, or computers.

Teachers in charter schools must have a college degree and a current teacher certification. In addition, specific "core" subjects must be taught for a specified number of days and hours each year.

The charter school movement is growing fast, but it has had its share of growing pains. Charter schools are still experimental schools, and some have had trouble surviving due to problems with finances and internal management.

Could a charter school be created for students of a particular religion?

No. In 1994 the Supreme Court ruled in the case of *Village of Kiryas Joel V. Grumet* that a public school created for Hasidic Jews in New York was a violation of the First Amendment's Establishment Clause. This ruling is consistent with the Court's rulings in earlier Establishment Clause cases.

What is a voucher program?

A voucher program is a state educational program giving parents the equivalent of tuition payments for a child's education in either a public or private school. Supporters of voucher programs claim they create competition, which they believe should improve public education overall. They point out that the state's role is to do more than support an educational system—that it must also provide a good one.

Voucher programs are a hot political issue in many states.

Is home schooling legal in every state?

It is now legal in almost every state, and some regulate home schools more closely than others. In many states a parent (or related individual) who teaches his or her children at home must have a college degree and also a current teacher certification. State laws always require that certain subjects be taught for a specific number of days and hours each year. In some states only grade schoolers can be home schooled.

States authorizing home schooling usually require that the parents permit home visits by school personnel. If a home school teacher refuses to permit inspection of his or her curricula and school records or doesn't require the home-schooled student to take certain standardized tests, the parents can be charged with a criminal offense.

NOTE

1. Fred H. Cate, *The Internet and the First Amendment: Schools and Sexually Explicit Expression* (Bloomington: Phi Delta Kappa Educational Foundation, 1998), p. 87.

FOR FURTHER READING

In General

Cary, Eve, et al. *The Rights of Students: The Basic ACLU Guide to Student's Rights*. Carbondale: Southern Illinois University Press, 1988.

Cary, Eve, et al. *The Rights of Students: The ACLU Handbook for Young Americans*. New York: Puffin Books, 1997.

Fischer, Louis, et al. *Teachers and the Law*. 4th ed. White Plains, NY: Longman Publishers, 1995.

Isaac, Katherine, and Ralph Nader. *Ralph Nader's Practicing Democracy 1997: A Guide to Student Action.* New York: St. Martin's Press, 1997.

Jacobs, Thomas A. *What Are My Rights?* Minneapolis: Free Spirit Publishing, Inc., 1993.

First Amendment Issues

Agre, Philip E., and Marc Rotenberg, eds. *Internet: Technology and Privacy.* Cambridge: The MIT Press, 1998.

Cate, Fred H. *The Internet and the First Amendment: Schools and Sexually Explicit Expression.* Bloomington, IN: Phi Delta Kappa Educational Foundation, 1998.

Gora, Joel M., et al. *The Right to Protest: The Basic ACLU Guide to Free Expression.* Carbondale: Southern Illinois University Press, 1991.

Johnson, John W. *The Struggle for Student Rights: Tinker v. Des Moines and the 1960s.* Lawrence: University Press of Kansas, 1997.

McWhirter, Darien. *Freedom of Speech, Press, and Assembly.* Phoenix, AZ: Oryx Press, 1996.

School Newspapers

Fuller, Sarah Betsy. *Hazelwood v. Kuhlmeier: Censorship in School Newspapers.* Springfield, NJ: Enslow Publishers, Inc., 1998.

Osborn, Patricia. *School Newspaper Adviser's Survival Guide.* New York: Center for Applied Research in Education, 1998.

School Prayer

Alley, Robert S. *Without a Prayer: Religious Expression in Public Schools.* Amherst, NY: Prometheus Books, 1996.

Andryszewski, Tricia. *School Prayer: A History of the Debate.* Springfield, NJ: Enslow Publishers, Inc., 1997.

Stronks, Julia K., and Gloria Goris Stronks. *Christian Teachers in Public Schools: A Guide for Teachers, Administrators, and Parents.* Grand Rapids, MI: Baker Book House, 1999.

Whitehead, John W. *The Rights of Religious Persons in Public Education.* Wheaton, IL: Crossway Books, 1994.

Discipline and Due Process

Bittle, Edgar H. *Due Process for School Officials: A Guide for the Conduct of Administrative Proceedings.* Dayton, OH: Education Law Association, 1987.

Rossow, Lawrence F., and Jacqueline A. Stefkovich. *Search and Seizure in the Public Schools*. Dayton, OH: Education Law Association, 1996.

Schliefer, Jay. *Everything You Need to Know about Weapons in School and at Home*. New York: Rosen Publishing Group, Inc. 1994.

Van Dyke, Jon M., and Melvin M. Sakurai. *Checklists for Searches and Seizures in Public Schools*. Deerfield, IL: Clark, Boardman, Callaghan, 1996.

Sports

Koehler, Mike. *Athletic Director's Survival Guide*. New York: Prentice Hall, Inc., 1997.

Newton, David E. *Drug Testing: An Issue for School, Sports, and Work*. Springfield, NJ: Enslow Publishers, Inc., 1999.

Hastings, Penny. *Sports for Her: A Reference Guide for Teenage Girls*. Westport, CT: Greenwood Press, Inc., 1999.

Students with Disabilities

Anderson, Winifred, et al. *Negotiating the Special Education Maze: A Guide for Parents and Teachers*. Bethesda, MD: Woodbine House, 1997.

Thomas, Stephen B., and Charles J. Russo. *Special Education Law: Issues and Implications for the '90s*. Dayton, OH: Education Law Association, 1995.

Wright, Peter W. D., and Pamela Darr Wright. *Wrightslaw: Special Education Law*. Hartfield, VA: Harbor House Law Press, 1999.

Private and Alternative Schools

Sarason, Seymour Bernard. *Charter Schools: Another Flawed Educational Reform?* New York: Teacher's College Press, 1998.

Shaughnessy, Mary Angela. *Catholic Schools and the Law: A Teacher's Guide*. 2nd ed. Mahwah, NJ: Paulist Press, 2000.

OTHER INFORMATION SOURCES

Organizations

American Civil Liberties Union for Students
125 Broad Street, 18th Floor
New York, NY 10004

(212) 549–2500
E-mail: aclu@aclu.org
Home page: www.aclu.org/students/students

Institute for First Amendment Studies
Box 589
Great Barrington, MA 01230
E-mail: comments@ifas.org
Home page: www.ifas.org

National Center for Youth Law
405 Fourteenth Street, Ste. 1500
Oakland, CA 94612
(510) 835–8098
E-mail: info@youthlaw.org
Home page: www.youthlaw.org

Student Press Law Center
1815 Fort Myer Drive, Ste. 900
Arlington, VA 22209
(703) 807–1904
E-mail: splc@splc.org
Home page: www.splc.org

Online Sources

Coalition for the Separation of Church and State
Home page: www.coalition.freethought.org

English as a Second Language (ESL)
Home page: www.lang.uiuc.edu/r-li5/esl/

Homeschooling Zone
E-mail: webmaster@homeschoolzone.com
Home page: www.homeschoolzone.com

Student Association for Freedom of Expression
Home page: www.mit.edu:8001/activities/safe/home.html

Y-RIGHTS Home Page (school privacy issues)
E-mail: mail to:
listserv@SJUVM)STJOHNS)EDU
body: subscribe y-rights firstname
lastname

—3—

At Home

How much authority do parents have over their children?

Parents have the right to make decisions about what their children eat, wear, read, access on a computer, and watch on TV. They have the right to determine where their children will attend school, what kind of religious training they receive, and who they hang out with. Parents have broad authority to decide how to discipline a minor child. Within certain limits, they can use corporal punishment.

This chapter takes up the rights of young people at home and the extent of their parents' authority.

Why do parents have so much control?

Because the right to have children and to raise them without substantial interference is a paramount right in America. Parents are the "natural guardians" of their children. Over the years, both Congress and the Supreme Court have gone to great lengths to preserve the parent-child relationship.

Minor children are inexperienced and vulnerable to exploitation, and parents are expected to protect them from life's sinister forces. But state and local governments watch out for young people as well. School attendance laws, child labor laws, antipornography legislation, statutory rape laws, and juvenile courts exist to protect minors—from their parents. These types of laws affect the parent-child relationship, regardless of a particular parent's opinions about work, school, sex, "porn," or parental authority.

For more about school attendance laws see Chapter Two, "At School." For more about child labor laws see Chapter Four, "On the Job," and for more about statutory rape see Chapter Eight, "Your Sexual Life."

TEENS, PARENTS, AND MONEY

Does a teen have a right to an allowance?

No. But parents are responsible for a minor child's support until the child reaches the age of majority, and children have a corresponding right to be taken care of.

Does a minor have a legal right to have a part-time or summer job?

No. Parents can legally forbid an unemancipated teen to work for pay outside the home. (Emancipation is discussed in Chapter Five, "On Your Own.")

Are minors legally entitled to keep the money they earn?

Not necessarily. Because parents are entitled to the services of their children, in most states they have a legal right to their children's income. If this idea seems outdated or even wrong, it is because it evolved when children were considered a type of property—when each child was regarded as another hand on the farm. If the minor was earning money instead of contributing to the upkeep of the household, his or her earnings would be the parent's pay for providing care and shelter.

Many states now have laws permitting minors to keep their earnings unless the parents notify the employer that they want to claim the earnings separately. When this happens, the employer must pay the parents, and the parents must declare the earnings on their own tax returns.

If a teen controls his or her money, can the teen independently decide how to spend it?

Again, not necessarily. Parents also have the right to forbid a minor child to buy, for example, a particular book or magazine, video or computer game, or other amusement. They can forbid a child to go to a certain movie or rock concert. They can also make a child's purchase of certain styles of clothes or footwear off-limits.

Is there any way a minor can prevent a parent from taking his or her earnings?

Yes. Parents can agree, orally or in writing, that they have no claim to their child's earnings. Or the minor's right to his or her separate earnings can be understood, although not expressly stated. Nowadays this is almost always the case.

Are teenage children legally required to work in order to help support the family?

No. Parents are required to support their family without assistance from their children. But nothing prevents parents from requiring a teenage child to work at a part-time job. If the teen refuses to look for one, nothing in the law prohibits parents from punishing the teen in a manner that doesn't constitute abuse or neglect.

DISCIPLINE

Can a parent legally throw a teen out of the house?

No. Parents have a legal responsibility to provide for their minor children, including hard-to-handle teens. They must give each child adequate food, shelter, clothing, schooling, and medical care. Parents may never discipline a child in a manner that constitutes physical, sexual, or psychological abuse or use neglect as a form of punishment. In other words, teens have a right to live at home.

If parents don't live up to their responsibilities—if, for example, they force a child to live on the streets—the state can enforce the teen's rights in "abandonment" proceedings in family court. (Abandonment is discussed later in this chapter.)

What should a minor do if his or her parents' discipline methods are obviously too harsh?

Discuss the matter with a teacher, minister, medical person, or adult friend, or call the state child protective agency. Action should be taken immediately.

Can parents legally prevent a child from calling the police in a family violence situation?

No. Anyone can call the police when violence erupts, although sometimes it's impossible to get to the phone before somebody gets hurt. To prevent injury and to subdue the violent family member, the police should always be called—by another family member or by someone outside the family such as a neighbor or relative.

For more information about abuse and neglect at the hands of parents and relatives see Chapter Ten, "Your Right to Be Healthy and Safe from Abuse."

If a minor's parents are divorced, who is legally responsible for the minor's discipline?

Both parents remain responsible. However, unless the parents have joint custody, day-to-day decisions regarding the child are made by the custodial parent. With joint custody, the parents continue to share these responsibilities.

For more about the rights of young persons when parents split up, see Chapter Seven, "If Your Parents Divorce."

If a minor's parents have never married, which parent is responsible for the minor's discipline and care?

Both are, in every state.

Are grandparents or brothers and sisters ever legally responsible for a minor?

Only if the minor's grandparents or his or her siblings have agreed to be responsible. This often happens when a minor's parents are elderly.

TOBACCO

At what age can teens buy tobacco products—cigarettes, chewing tobacco, and snuff?

In most states a person must be age 18 to buy any form of tobacco. Although some states prohibit minors from using tobacco in public places, it usually isn't illegal for a minor just to possess or use it.

Tobacco products are known to cause cancer and other serious diseases, and high schoolers are foolish to spend their earnings on them. It might be wiser to save the money for college, for this reason. In a recent survey the American Cancer Society established that the less education a person has, the more likely he or she is to be a cigarette smoker. An estimated 29.8 percent of those who finish just 12 years of school are smokers. But among those who finish 16 years of school, only 12.3 percent smoke.[1]

ADULT BOOKS AND ADULT MOVIES

Why aren't laws prohibiting the sale of pornography to minors a violation of the First Amendment?

Courts have said that society has a strong interest in preventing children from seeing materials that primarily appeal to "shameful or morbid interests." In the 1968 case of *Ginsburg v. New York*, the Supreme Court upheld a New York law prohibiting the sale of pornographic materials to persons under age 17, even though some of the materials reviewed in the case weren't considered obscene for adults. The Supreme Court said that although there is no sure way to prove that a minor's exposure to pornography is harmful, New York could assume that such a link exists.

Every state controls the sale of "porn" to minors. Furthermore, every state prohibits the production and sale of child pornography, which is visual or printed material that depicts explicit sexual conduct involving children. This type of pornography is often called "kiddie porn." (Some states even make viewing child pornography illegal.)

As a practical matter, isn't a term like "pornography" rather difficult to define?

Yes. A prudish person might consider even mildly suggestive materials to be utterly pornographic, and yet a looser individual might find the same materials harmless or even artistic. In essence, the words "pornography" and "obscene" mean many things to many people.

This range of meaning raises an important legal issue. A law that simply prohibits the sale of "pornography" or "obscene materials" might be too broad to satisfy the First Amendment. Because of the dozens of meanings assigned to these terms, such a law might have the effect of prohibiting the sale of materials that countless citizens, young and old, don't consider obscene at all.

The Supreme Court considered this issue numerous times during the 1960s and 1970s. Ultimately it crafted a definition of pornography in relation to minors. For material to be pornographic to underage persons, the Court said it must (a) primarily appeal to shameful or morbid interests of minors, (b) be offensive to adults with respect to what is proper for minors, and (c) be without any positive social value.

This definition still applies in First Amendment cases relating to the sale of pornography to young people. Incidentally, one justice on a leading pornography case is rumored to have said that he probably couldn't define pornography, but he certainly recognized it when he saw it!

Can minors buy or rent obscene and so-called "slasher" videos?
States and cities can legally prohibit this also.

For more about First Amendment rights under the federal Constitution see Chapter Two, "At School."

Can a minor go to an X-rated movie?
Communities usually have laws prohibiting minors from attending X-rated films, but these laws aren't always vigorously enforced. Furthermore, a theater will rarely turn away a minor because a film is violent or sexually explicit but not X-rated. Parents do, however, have the power to forbid their children to go to all types of movies under their authority as parents.

X-rated films are sometimes referred to as NC-17-rated films.

THE AGE OF MAJORITY

What is meant by the term "the age of majority"?
It is the age at which a person legally becomes an adult. The age of majority is 18 in every state except Alabama, Mississippi, Nebraska, and Wyoming.[2]

When a young person reaches the age of majority, does all parental authority end?
Yes, but this doesn't mean the young person is entitled to all the rights of adulthood. For example, it is illegal in most states to purchase or drink alcoholic beverages before age 21, regardless of the state's legis-

lated age of majority. In addition, states have the power to set a higher legal age for special activities such as voting in local elections and serving on a jury.

What rights does a young person gain at the age of majority?

The right to work at almost any job, marry or enlist in the armed forces without parental consent, enter into all types of contracts, consent to all types of health care, and buy adult books. On the other hand, at the age of majority a minor no longer is subject to the "jurisdiction" of the juvenile court.

Can parents' legal responsibilities toward their children ever extend beyond the age of majority?

Yes, but these extensions occur in connection with divorce decrees and custody agreements and not by virtue of public laws. For example, a custody decree might require a parent to pay for a child's college education through age 24.

In a recent Ohio case a divorce court made a well-to-do father pay for his 19-year-old son's $17,000 education at a local technical school. The court interpreted the divorce decree to require this, even though it stated that the father had to pay for his son's *college* education.

A young person with divorced parents is rarely in a position to make the parents pay for college if the divorce decree doesn't order it. This is partly because a young person usually can't afford a lawyer. However, a divorced parent might be willing to co-sign or guarantee for a higher education loan.

LEGAL GUARDIANS

If parents can't care for their minor children, who helps out?

Usually it depends on factors such as the age of the children and the parents' financial worth. If the parents don't have much in savings, the children are often cared for by relatives, particularly if the children are older. Sometimes this type of relationship presents difficulties if parental consent is needed for medical care.

If a minor child is quite young or needs special treatment, a family court might appoint a "legal guardian" to be responsible for the child.

The adult files a petition in the local family court to obtain his or her appointment. The petitioner is often a sibling or other relative.

Once appointed, the guardian makes decisions about the minor's overall care and discipline, plus his or her education, medical care, and religious life. The "ward" almost always lives with the guardian. The appointment doesn't relieve the parents of their legal duty of support, however, and usually the guardian is entitled to be paid for serving.

Unlike a court-appointed foster parent or custodian in abuse or neglect cases, neither the parents nor the child need to have gotten in trouble for a guardian to be appointed. Guardians also serve when parents have died, can't be found, or don't reside with the child for some other reason.

Again in contrast to custody proceedings involving a child either at risk or in trouble with the law, the state's involvement in a guardianship diminishes after the appointment is made. This means the legal guardian isn't under the continuing supervision of the family court. Even so, a guardian is considered an "officer of the court" and must act in "the best interests of the child."

Does a minor have to obey a guardian?

Yes, unless the guardian asks the minor to do something illegal. The specific powers of legal guardians are always spelled out in state law.

How long does a guardianship last?

Until the minor reaches the age of majority, unless the court believes it should continue longer. A guardianship might be extended beyond the age of majority if, for example, the young person can't manage in the adult world because of a physical or mental disability.

Can a teen arrange for an elderly parent's medical care?

No. As a rule, a doctor can't treat a sick or injured adult without his or her consent. If a parent is unable to consent to treatment, only a spouse or adult child may legally do so. But nothing prevents a minor from calling an emergency medical team to help a sick or injured parent, and nothing prevents a minor from arranging for a parent to be taken to the emergency room for immediate care.

If a person, young or old, needs emergency treatment, that person's consent is legally *presumed*. This is why doctors and medics may give treatment in an emergency without obtaining consent from anyone.

TERMINATION OF PARENTS' RIGHTS

In cases of serious abuse or neglect, can parental rights be terminated completely?

Yes, although to do so, the situation at home must appear hopeless. When parental rights are terminated, the parent-child relationship ends by court order. Once this happens, a parent has no legal right to see his or her child or know the child's whereabouts. This makes termination of parental rights dramatically different from custody and foster parent arrangements. (For more about the circumstances in which the state can take custody of a minor, see Chapter Ten, "Your Right to Be Healthy and Safe from Abuse.")

Parents' rights are most often terminated when they have abused, neglected, or abandoned a minor child on a consistent basis.

What is abandonment?

In contrast to "neglect," abandonment is a *conscious* failure to perform parental responsibilities. Examples of abandonment include failing to keep in contact with a minor child; failing to provide care, love, and affection for a child; leaving a child with another person for a long time for no good reason; failing to provide support for a child; and totally ignoring a child in foster care. Abandonment most definitely is a cause for terminating parental rights.

Abandonment doesn't require that a parent have left the child on the steps of the local orphanage. (Only a few orphanages still exist in the U.S. in any event.) In fact, family courts are more willing to declare an abandonment than in years past. They now look for facts showing "disinterest and total lack of concern" for the child. Courts are less likely to hold parental rights sacred when the parents have obviously and deliberately ceased to care. Claims of parental love and affection don't hold much weight in such circumstances.

Sometimes a parent isn't really at fault for the unfortunate situation. A serious physical or emotional illness might explain the apparent lack of concern. When this happens, foster care or a legal guardianship is frequently the court's first course of action.

Will a court only terminate parental rights when the child is an infant?

No. It often happens in the case of teens.

Can the state seek to terminate the parental rights of one parent but not the other?

Yes. This often happens.

Why might the state seek to terminate parental rights in some cases but not others?

Because the focus of a termination case isn't just a parent's current inability to provide care, but whether his or her obligations can be fulfilled in the years ahead. If the parent's problem is serious but not hopeless, the child protective agency might take custody of the child and possibly make a foster care placement.

Must the state assist a family with its problems before it can terminate parental rights?

Yes. Usually the family court or child protective agency will require the parent (or parents) to undergo counseling or take parenting classes. Here the goal is to keep the family intact. If the parent fails to cooperate or rehabilitation doesn't prove worthwhile, the state can initiate termination proceedings in family court. Counseling can be skipped if it would obviously be a waste of time.

In most states a family court will terminate parental rights only if the parent has already been separated from the child for six months to one year.

Does a parent have any constitutional rights in a termination case?

Yes. Parental rights can be terminated only if "due process of law"—a full hearing in family court—has been provided. Furthermore, the parent must receive plenty of advance notice of the hearing in order to have time to prepare a case opposing the termination. Of course, the parent's goal will be to retain or resume custody of the child.

Most states provide legal counsel for poor parents in termination cases. However, the right to counsel may depend on the complexity of the case and whether the parent faces criminal charges (such as abuse or neglect charges) in connection with the parent-child relationship.

What must the state prove in order to terminate parental rights?

It must present facts establishing one or more of the following situations: extreme disinterest in a child, extreme or repeated neglect or abuse, severe deterioration of the parent-child relationship, failure to show an ability to care about the child, and failure to improve an already serious family situation. Also, the state must prove that severing the bonds between parent and child are in the best interests of the child. The state must prove its case by "clear and convincing evidence," which is a higher burden of proof than in most other civil cases.

Obviously, a state can only sever these bonds in very grave cases. In most, the state will already have the child in custody or foster care, and it probably will have intervened on previous occasions. In fact, revoking parental rights of one or both parents after a first incident is unusual, and in some states it is illegal. Again, see Chapter Ten to read about "dependency" actions to protect young people.

Is a minor entitled to a lawyer in a termination of parental rights case?

In certain states, yes.

Can parents give up parental rights voluntarily?

Yes. This actually is the way parental rights are most often terminated. When a minor child is placed for adoption, the child's "birth parents" already will have agreed to give up parental rights.

Can parental rights be terminated because the parents don't have enough money—are too "indigent"—to raise the child?

The rights of indigent parents can be terminated only if there is a serious reason besides poverty to justify terminating their rights. Such a reason might be abandonment or consistent abuse. Failure to support a minor child will rarely be the sole reason for terminating parental rights, especially if the parent and child are close.

Can parental rights be terminated because the parent has been convicted of a serious crime?

Yes. Some states also permit parental rights to be terminated if a parent has been convicted in adult court of "debauchery" or "fornication" or if the parent has been involved in prostitution.

Can parental rights be terminated because a parent is mentally ill or has some other emotional disability?

In some states, yes, but only if the mental problem is so serious that the parent is unable to care for the child. These days, many mental disorders (even grave ones such as schizophrenia) can be treated with medications and therapy. For this reason, a family court's ruling that a parent is mentally disabled, without strong proof that he or she isn't fit to parent, won't be sufficient to terminate parental rights.

Can the parent-child relationship be terminated because the minor child would be better off in another situation such as a calmer household with fewer problems?

This is a tough question. Family courts don't exist to find perfect homes for minors—their purpose has always been to protect young persons in danger. Parents have a fundamental right to raise their children; they don't have a legal obligation to be models of parenthood.

Even so, courts in some states have considered using the child's "best-interests" as the only basis for terminating parental rights. When this approach is used, the state doesn't have to show that a parent repeatedly committed a serious wrong such as child abuse or abandonment. It has to prove only that the child would be better off in other circumstances.

Earlier Supreme Court decisions suggest that states may violate the federal Constitution if they allow parental rights to be terminated without proof that the parents truly are unfit. Before long, the Supreme Court may have to decide whether parental rights can be lawfully terminated simply because the child's "best interests" aren't being served.

OTHER FAMILY ISSUES

Can a minor carry or use a firearm or other weapon with parental consent? Without parental consent?

The answer to the first question is a qualified yes. Federal, state, and local laws govern the possession and use of weapons. Federal law prohibits the sale of handguns to persons under age 21 and the sale of rifles and shotguns to persons under age 18. A minor can receive a handgun as a gift but can't legally buy ammunition until age 21.

States and cities regulate weapons within their borders, and the scope of their laws always includes the possession and use of firearms by young people. In most states a minor can carry a handgun only if he or she has written permission from a parent. But even in these states, if a law forbids weapons in certain places such as a retail store or public auditorium, or if a high school forbids weapons on school grounds, parental permission will never make the weapon legal.

Recent illegal uses of handguns and other firearms by minors have focused national attention on the weapons issue. As a result of tragic incidents involving minors at school in the late 1990s, federal and state gun laws are likely to become more restrictive.

Can a minor legally take illegal drugs at home or elsewhere with parental permission?
Never.

NOTES

1. American Cancer Society, National Health Interview Survey, 1994.
2. In Alabama, Nebraska, and Wyoming, the age of majority is 19. In Mississippi it is 21.

FOR FURTHER READING

In General

American Bar Association Guide to Family Law. New York: Times Books, 1996.

Barber, Nigel. *Why Parents Matter: Parental Investment and Child Outcomes*. Westport, CT: Bergin & Garvey, 2000.

Forman, Deborah. *Every Parent's Guide to the Law*. New York: Harcourt, Brace & Company, 1998.

Guggenheim, Martin, et al. *The Rights of Families: The Authoritative Guide to the Rights of Family Members Today (ACLU)*. Carbondale: Southern Illinois University Press, 1996.

Packer, Alex J. *Bringing Up Parents: The Teenager's Handbook*. Minneapolis: Free Spirit Publishing, 1992.

Wolf, Anthony E. *Get Out of My Life: A Parent's Guide to the New Teenager*. New York: Noonday Press, 1992.

Money

Bijlefeld, Marjolijn, and Sharon K. Zoumbaris. *Teen Guide to Personal Financial Management*. Westport, CT: Greenwood Press, 2000.

Bodnar, Janet. *Dollars and Sense for Kids*. New York: Kiplinger Books, 1999.

Covey, Sean. *The 7 Habits of Highly Effective Teens: The Ultimate Teenage Success Guide*. New York: Simon & Schuster, Inc., 1998.

Erlbach, Arlene. *If Your Family Is on Welfare*. New York: Rosen Publishing Group, Inc., 1998.

Tobacco

Griffin, Patrick. *Let's Ban Smoking Outright!* Berkeley: Ten Speed Press, 1995.

Wekesser, Carol. *Smoking*. San Diego: Greenhaven Press, 1996.

Adult Books and Movies

Jasper, Margaret C. *The Law of Obscenity and Pornography*. Dobbs Ferry, NY: Oceana Publications, Inc., 1996.

Hawkins, Gordon J., and Franklin E. Zimring. *Pornography in a Free Society*. New York: Cambridge University Press, 1991.

Hixson, Richard F. *Pornography and the Justices: The Supreme Court and the Intractable Obscenity Problem*. Carbondale: Southern Illinois University Press, 1996.

Legal Guardians

Field, George W. *Legal Relations of Infants, Parent and Child and Guardian and Ward*. New York: William S. Hein & Company, Inc., 1981.

Shapiro, Michael. *Solomon's Sword: Two Families and the Children the State Took Away*. New York: Times Books, 1999.

Guns

Gottlieb, Alan M. *Gun Rights Fact Book*. Bellevue, WA: Merril Press, 1998.

Kates, Don B., Jr., and Gary Kleck. *The Great American Gun Debate*. San Francisco: Pacific Resource Institute for Public Policy, 1997.

Roleff, Tamara. *Gun Control: Current Controversies*. San Diego: Greenhaven Press, 1997.

Schliefer, Jay. *Everything You Need to Know about Weapons in School and at Home*. New York: Rosen Publishing Group, Inc., 1994.

OTHER INFORMATION SOURCES

Organizations

Americans for a Society Free from Age Restrictions (ASFAR)
E-mail: asfar@oblivion.net
Home page: www.asfar.org

National Guardianship Association, Inc.
1604 North Country Club Road
Tucson, AZ 85716
(520) 881–6561
Home page: www.guardianship.org

Parents Anonymous
675 West Foothills Boulevard, Ste. 220
Claremont, CA 91711
(909) 621–6184
E-mail: mailto:
parentsanon@msn.com
Home page: www.parentsanonymous-natl.org

Teens 411—National Help Resources
Streetcats Foundation
Box 191396
San Francisco, CA 94119
Home page: www.child.net/teenhelp

Online Sources

Parenting Today's Teen
Home page: www.parentingteens.com

U.S. Bureau of Alcohol, Tobacco and Firearms
Home Page: www.atf.treas.gov

— 4 —

On the Job

At what age can a young person work outside the home?

It depends on the type of work. At age 18, any person can be employed at any job. However, federal and state child labor laws regulate the types of work that persons under 18 can legally perform.

Young people under age 18 can't be hired for work that is hazardous, such as work in mines, steel mills, quarries, foundries, and butcher shops. Working with explosives, dangerous chemicals, radioactive materials, power-driven machinery, and earth-moving equipment is also off limits for those under 18.

Persons under age 16 almost always are prohibited from working in factories unless the job involves office work. Teens between the ages of 14 and 16 are permitted to work only after school, on weekends, and during vacation and aren't allowed to hold jobs that are dangerous or unhealthy. They can do office and sales work, wait on tables, be shelvers and baggers at retail stores, and hold similar positions.

Minors above age 12 (above age 10 in some states) can have newspaper routes and work as golf caddies, but only during nonschool hours. They can also do yard work, babysit, and perform certain types of nonhazardous farm work. As a rule, children under age 12 can't work outside the home, although special child labor laws in each state permit minors of any age to do stage and screen work.

Can a minor work full-time?

In most states, minors between 14 and 16 are prohibited from working more than 40 hours per week. Furthermore, this age group can't work for more than three hours on school days and more than eight hours on nonschool days and during the summer.

Minors between the ages of 14 and 16 also are prohibited from working the "graveyard shift"—between 9:30 P.M. and 7:00 A.M. In some states, however, teens can work these hours if school isn't in session the next day.

Couldn't a teen just lie about his or her age to be hired for a particular job?

No, because in most states, job applicants under age 16 (under age 18 in some states) must present an "employment certificate" or other proof of age in order to be hired.

Who issues employment certificates?

If state law requires them, the superintendent of schools usually is the issuer. To obtain an employment certificate, the minor must be able to produce:

1. a statement from the prospective employer describing the type of work;
2. a statement that the minor's parents don't object to the job;
3. a birth certificate or other proof of age; and
4. a statement, signed by a doctor, that the minor is physically fit for the job.

Employment certificates are called "work permits" in some states.

Is it illegal for a minor to work without an employment certificate?

If one is required, yes. In states that require them, an employer can't hire a young person who is unable to produce one.

Who, then, is regulated by child labor laws—the minor or the employer?

The employer. When a federal or state child labor law is violated, the employer commits the offense.

Can the government punish a minor for working without an employment certificate—or for working underage if a certificate isn't required?
No.

What kinds of jobs don't require an employment certificate?
An employment certificate isn't needed for farm work, babysitting, yard work, selling newspapers, and golf caddying.

Can an employment certificate be revoked?
Yes, if the minor's job interferes with school work or adversely affects his or her physical or mental health. The school principal usually is the person with the power to revoke.

Does a minor need a Social Security card to work outside the home?
Yes. A person's Social Security card shows his or her lifetime Social Security number. Employers need their employees' Social Security numbers to make advance Social Security payments and income tax deposits to the federal government in their employees' behalf. Employers are legally required to make these payments, which is why they always ask for a person's Social Security number at the time of hiring.

Who issues Social Security cards?
The local Social Security Administration office. To obtain a card, call the closest office and ask to be sent a Social Security card application. Fill it out, have a parent sign it, then send it back with an original copy of your birth certificate and one of the other forms of identification requested on the application. Your Social Security card will arrive in about two weeks.

Can minors who aren't U.S. citizens legally work here?
It depends on whether the minor has the required legal documentation. To be legally eligible for work, a person born abroad—an "alien"—must at least have a "visa." The various types of visas are issued by the Immigration and Naturalization Service, or INS.

An INS immigrant visa permits an alien to live in the United States for a work-related purpose. Obtaining this type of visa is often an alien's first step towards getting a "green card." Because there are many types of visas, an alien who wants to work here should consult an INS agent or other immigration expert to determine the best visa for his or her job skills.

It is a violation of federal law to hire an illegal alien. However, it is also a violation of federal law for an employer to discriminate on the basis of nationality or noncitizen status, provided the alien has a right, by virtue of his or her visa or green card, to work in this country.

What is a "green card"?

A green card is the document needed by aliens to travel to and from the U.S. and to work here legally and without restrictions. Although its official name is the "Alien Registration Receipt Card," everybody uses the term "green card." When it was introduced in the 1940s, the ID card with the alien's photo, registration number, birth date, entry date, and port of entry was green. However, the cards were changed to blue in the 1960s and 1970s, to white in the 1980s, and in the 1990s they became pink. Even so, it's still a "green card."

THE MINIMUM WAGE

Are minors entitled to the minimum wage?

Yes. Congress increased the minimum wage to $5.15 per hour in 1997. However, the 1997 legislation provides that anyone under age 20 may be paid $4.25 per hour as a training wage for three months. The Fair Labor Standards Act, or FLSA, makes these requirements.

Most states have minimum wage laws as well. When an employer is covered by both federal and state minimum wage laws, employees must be paid the higher of the two minimum wages.

Are certain jobs outside the minimum wage laws?

Yes. "Exempt" positions such as executive and professional positions aren't covered because persons with these types of jobs usually aren't paid by the hour. Certain administrative positions are also exempt. The best way to find out whether a job is exempt is to call the local Wage and Hour Division of the Department of Labor.

Do people have to work full-time to receive the minimum wage?
No.

Are tips treated as wages under the minimum wage laws?
In some cases, yes. If a worker normally receives more than $30 per month in tips, the employer may credit the worker's total tips toward his or her pay. But this "tip credit" can't exceed 40 percent of the minimum wage, multiplied by the number of hours the worker put in during the month.

Can minors draw overtime pay?
No, but this is because most minors can't legally work more than 40 hours per week.

Under the FLSA, hourly employees must be paid extra for each hour worked over 40 in any week. The overtime rate is 1½ times the worker's regular hourly rate. But under state child labor laws, persons under age 16 can't work more than 40 hours per week, and persons under age 18 who attend school can't work more than 3 hours on school days and 8 hours on nonschool days. Because of these limits, minors usually don't qualify for overtime pay.

SUMMER JOBS

Can teens work full-time during the summer?
Yes, but only up to 40 hours per week under federal and state child labor laws. Although the FLSA's minimum wage and overtime rules don't apply to certain seasonal work such as jobs at resorts, summer camps, and swimming pools, the 40-hour-per-week limit nevertheless does.

For more about part-time and summer jobs see "Teens, Parents, and Money" in Chapter Three.

THE OBLIGATIONS AND BENEFITS OF EMPLOYMENT

What do employee and employer "owe" one another?
Every employee has a duty to work hard, be loyal, follow the employer's rules and directions, and work for the employer and no one else

while on the job. In return, the employer must pay the employee for performing his or her job and refrain from discriminating against the employee because of race, color, nationality, gender, age, or religion with respect to pay, promotions, and working conditions. These duties and obligations apply across the board—to teens as well as adults.

What are "fringe benefits"? Are minors entitled to them?

A fringe benefit is any benefit other than pay that an employee receives for working. Examples of fringe benefits are paid holidays, paid or unpaid vacation time, maternity and sick leave, and pensions.

If an employer provides fringe benefits to adult workers, minors are entitled to them also. But employers usually restrict fringe benefits to full-time nonseasonal employees, so most minors aren't able to qualify for them.

What is a pension? Can a minor be in a pension plan?

A pension is a payment from a "pension plan" or "retirement plan," which is, in turn, a company program for setting aside money for employees and their spouses for their later years. The federal Social Security program is a retirement program. Because employers aren't required to established and maintain their own pension or retirement plans, Social Security is the only retirement program that many American workers ever participate in.

Company pension plans are governed by complex federal laws. Under a company plan, either the employer makes a yearly contribution to the employee's pension account or the employee makes a yearly contribution and the employer matches it. The accounts are invested and reinvested over the years. Unless the employee quits, he or she doesn't receive any payments from the pension plan until retiring.

Nothing prohibits an employer from including minors in a pension plan. But if eligibility in the plan is based on age and length of service (as almost always happens), under federal law the employer doesn't have to let employees participate until they reach age 25 and work at least 1,000 hours in 12 months. This means that although the law doesn't prohibit minors from participating, the terms of the plan rarely permit it.

Is health insurance a fringe benefit? Are employers required to provide health insurance for their employees?

Health insurance is indeed a fringe benefit, and a very important one. It pays an employee's medical expenses (or a large part of them) and often pays the medical expenses of the employee's family. An illness or injury doesn't have to be job-related to be covered by employer-provided health insurance.

Although employers aren't required to provide health insurance for their workers, many believe that federal law should require employers to cover at least their full-time people.

What is workers' compensation?

It is a payment from an employer that "compensates" an employee for medical expenses and time off due to a job-related injury or illness. In this respect it differs from employer-provided health insurance.

The amount of wage compensation normally is a percentage of the disabled person's regular pay. If a job-related injury results in the loss of a body part such as a hand or foot, the employee usually receives a lump sum based on a payment schedule. The more serious the loss, the greater the lump sum.

Workers' compensation is "no-fault," which means that an employee can qualify for it regardless of who, if anyone, was at fault for the injury or illness. The problem—the "disability"—just has to be job-related. But the employer also benefits: under a workers' compensation program, an employee cannot demand and receive additional payment for "pain and suffering" and can't receive "punitive damages." For more about damages resulting from an injury or illness see Chapter Seventeen, "Taking Matters to Court."

The laws of most states provide workers' compensation. Depending on the state, workers' compensation payments are made by an insurance company, the employer, or the state where the employee works.

Are minors entitled to workers' compensation benefits?

Minors as well as adults can receive workers' compensation. Extra benefits are often payable if the injured person is a minor who was employed in violation of a child labor law.

What should a minor do if he or she is injured on the job?

Report the accident to the employer right away. In turn, the employer must report it to the state workers' compensation board. All employers are required by law to post reporting and filing requirements at an easy-to-find location at work.

IF YOU LOSE YOUR JOB

Can an employer fire an employee for "no good reason"? Does it depend on whether the employee is a minor?

If an employee hasn't entered into a written contract with the employer to work a certain length of time or for a specific purpose, that person is an "employee at will." Employees at will can be fired or laid off for any reason and at any time, so long as the reason doesn't violate "public policy." In fact, an employee at will can be fired for no apparent reason at all.

These rules apply to employees of all ages. But since minors are almost always hired as employees at will, they usually can be fired for what may seem like no good reason.

Does the law ever prohibit an employer from firing an employee?

Yes. Title VII of the Civil Rights Act of 1964 prohibits employers from dismissing an employee solely for reasons of race, color, gender, age, national origin, or religion. If an employee is in any one of these "protected classes," Title VII requires that if the employee is discharged, it must be for the same reason or type of conduct that workers not in a protected class can be discharged for.

Three other landmark items of legislation also prohibit employers from firing an employee. First, the Americans with Disabilities Act prohibits discrimination in hiring and firing for no other reason than the existence of a disability; second, the Age Discrimination in Employment Act prohibits an employer from firing an employee for no other reason than that the employee is over age 40; and third, the National Labor Relations Act prohibits an employer from firing an employee for either joining a union or refusing to join one. Also, an employee can't be fired for refusing to perform an unlawful act at work, for reporting a violation of the law, or for filing a workers' compensation claim.

Discrimination on the job is discussed later in this chapter.

If a minor gets fired, can he or she collect "unemployment"?

In some cases, yes. Unemployment compensation is a weekly payment that is meant to hold people over until they find another job. Unemployment compensation is a matter of federal law, although the states administer the system.

Some unemployed persons simply don't qualify. To be eligible, an applicant must have held a job for a specific number of weeks before being let go, and he or she must be actively looking for new work. In addition, the employee cannot have quit or have been fired for misconduct.

Minors aren't prohibited from receiving unemployment compensation, but part-time employees and persons under age 14 don't qualify. (Part-time work includes work after school and during summer vacation.) For this reason, minors who are still in school usually can't collect it.

Each state has an unemployment office with detailed information available about how the system works.

INCOME TAXES

Do minors have to pay income taxes?
Yes. Everyone who has an income may have to pay income taxes, even babies. A person's income may take the form of wages, dividends from corporate stock, or a debt that has just been forgiven.

Income taxes are imposed by the federal government and most states. Annual federal and state tax returns for the previous calendar year and any unpaid taxes are due from every individual taxpayer on April 15.

To ensure that income taxes are paid, both the federal government and the states require employers to "withhold" certain amounts from their employees' pay. The employer then pays the withholding amount to the government. The payment serves as an advance deposit against income taxes owed by the employee.

Employers must withhold Social Security (FICA) taxes and federal unemployment (FUTA) taxes in addition to state and local income taxes. These withholding amounts are paid to the federal government.

Does this mean a minor's pay is subject to withholding?
Unfortunately, yes.

What happens if the taxes withheld during the year turn out to be more than the total taxes owed?
The taxpayer shows the amount of the overpayment on his or her annual tax return. If the "taxing entity" agrees with the taxpayer, the excess is refunded. So even if a person doesn't earn enough in a calendar

year to have an income tax liability, returns are required in order to obtain the refunds owed.

Are FICA and FUTA withholdings ever refundable, either in whole or in part?
No.

Is babysitting money taxable? How about money earned delivering newspapers?
Although earnings from babysitting and paper routes are types of income that are taxable under federal and state tax laws, most teens don't earn enough from these pursuits to have to pay taxes on the money they take in. Even so, teens should let their parents know when their earnings from babysitting, delivering newspapers, and similar part-time jobs have exceeded $500 in any single year.

PRIVACY

Can a minor be required to submit to a drug or urine test as a condition of employment?
Yes. A private employer can require all job applicants to be tested for drugs and also can make periodic, random drug testing a condition of continued employment. But employers can't legally test either employees or job applicants for human immunodeficiency virus/acquired immunodeficiency syndrome (HIV/AIDS) without their explicit permission.

Government employees enjoy greater privacy protections. A drug or urine test by a governmental employer would be considered a "search and seizure" under the federal Constitution and would therefore need to satisfy the Fourth Amendment's "reasonableness" standard in order to be legal.

The results of drug and urine tests must remain confidential.

Can an employer legally require an employee to submit to a search?
Yes. Employers sometimes search employees or their personal belongings to prevent theft, seek evidence of suspected theft, or prevent

drugs and weapons from coming onto company property. On-the-job searches are usually legal. There isn't much an employee can do about a search provided it isn't too "invasive."

Both minors and adults can be searched. Again, government employees enjoy more privacy protections, due to the Fourth Amendment's search and seizure rules.

Can an employer legally enforce rules relating to employees' clothes or hairstyles?

Yes. It is almost always legal for an employer to forbid a certain style of dress or hairstyle, provided the rule doesn't discriminate on the basis of gender. An employer can require a particular uniform and type of footwear for the job, can prohibit excessive jewelry, and can require that tattoos be covered up. For more about related issues see Chapter Six, "Your Personal Appearance."

Can an employer legally use a video camera to monitor a working employee? Can an employer legally monitor telephone conversations between its employees and third parties?

The answer to both questions is yes.

Can an employer legally access an employee's e-mail, voice mail, or private computer files?

At present, no federal laws limit an employer's activities in these areas. However, state legislatures have begun to look at these issues extensively.

Many employers address the issues of e-mail, voice mail, and computers in their employee handbooks, particularly when these technologies are able to be used by employees for personal matters as well as for work. To learn about your employer's position on these issues, look first to the employee handbook. If the answers to your questions aren't addressed, don't be afraid to pose them to a supervisor or human resource person.

On the other hand, it wouldn't be wise to test the legal waters by sending a sexually explicit electronic message to someone from your computer at work.

DISCRIMINATION IN EMPLOYMENT

What, if anything, prevents an employer from discriminating against employees and job applicants?

Important federal legislation, including Title VII of the Civil Rights Act of 1964 and the Americans with Disabilities Act or ADA. These laws make it illegal for employers to discriminate at work on the basis of race, color, religion, gender, age, national origin, or disability. Title VII and the ADA apply to hiring, firing, promotions, pay, and benefits.

But Title VII and the ADA don't require employers to hire people who aren't qualified for a particular position or to keep people who can't handle the work. Nor do these laws prohibit employers from basing differences in pay on job performance or length of service. Pay differences based on these reasons are actually examples of *lawful* discrimination.

For Title VII to be violated, must the employer have intended to discriminate against the job applicant or employee?

No. For example, if an employer requires all applicants to take a test to determine who has a particular job skill, and members of a racial minority consistently perform worse than others, a court may declare the test discriminatory because it has the effect of screening out a Title VII "protected class." The impact of the test would be illegal, even if it appeared fair on its face.

In this situation the employer must prove that a job-related purpose justifies the test—that the skills being tested for are needed for the successful operation of the business. In addition, the employer must show that no other testing method would have a less discriminatory impact. If this can't be proved—if the employer can't carry its "burden of proof"— the test must be either revamped or discontinued.

Is it illegal to discriminate against young persons on the basis of age?

No. Federal law doesn't prohibit discrimination against persons under age 40. The reason is that young people don't have a history of being unfairly discriminated against—in contrast to women, the elderly, and racial and ethnic minorities. However, some state laws prohibit discrimination against age groups that aren't covered by federal legislation.

What racial groups are protected by Title VII?

All racial groups, including blacks, whites, Asians, Hispanics, and American Indians.

What is "reverse discrimination"? Is it legal?

Reverse discrimination occurs when an employer gives an unfair advantage to a class of people who have historically been discriminated against—blacks or women, for example. It occurs when a person is hired for a job or promoted because of minority status and not because he or she is the best candidate or has the best job record.

Reverse discrimination is prohibited under Title VII when it illegally favors a Title VII protected class. For more about discrimination issues see Chapter Thirteen, "Age, Race, and Sex Discrimination."

What then is "affirmative action"?

Affirmative action occurs when an employer hires or promotes an employee in a manner that *legally* favors a protected class. For example, it would be legal for an employer to recruit black candidates to *compete* for a particular job, or set hiring goals to place women in positions in which they have been underrepresented.

Can a woman be discriminated against because she is pregnant? Because she is pregnant and unmarried?

The answer to both questions is no. A 1978 amendment to Title VII makes it illegal to discriminate at the workplace on the basis of pregnancy, childbirth, or a related medical condition such as abortion. In other words, and employer must treat a pregnant woman or a woman with a related condition the same as other employees, based on her ability to work.

These rules apply to minors as well as adults.

Can a teenage parent take paternity or maternity leave without placing his or her job at risk?

It very much depends on the circumstances. The federal Family and Medical Leave Act, or FMLA, permits a parent—either a father or mother—to take leave from work to care for a newborn child or tend to a family medical emergency, under certain conditions.

Under the FMLA, if an employee has worked at least 1,250 full-time hours for the employer in the last 12 months, he or she may take up to 12 weeks of unpaid leave to care for a newborn without losing his or her job. The employer must employ at least 50 people for the FMLA to apply. Because of these conditions, many teenage parents fail to qualify for leave in connection with the birth of a child and therefore risk their jobs if they take time off.

However, a father does not have to be married to the newborn's mother to take paternity leave under the FMLA.

Some states have their own laws regarding maternity and paternity leave that apply when the FMLA doesn't. Check with a librarian to learn more about state laws relating to family leave.

What is sexual harassment?

It is any unwelcome sexual advance, a request for a sexual favor, or any other words or actions of a sexual type that interfere with work, especially if submitting to or rejecting the advance or request becomes the basis for a job-related decision. If the behavior is really unwelcome, it doesn't matter that the employee may have eventually decided to put up with it to save his or her job.

Sexual harassment is illegal discrimination under Title VII.

Consider this clear example of illegal sexual harassment. In a 1987 Colorado case, a court found that a woman had been illegally harassed by a job supervisor after he reached across her lap when they were in a company car, rubbed her thigh, and said, "I think you're going to make it here." Not long after, another supervisor at the same job approached the woman, patted her on the buttocks, and said, "I'm going to get you yet."

If an employer knows or has reason to know that sexual harassment of an employee is going on and doesn't do anything about it, both the person causing the harassment and the employer can be found responsible.

Consider another example. In a 1991 California case a woman who was being bothered by a male co-worker received a note from him that read:

I cried over you last night and I'm totally drained today. I have never been in such constant term oil [sic]. Thank you for talking with me. I could not stand to feel your hatred for another day.

After the woman complained, the co-worker was transferred out of town. But a few months later he was transferred back to the local office and began harassing her again. Finally the woman brought sexual harassment charges against her employer (which happened to be the Internal Revenue Service), as well as the co-worker.

Can discriminatory sexual harassment occur between persons of the same sex?

For years this area of the law was unsettled. In 1998, however, the Supreme Court ruled in *Oncale v. Sundowner Offshore Services, Inc.* that discriminatory sexual harassment on the job can occur between persons of the same sex.

If a young person believes he or she has been discriminated against at work or in applying for a job, what can be done?

Sometimes the matter can be resolved by talking to the hiring person, the supervisor, or another individual in charge. If this doesn't help, the "complainant" may file a charge against the employer with the local Equal Employment Opportunity Commission or state civil rights office. Many cases are settled at this level. If no settlement is reached, the complainant at that point is granted the right to sue the employer in court.

If a young person is being sexually harassed at work, he or she should tell the harasser to stop. Also, he or she should keep an accurate written record of the harassing incidents including the date, time, and place they occurred and the names of any witnesses. Again, the supervisor should be notified.

This area of law is complex, and it constantly changes. If a person, regardless of age, believes he or she has been illegally discriminated against in connection with work or sexually harassed, it is best to discuss the matter with a parent, who may want to contact a lawyer versed in employment law. This can be expensive, so most communities have legal service organizations that provide help with discrimination and civil rights cases at low cost.

What does a complainant have to prove in order to win a Title VII job discrimination case (other than a sexual harassment case)?

These four things:

1. That the complainant belongs to a "protected class"—an ethnic minority, for example.

2. That the complainant applied for and was qualified for a position that the employer wanted to fill, or for a promotion.

3. That despite these qualifications, the complainant was denied the position or the promotion.

4. That after the person was rejected, the employer continued to seek applications, and didn't change the job qualifications.

JOB SAFETY

Are employers required to provide a safe place to work?

Yes, although this wasn't always the case. Under the federal Occupational Safety and Health Act or OSHA, and also under state laws, employers must maintain a workplace that is safe and healthy for employees.

What should a person do if working conditions on the job appear unsafe?

Workers exposed to health or safety hazards have the right under OSHA to ask the employer to correct the problem, or to report it to the closest OSHA office. Workers also have the right to talk privately to OSHA inspectors about what appear to be health and safety hazards. Under federal law, it is illegal for an employer to punish or discriminate against any worker who exercises these rights.

FOR FURTHER READING

In General

Clymer, John F. *The Triangle Strike and Fire.* New York: Harcourt, Brace & Company, 1997.

Covington, Robert N., and Kurt H. Decker. *Individual Employee Rights.* St. Paul: West Publishing Company, 1995.

Fick, Barbara J. *The American Bar Association Guide to Workplace Law.* New York: Times Books, 1997.

Friedan, Betty, and Brigid O'Farrell. *Beyond Gender: The New Politics of Work and Family.* Baltimore: Woodrow Wilson Center Press/Johns Hopkins University Press, 1997.

O'Neil, Robert M. *The Rights of Public Employees (ACLU).* 2nd ed. Carbondale: Southern Illinois University Press, 1994.

Outten, Wayne N., et al. *The Rights of Employees and Union Members: The Basic ACLU Guide*. Carbondale: Southern Illinois University Press, 1994.

Steingold, Fred S. *The Employer's Legal Handbook*. 2nd ed. Berkeley: Nolo Press, 1997.

Immigration

Connolly, Norma C. *Bilingual Dictionary of Immigration Terms*. Longwood, FL: Gould Publications, Inc., 1997.

Lewis, Loida Nicolas, et al. *How to Get a Green Card: Legal Ways to Stay in the U.S.A.* 4th ed. Berkeley: Nolo Press, 1999.

Privacy

Alderman, Ellen, and Caroline Kennedy. *The Right to Privacy*. New York: Vintage Books, 1997.

Hendricks, Evan, et al. *Your Right to Privacy: A Basic Guide to Legal Rights in an Information Society (ACLU)*. Carbondale: Southern Illinois University Press, 1990.

Discrimination/Sexual Harassment

Bernbach, Jeffrey M. *Job Discrimination II: How to Fight, How to Win*. Englewood Cliffs, NJ: Voir Dire Press, 1998.

Callender, Dale. *Sexual Harrassment Claims, Step-by-Step*. Hauppage, NY: Barron's Educational Services, Inc., 1998.

Petrocelli, William, and Barbara Kate Repa. *Sexual Harassment on the Job: What It Is and How to Stop It*. 4th ed. Berkeley: Nolo Press, 1998.

Sack, Steven Mitchell. *Getting Fired: What to Do If You're Fired, Downsized, Laid Off, Restructured, Discharged, Terminated, or Forced to Resign*. New York: Warner Books, 1999.

Disability Issues

Crockett, Paul Hampton. *HIV Law*. New York: Three Rivers Press, 1997.

Hermann, Donald H. J. *Mental Health and Disability Law*. St. Paul: West Publishing Company, 1997.

OTHER INFORMATION SOURCES

Organizations

American Immigration Lawyers Association (AILA)
1400 Eye Street NW, Ste. 1200

Washington, DC 20005
(202) 216–2400
Home page: www.aila.org

Americans United for Affirmative Action
1201 Peachtree Street NE
Atlanta, GA 30361
(404) 870–9090
Home page: www.auaa.org

National Organization for Women (NOW)
733 Fifteenth Street NW, 2nd Floor
Washington, DC 20005
(202) 628–8NOW
E-mail: now@now.org
Home page: www.now.org/issues/affirm

Online Sources

Disability Hotline.com
(800) 786–6202
Home page: www.disabilityhotline.com

EDLAW, Inc. (disability law)
Home page: www.edlaw.net

Legal Information Institute (LII)
Home page: www.law.cornell.edu/topics/employment_discrimination

U.S. Department of Justice—ADA Homepage
www.doj.gov/crt/ada

U.S. Department of Labor—Women's Bureau
(800) 379–9042
Home page: www.dol.gov/dol/wb

— 5 —

On Your Own

EMANCIPATION

Can minors legally live beyond their parents' control?

In certain cases, yes. Minors can be "emancipated" from their parents under the laws of most states.

What exactly is "emancipation"?

It is an act or course of conduct that terminates the right of parents over a minor child, and also terminates the child's right to be taken care of.

Parents usually seek emancipation. When it occurs, it is often because a judge confirms or denies its existence as part of a larger issue in a court case. But a court won't declare an emancipation simply because a minor can't stand his or her folks or because they can't stand their child. It only happens if a minor already has been living apart from his or her parents and is clearly self-sufficient—if the minor's emancipation already has been "implied."

Consider the following situation. An Iowa doctor went to court to recover payment from the father of a teenage girl after having given her extensive medical treatment. The young woman had previously left home, with her father's permission, to live and work in another town. She supported herself and paid her bills until she contracted typhoid fever.

The young woman's father argued that his daughter had been emancipated, so he shouldn't have to pay her medical bills. After reviewing the facts of the case, the Iowa court said there was no emancipation. Its ruling meant the young woman's father continued to be responsible for her medical costs.

This case was decided in 1890, and the daughter was only 14 years old when she left home, but it demonstrates what emancipation really means.

If parents throw a teen out of the house, is his or her emancipation automatic?

Not in the vast majority of cases, because the teen usually won't have the income or maturity to live independently. Emancipation doesn't happen unless it's clear that the child is living an independent life and will be able to do so in the future. If this can't be shown, the child remains the parents' responsibility and continues to be under their authority.

If a minor runs away from home, is he or she emancipated?

Not usually. Parents are responsible for their minor children, including runaways. But if parents allow a runaway child to live independently for a long time and the child develops a reliable means of support or completely abandons the parents, a court may decide that emancipation has been implied.

These days, why might parents seek to establish emancipation?

Often it will be in relation to a child support order in a divorce settlement. For example, in one case a divorced mother went to court to collect past due child support from her former husband. After their daughter was age 15 she briefly lived with her mother, but sometimes she lived with friends, worked odd jobs, and was even jailed on two occasions. Neither parent knew where she was, although both had tried to help her by offering special schooling and psychiatric care.

The mother wanted past due support payments because she had legal custody of the runaway daughter. The court refused, stating that the daughter was legally emancipated because she had completely abandoned both parents.

For more about divorce and child support see Chapter Seven, "If Your Parents Divorce."

What factors will a court use to decide whether a minor is emancipated?

Some important ones are:

1. whether the minor still lives at home;
2. whether the minor pays room and board at home;
3. whether the minor has a job, and whether the minor is allowed to spend his or her earnings without parental interference;
4. whether the minor owns a car or house;
5. whether the minor pays his or her own debts; and
6. whether the minor is being claimed as a dependent on his or her parents' tax return.

If a minor is emancipated, does he or she gain all the rights of adults?

Not usually. Traditionally, emancipation didn't enable a minor to manage or convey property, bring a lawsuit, vote, change his or her name, or consent to medical care—the emancipated minor was still too young to engage in these adult activities. In recent years, however, many states have given teens these rights when emancipation can be established by the parents or is evident in the minor's actions and lifestyle.

When a minor marries, is he or she instantly emancipated?

Yes, provided the marriage is legal. In most states a person under age 18 must obtain parental consent and must be at least age 16 in order to marry.

Does enlisting in the armed forces constitute automatic emancipation?

Yes. Serving in the armed forces is said to be inconsistent with the idea of parental control. To enlist in any branch of the armed forces except the Army, a high school diploma currently is needed.

If a minor is emancipated, is he or she still required to obey the state's school attendance laws?

Yes, except in cases in which marriage was the basis for emancipation.

Once a minor is emancipated, are the parents relieved of liability for the child's negligent or reckless acts?

Not in every case. In California, for example, parents are responsible for a minor's negligent or reckless acts while driving, even if emancipation has occurred. For more about the responsibility of parents for a child's negligence while driving see Chapter One, "Behind the Wheel."

Can a minor be emancipated and still live at home?

The answer to this question is unclear. But if a minor pays room and board and has an independent source of income, a court might declare an emancipation. As a rule, it depends on the nature of the particular case.

HAVING YOUR OWN APARTMENT

Can a teenager legally rent an apartment?

Teens may enter into contracts, and this includes lease and rental contracts. But many landlords refuse to rent to them—they don't want teens as tenants.

Although minors can walk away from or "disaffirm" contracts they enter into, this probably isn't the reason why landlords refuse to rent to them. Many landlords figure that teens who want their own apartments must be troublemakers, "party animals," or drug dealers—otherwise they wouldn't be living away from home. On the other hand, some landlords will rent to a teen if a parent or guardian co-signs the lease or rental agreement.

Age discrimination against a minor who wants to rent an apartment isn't against the law, although refusing to rent to someone on the basis of race, color, gender, religion, nationality, or handicap clearly is. Some state constitutions or state laws prohibit landlords from renting to "adults only" because such policies discourage families from living together. To date, however, no state prohibits landlords from refusing to rent to teens.

In early 1999, however, a federal appeals court upheld the right of a landlord to refuse to rent to an unmarried couple, saying it interfered with the landlord's right to the free exercise of his religion as well as his property rights and free speech rights. The ruling overturned Alaska's ban on housing discrimination based on marital status.

If you do succeed in finding an apartment to rent or lease, don't be surprised if the landlord requires you to prepay both the first and last month's rent and also make a security deposit. For more about teens and contracts see Chapter Sixteen, "Entering into Contracts."

SERVING YOUR COUNTRY

Do men still have to register for the armed forces? Do women have to register?

With narrow exceptions, all men who are U.S. citizens and all foreign-born males living in the United States and its territories must register for the draft within 30 days of their eighteenth birthday. Women aren't required to register but may enlist.

What is the procedure for registering for the draft?

Each registrant must complete and return a Selective Service draft registration form, available at any post office. Registrants receive notice within 90 days of the date the Selective Service receives it.

Does everyone who registers for the draft end up in the armed forces?

No. The last year anyone was drafted in the United States was 1973. We now have a stand-by draft and voluntary service. No one can be drafted involuntarily unless Congress and the president determine that inducting persons previously registered is needed because of war or other national emergency.

When can a young person volunteer for the armed forces?

At age 18, and persons under 18 may enlist if they have parental consent. Most branches of the armed forces require a high school diploma, however, and some won't consider an applicant who has a juvenile record. To find out more about the Army, Navy, Air Force, Marines, Coast Guard, or National Guard, contact your local armed forces recruiter.

What is a conscientious objector?

It is a person who holds a sincere religious, moral, or ethical opposition to war. If the person's objection is only to participating in combat, he is assigned noncombat military duties if called to serve. If the person's objection is to participating in all military service, he may be excused from active or combat duty but may be required to perform civilian work relating to the national interest.

THE RIGHT TO VOTE

What is the legal voting age?

For national elections it is age 18, and for state and local elections it is usually age 18 as well.

HOLDING PUBLIC OFFICE

Can a minor run for public office?

It depends on the minor's state of residence because age and residency requirements for particular offices vary from state to state. For example, state constitutions typically require that a person be at least age 24 to hold a seat in the state legislature. City laws (called "ordinances") often require a person to be at least age 21 to sit on the city council. In addition, state laws usually require that a person be 35 to be installed as a judge.

FOR FURTHER READING

On the Streets

Greenberg, Keith Elliot. *Runaways*. Minneapolis: Lerner Publishing Group, 1995.
Switzer, Ellen. *Anyplace but Here: Young, Alone, and Homeless*. New York: Atheneum Press, 1992.
Salinger, J. D. *The Catcher in the Rye*. New York: Little, Brown & Co., 1951.
Schaffner, Laurie. *Teenage Runaways: Broken Hearts and "Bad Attitudes."* Binghamton, NY: Haworth Press, Inc., 1999.

Your Own Place

Ihara, Toni, Ralph Warner, and Frederick Hertz. *The Living Together Kit: A Legal Guide for Unmarried Couples*. 9th ed. Berkeley: Nolo Press, 1999.

Portman, Janet, and Marcia Stewart. *Renters' Rights*. Berkeley: Nolo Press, 1999.

The Armed Forces

Disher, Sarah Hanley. *First Class: Women Join the Ranks at the Naval Academy*. Annapolis: Naval Institute Press, 1998.

Johnson, R. Charles. *Draft Registration and the Law: A Guidebook*. Berkeley: Nolo Press, 1985.

Simons, Donald L. *I Refuse: Memories of a Vietnam War Objector*. Metuchen, NJ: Broken Rifle Press, 1992.

Steffan, Joseph. *Gays and the Military: Joseph Steffan Versus the United States*. Princeton, NJ: Princeton University Press, 1994.

Public Office

Inouye, Daniel Ken, and Lawrence Eliot. *Journey to Washington*. New York: Prentice Hall, Inc., 1967.

Christian, Spencer. *Electing Our Government*. New York: St. Martin's Press, 1996.

OTHER INFORMATION SOURCES

Organizations

Rock the Vote
10950 Washington Boulevard, Ste. 240
Culver City, CA 90232
(310) 237–2000
E-mail: field@rockthevote.org
Home Page: www.rockthevote.org

Selective Service System
Box 94732
Palatine, IL 60094
(847) 688–2576

Online Sources

About Elections and Voting
Home page: www.fec.gov/pages/electpg

U.S. Military
Home page: usmilitary.about.com

Hotlines

National Runaway Switchboard
(800) 621–4000
(800) 621–0394 (TDD)

— 6 —

Your Personal Appearance

AT HOME

Do parents have a right to decide how their children can dress and style their hair?

Yes. Although most parents give their children plenty of leeway when it comes to personal appearance, they do have the right to forbid particular types of clothes and hairstyles. Parents can forbid a teen to shave his or her head, use hair dye, or wear torn jeans or revealing tops. They can also forbid tattooing and any kind of body piercing.

What happens if a minor ignores his or her parents' requirements in matters of personal appearance?

Nothing in the law prevents the parents from punishing the minor. However, as discussed in Chapter Ten, "Your Right to Be Healthy and Safe from Abuse," parents may never punish children in a manner that amounts to abuse or neglect. If they do, the state can take them to court.

AT SCHOOL

Can a school legally enforce a dress code?

Yes, unless the provisions of the dress code truly don't promote discipline or good health, or don't serve some other worthwhile purpose. If a school can offer a plausible reason for the rule, it will usually stand.

In the last 25 years the issue of whether high school dress codes are legal has been argued in the courts countless times. Some states place the "burden of proof" on the *student* to show that the rules don't serve any useful purpose. In these states the students must prove that the rules are "arbitrary"—that they don't make any sense. Others place the burden of proof on the *school* to show that the regulation is related to a source of discipline problems or poor academic performance. The first type of case is difficult for students to win. The second type is tough for the school to win and is therefore more favorable to student rights.

In a case decided in 1984, students at an Alabama high school challenged a rule prohibiting males who participated in sports from wearing beards, sideburns, and long mustaches. The Alabama court ruled that the rule was a reasonable way to further personal hygiene and compel uniformity among the athletes. Since the students couldn't prove that the rule was arbitrary, they lost.

Earlier, an Illinois court was faced with the same type of rule, but in this case the rule applied to the entire student body. Here the students won because the school couldn't prove that hairstyles bore any sensible relation to the students' behavior or academic performance.

For a discussion about clothes as a personal or political expression at school see Chapter Two, "At School."

AT WORK

Can an employer require employees to follow a dress code?

Yes, provided the regulations have a reasonable business purpose. Courts rarely interfere with business policies relating to dress and hairstyle unless the policies are shown to discriminate on the basis of gender or race.

A New York court ruled in 1981 that an airline could legally prohibit employees of both sexes from wearing their hair in "corn-rows." The court sided with the airline after it argued that having its employees project a conservative image was a sensible business policy. Likewise, an airline—or a McDonald's—can legally require all employees who work with the public to wear the company uniform.

What if a certain provision in a company dress code only applies to women?

In most cases it discriminates illegally. The Illinois supreme court ruled in 1979 that a bank illegally discriminated on the basis of gender when it tried to enforce a rule requiring all the women to wear the same color, but permitted the men to wear any color of suit, jacket, shirt, or tie. Rules requiring women employees to wear makeup or making women flight attendants stay below a certain body weight also discriminate illegally, unless the employer can prove the rule serves a very important business purpose.

IN PUBLIC

Can a restaurant legally refuse to serve persons who aren't dressed in a certain manner?

In most states a business can require a particular type of dress only if the rule doesn't discriminate on the basis of gender. In 1977 a California man brought a sex discrimination suit against a restaurant with a formal dress code after it refused to seat him for dinner. The man was wearing a polyester leisure suit—and no tie. He argued that all the women in the restaurant were at least as casually dressed as he. The California supreme court ruled in his favor, stating that the restaurant's "no tie, no service" rule discriminated on the basis of gender in violation of the California constitution.

Are "no shoes, no shirt, no service" policies legal?

Yes, because a rule at a business establishment forbidding bare feet and bare chests promotes cleanliness, which is considered a good business policy. In addition, such rules promote a positive business image and don't discriminate on the basis of gender. (Woman dressed "topless" would be subject to the rule as well.)

Can a store or restaurant legally keep out "longhairs" or "biker types"?

Under federal law, yes, because the rule doesn't discriminate on the basis of gender, color, religion, national origin, or handicap. A state or local law would have to protect the customer in this type of situation. For more about discrimination see Chapter Thirteen, "Age, Race, and Sex Discrimination."

Is public nudity legal?

Not in very many places. States, cities, counties, and other legal subdivisions may legally forbid public nudity at beaches and parks as both a health measure and a means of upholding community standards of morality. However, California and Florida do have a few nude and top-less beaches.

FOR FURTHER READING

Books

Hewitt, Kim. *Mutilating the Body: Identity in Blood and Ink.* Bowling Green, OH: Bowling Green State University Press, 1997.

Reybold, Laura. *Everything You Need to Know about the Dangers of Tattooing and Body Piercing.* New York: Rosen Publishing Group, Inc., 1998.

Rollin, Lucy. *Twentieth-Century Teen Culture by the Decades.* Westport, CT: Greenwood Press, 1999.

Articles on Dress

"Dress Codes." *American Girl*, September/October 1999:10.

Fisher, Anne. "Casual Dress Codes, and Jobs for the Disabled." *Fortune*, April 26, 1999:428.

Nafisi, Azar. "The Veiled Threat." *The New Republic*, February 22, 1999:24.

Sack, Kevin. "Schools Look Hard at Lockers, Shirts, Bags and Manners." *The New York Times*, May 24, 1999:A1.

Wingert, Pat, and Esther Pan. "Uniforms Rule." *Newsweek*, October 4, 1999: 72.

Articles on Tattoos and Body Piercing

Brody, Jane E. "Fresh Warnings on the Perils of Piercing." *The New York Times*, April 4, 2000:D8.

Goodman, Elizabeth. "Post-Tattoo Blues." *Cosmopolitan*, March 1999:122.

"Piercing Concern." *Seventeen*, May 1999:88.

Tang, Alisa. "Lurking Perils on the Tip of the Tongue." *The New York Times*, January 26, 1999:F7.

OTHER INFORMATION SOURCES

Online Sources

Tattoos.com
Home page: www.tattoos.com

— 7 —

If Your Parents Divorce

CUSTODY

If a minor's parents plan to divorce, who decides where the minor will live after the divorce is final?

Usually the parents—they determine who will have "primary custody" of the child.[1] If they can't decide on their own, the court decides for them. Its decision must be in "the best interests of the child," a term often applied in relation to legal matters involving young people.

Married parents have both "physical" and "legal" custody of their minor children. Physical custody means the parents are responsible for their children's immediate personal needs such as food, clothing, and shelter; legal custody means they are responsible, legally and financially, for their children's safety, education, and actions with respect to others. When parents divorce, one parent—the "custodial parent"—usually receives both primary physical custody and primary legal custody of the children, except when the parents agree to share physical custody, legal custody, or both.

What do divorce courts consider in determining which parent should be the custodial parent?

As a rule, they consider the child's physical, mental, and financial needs; the parents' physical, mental, and moral fitness; and the parents' love and concern for the child. In addition, they take into account who has most recently been the primary custodian for the child and whether that situation has been in the child's best interests.

Custody decisions can be a close call. In a 1982 Virginia case, a judge awarded custody of twins to a father even though both parents were fit. The judge thought the father's home would be better because the children had been living with him for over three years and, because he had remarried, they wouldn't have to stay with a babysitter while he was at work.

Does a young person have a right to a lawyer at his or her parents' divorce?

Many states permit their courts to appoint a special representative for a child when parents disagree on custody, and many of these states require the representative to be an attorney. The representative can assist the child in expressing which parent he or she prefers to live with, can be effective at mediating problems, and can collect important information for the court. In some states the representative can also bring a support action on the child's behalf if a parent isn't obeying a child support order. The parents pay for the representative in most of these states, although the state or county will pay if they can't afford it.

Does a child of divorcing parents have a right to choose which parent he or she wants to live with?

Not usually. Even so, divorce courts in many states are required to take the child's preference into account. The older and more mature the child, the more weight his or her preference is likely to receive, especially if the child can give a good reason for preferring one parent to the other. For example, if an older child has been living with a grandparent and wants to continue to do so, his or her preference is given serious weight.

In Ohio, a child age 12 or older can choose which parent he or she wants to live with—its courts will respect the child's preference unless living with the chosen parent isn't in the child's best interests. Georgia's divorce courts have been taking the child's preference into account for decades.

Isn't it true that the mother usually wins custody in a divorce?

Yes. In years past, courts almost always resolved custody disputes in favor of the mother. These decisions were based on the notion that mothers are better able to care for children day in and day out, especially when the children are quite young. (On the other hand, teenage boys often lived with their fathers.) Although this "maternal preference" is no longer part of most states' divorce laws, courts still tend to award primary custody to mothers in situations that don't involve "joint custody." For more about the maternal preference see Chapter Nine, "Marrying and Having Children."

What is "joint custody"?

It is a type of custody arrangement in which the divorced parents continue to share physical custody, legal custody, or both. Joint custody gained popularity in the 1980s. The child might spend weekdays with one parent and weekends with the other, or live with one parent during the school year and stay with the other during summer vacation. When the parents share both legal and physical custody, both continue to make important decisions about the child's education, religious upbringing, and extracurricular activities. Sometimes both parents will be awarded joint legal custody but just one will have physical custody.

Joint custody arrangements are usually more flexible than traditional custody arrangements, and most experts believe that joint custody cushions children against the traumas often associated with their parents' divorce. Also, many contend that joint custody cuts down on parental kidnapping (discussed later in this chapter).

But joint custody has its critics. They ask, if the parents couldn't get along during their marriage, how will they ever be able to agree on what is best for their child once they split up? This can be a problem—one that sometimes requires the divorce court to act as the parties' referee.

Can parents continue to have legal custody over a person who is over the age of majority?

No, because that is the age at which a young person can live independently. Under the terms of a support decree, however, parents can be required to support a child who is beyond the age of majority. (Child support is discussed later in this chapter.) In addition, some states allow minors to be legally emancipated when their parents divorce if the minor is self-supporting. For more about the age of majority see Chapter Three, "At Home," and for more about emancipation see Chapter Five, "On Your Own."

In custody matters, is a parent's sexual behavior relevant?

It can be, although most courts don't give sexual conduct excessive weight unless the parent's behavior is likely to have an adverse impact on the child. For example, a Missouri court recently awarded custody to a child's father because the mother was having extramarital affairs on a regular basis.

Will a divorce court award custody to a gay or lesbian parent?

Each case of this nature is judged on its own merits. In resolving custody a court might ask, is the gay or lesbian parent living in a same-sex relationship? If so, is the relationship stable and discreet?

Will a divorce court award custody to a parent who is handicapped or disabled?

They certainly may—and often do. Again, "the best interests of the child" is the standard to be applied. A physical handicap—even a mental handicap—would be just one factor to weigh, although if the handicap is substance abuse, the best interests of the child might motivate a court to award custody to the nonabusing parent.

If one parent stands to become wealthier—through employment or perhaps an inheritance—is that parent more likely to obtain primary custody?

Not necessarily. Although divorce courts take the separate financial status of the parents into account, this isn't a controlling factor. Even a parent's poverty won't determine who receives custody unless the lack of money or steady income has resulted in child neglect.

Can a young person "divorce" his or her parents—bring a lawsuit to terminate their parental rights?

In 1992 a Florida judge permitted a young boy to go to court to do just this. The boy had been in foster care, and life at the foster home was stable. His foster parents wanted to adopt him, so he filed a lawsuit to terminate parental rights in order to clear the way for adoption proceedings. The boy won. This case is important because it is the first time a court permitted a young person to *personally* seek a termination of parental rights. As Chapter Three explains, the *state* normally seeks to terminate parental rights.

Does a child of divorced parents have a legal right to visit the parent he or she isn't living with?

Not exactly. Visitation rights belong to the noncustodial parent, not the child. Courts grant visitation to the noncustodial parent except in cases in which it wouldn't be in the child's best interests.

What happens if a child doesn't want to see the noncustodial parent?

In most situations the child can be required to, particularly if the custodial parent has turned the child against the other parent. In a 1983 Pennsylvania case a court permitted a father to visit his 11-year-old daughter against her wishes after the court declared that the mother had been "poisoning her daughter's mind against her father."

Will a court forbid a noncustodial parent to visit a minor child because that parent is "living with someone"?

Not for that reason alone. Courts will forbid a parent to have contact with a child only if spending time together isn't in the child's best interests. These days, very few judges would limit visitation rights solely because the noncustodial parent lives with someone outside of marriage.

If it appears that the noncustodial parent might not return the child at the end of a visit, the court has the power to suspend the parent's visitation rights or revoke them altogether. Courts will also suspend or revoke visitation rights if the noncustodial parent physically injures the child or threatens to. If the noncustodial parent abused a child during marriage, his or her visits usually are both short and supervised.

Many states regard sexual promiscuity of the noncustodial parent as grounds for denying visitation.

In custody determinations, does a young person have the right to continue living with his or her siblings?

No, but courts try to keep brothers and sisters together unless there is an important reason not to.

CHILD SUPPORT

Are both parents legally required to support their minor children after a divorce?

Yes, unless the parental rights of one or both parents have been terminated in a separate court case. For more about terminating parental rights see Chapter Three, "At Home."

What is child support?

It is an amount of money that the noncustodial parent is required to pay to fulfill his or her legal support obligations. Usually these payments are made to the custodial parent, although they may be made through the divorce court. Child support must cover food, clothing, shelter, medical expenses, and education.

Who decides how much child support the noncustodial parent must pay?

Usually the divorce court. The actual amount depends on how much each parent earns, the number of children in the family, its standard of living, and any child's unique physical, educational, and psychological needs. Each state has "child support guidelines" that set the appropriate amount. Parents can agree on a figure, but if they do, it must be court-approved.

If the court refuses to grant visitation rights to the noncustodial parent, is that parent relieved of his or her child support obligations?

No. Child support must be paid by the noncustodial parent regardless of whether visitation rights are granted.

Aren't most children worse off financially after their parents divorce?

Studies show that they are. The purpose of child support is to allow the children to enjoy the same standard of living that they enjoyed before the divorce, but even so, support is often inadequate. A famous study in the mid-1980s found that after a couple divorces, the average woman's spending money declines by 73 percent, but the average man's spending money increases by 42 percent.[2] Since most children live with their mothers after a divorce, their standard of living also drops. An earlier study argues that support awards are too low to pay even half the costs of child rearing.[3] Recent studies show that this situation has not really improved, even as more mothers enter and remain in the workforce.

Does the noncustodial parent have to pay child support if the custodial parent works outside the home?

Yes, although in some cases the amount the custodial parent earns will reduce the noncustodial parent's support payments.

Can child support continue after a child reaches the age of majority?

Yes. As part of many divorce settlements, one parent may be required to pay child support until each child reaches age 21 and may have to pay for each child's college education. In 1989 an Illinois court required a father who earned $77,000 annually to pay $11,000 each year for his son to attend a four-year private college.

Can a custodial parent take a noncustodial parent to court to enforce a child support order?

Absolutely. In addition, state child welfare agencies, with substantial help from the federal government, always pursue "deadbeat parents." Furthermore, a noncustodial parent's income tax refund can be seized for nonpayment of child support. In some states (and in narrow and extreme circumstances), courts can even hold a nonpaying parent "in contempt of court." This means the noncustodial parent can be ordered to sit in jail until he or she pays up.

Can a young person take a parent to court to recover child support?

Only if he or she is above the age of majority and continues to be entitled to support (such as tuition for a college education) under the parents' divorce decree.

Are there any special ways to track down deadbeat parents in order to enforce current or overdue support obligations?

Yes. Special laws help parents collect child support from noncustodial deadbeats who live within the state's boundaries. In addition, the federal government assists state welfare agencies to locate absent, nonpaying parents out-of-state.

What's the difference between child support and alimony?

Alimony or "maintenance" is a payment made by one former spouse to the other to reduce the latter's financial hardships after a divorce. Women who have never worked outside the home during a lengthy marriage often are awarded monthly or annual alimony after divorcing. The recipient of the alimony doesn't need to have legal custody of minor children to receive it, as payments are separate and distinct from child support. Nothing prevents a court from awarding both child support and alimony, but these days it doesn't happen very often.

GRANDPARENTS AND STEPPARENTS

Do grandparents have a legal right to visit their grandchildren after the parents divorce?

Visitation by grandparents used to be decided by the custodial parent. But now every state has legislation authorizing grandparent visitation. In each case the court's decision to allow grandparent visitation is guided by the best interests of the child.

Do stepparents ever have parental rights over a stepchild?

Only if they've agreed to assume certain parental obligations. Accepting legal responsibility for a stepchild usually gives a stepparent legal rights similar to parental rights. The extent of those rights would depend on the responsibilities assumed. A typical example of an assumed obligation might be an agreement to provide for a young stepson or stepdaughter.

Do former stepparents have any legal rights?

Sometimes. Courts occasionally grant visitation rights to former stepparents after determining that visitation would be in the child's best interests.

OTHER ISSUES RELATING TO DIVORCE

What's the difference between a divorce and a legal separation?

A divorce legally dissolves the marriage. A legal separation doesn't dissolve all marriage ties, but it does declare that the couple no longer live as husband and wife. It also declares that they no longer will be responsible for each other's debts.

What is "child snatching"?

Child snatching, sometimes called "child kidnapping," occurs when a noncustodial parent unlawfully takes a child from the custodial parent or from the custodial parent's home. Children are often snatched to exact a promise from the custodial parent to accept less child support, or to pressure the custodial parent to change custody or visitation rights.

Child snatching is a crime. This means that a parent who is guilty of child snatching can be punished under state law. In addition, federal law requires state courts to enforce out-of-state custody orders. This means that if a child is taken across state lines in violation of a custody order, a state court must order the child returned to the custodial parent, regardless of how far away that parent happens to live.

If a young person thinks his or her parents should get a divorce, what can he or she do?

From a legal standpoint, nothing. However, the child should consider discussing the family situation with a trusted relative or minister.

NOTES

1. In 1990 there were 2,448,000 marriages in the United States and 1,175,000 divorces.

2. Lenore J. Weitzman, *The Divorce Revolution: The Unexpected Social and Economic Consequences for Women and Children in America* (New York: The Free Press, 1985).

3. Lenore J. Weitzman and Ruth B. Dixon, "Child Custody Awards: Legal Standards with Empirical Patterns for Child Custody, Support and Visitation After Divorce," 12 *University of California Davis Law Review* 473, 497–499 (1979).

FOR FURTHER READING

In General

American Bar Association Guide to Family Law. New York: Times Books, 1996.

Everett, Craig A., ed. *The Consequences of Divorce: Economic and Custodial Impact on Children and Adults.* Binghamton, NY: Haworth Press, Inc., 1996.

Johnson, Linda Carlson. *Everything You Need to Know about Your Parents' Divorce.* New York: Rosen Publishing Group, Inc., 1994.

Joselow, Thea, and Beth Baruch Joselow. *When Divorce Hits Home: Keeping Yourself Together When Your Family Comes Apart.* New York: Avon Books, 1996.

Leonard, Robin D., and Stephen R. Elias. *Family Law Dictionary.* Berkeley: Nolo Press, 1988.

Custody

Ross, Julia A., and Judy Corcoran. *Joint Custody with a Jerk.* New York: St. Martin's Press, 1996.

Spence, Simone. *1–800 DeadBeat: How To Collect Your Child Support.* New York: Eggshell Press, 1999.

Steinbreder, John, and Richard G. Kent. *Fighting for Your Children: A Father's Guide to Custody.* Dallas: Taylor Publishing Company, 1997.

Terkel, Susan Beibung. *Understanding Child Custody.* New York: Franklin Watts, Inc., 1991.

Truly, Tracy. *Grandparents' Rights.* Clearwater, FL: Sphinx Publishing, 1995.

Watnik, Webster. *Child Custody Made Simple: Understanding the Law of Child Custody and Child Support.* Claremont, CA: Single Parent Press, 1997.

OTHER INFORMATION SOURCES

Organizations

American Bar Association
Family Law Section
750 North Lake Shore Drive
Chicago, IL 60611
(312) 988–5603
E-mail: familylaw@abanet.org
Home page: www.abanet.org/family

Children's Rights Council
300 Eye Street NE, Ste. 401
Washington, DC 20002
(202) 547–6227
Home page: vix.com/crc/

DadsDivorce.com
10425 Old Olive Street Road, Ste. 7
Creve Coeur, MO 63141
(314) 983–0001
Home page: www.dadsdivorce.com

Grandparents Rights Center
723 West Chapman Avenue
Orange, CA 92868
(714) 744–8485
E-mail: info@grandparentsrights.com
Home page: www.grandparentsrights.com

Stepfamily Foundation
333 West End Avenue
New York, NY 10023
(212) 877–3244
E-mail: staff@stepfamily.org
Home page: www.stepfamily.org

— 8 —

Your Sexual Life

Do teens have a legal right to engage in all types of sexual activity?
No—the laws don't go this far. States legally regulate, or attempt to regulate, the sexual conduct of minors. Some forbid teens under a certain age to have sexual intercourse, including homosexual intercourse. Every state attempts to regulate teen sex through statutory rape laws, which are discussed later in this chapter.

A law regulating teenage sex is intended to preserve community standards of morality. The same type of law still makes it illegal in a few states for consenting but unmarried adults to have sex and for married adults to perform certain sexual acts such as oral sex. Overall, these laws don't violate the privacy protections of the Constitution.

BIRTH CONTROL

Are contraceptives legal?
Both nonprescription and prescription contraceptives are legal in the United States. At one time the laws of most states restricted the sale of contraceptives, although only Connecticut prohibited them altogether. These laws were challenged by individuals who wanted to use them and by doctors who wanted to prescribe them for their patients.

In 1965 the Supreme Court finally ruled that states interfere with special privacy rights protected by the Constitution when they pass laws banning the sale or use of contraceptives. It is now clear that states may not interfere excessively with an individual's personal decisions about reproduction.

Can teens legally use contraceptives?

Yes. The early contraceptive cases dealt with the right of married couples to make decisions about childbearing, but later cases established that all sexually active people have this right.

Do teens have a right to obtain contraceptives without parental consent?

Teens don't need parental consent to purchase nonprescription contraceptives such as foams, jellies, sponges, and condoms, and stores don't need to notify a teen's parents about these purchases. But prescription contraceptives such as birth control pills, diaphragms, interuterine devices (IUDs), cervical caps, and Norplant (a long-term contraceptive method) raise special legal issues.

As a rule, minors need parental consent for medical treatment, and this includes obtaining prescription drugs. Even so, in 24 states a minor is legally entitled to give consent for prescription contraceptives. In no state is parental consent explicitly required, although some states do specify an age above which parental consent is no longer needed.

Note also that the laws of 28 states explicitly allow a minor to legally consent to prenatal care for his or her child.

See Table 3 for state-by-state information on these issues. If you have additional questions about contraception, call a confidential information source such as your local Planned Parenthood office or clinic. Planned Parenthood's national hotline number is (800) 541–7800.

Would a public school be able to distribute condoms to minors without parental consent?

It's not likely. In 1994 a New York court ruled that because parents are legally in charge of their minor children's health, schools can't distribute condoms to students without at least one parent's consent. Other states have taken the same position on this issue.

Do teens have a legal right to obtain counseling and services from family planning agencies?

Yes. "Title X–funded clinics" make confidential family planning available to eligible persons at little or no cost. These clinics are federally

Table 3
Reproductive Health Care for Minors

State or Jurisdiction	Contraceptive Services	Prenatal Care	Abortion Services
Alabama	No Law	Minor May Consent	Parental Notice
Alaska	Minor May Consent	Minor May Consent	No Law
Arizona	No Law	No Law	No Law
Arkansas	Minor May Consent	Minor May Consent[1]	Parental Notice[2]
California	Minor May Consent	Minor May Consent[1]	No Law
Colorado	Minor May Consent	No Law	No Law
Connecticut	No Law	No Law	Minor May Consent
Delaware	Minor May Consent[3,4]	Minor May Consent[1,3,4,5]	Parental Notice[6]
D.C.	Minor May Consent	Minor May Consent	Minor May Consent
Florida	Minor May Consent[7]	Minor May Consent[5]	No Law
Georgia	Minor May Consent	Minor May Consent[1]	Parental Notice
Hawaii	Minor May Consent[4,8]	Minor May Consent[1,4,8]	No Law
Idaho	Minor May Consent	No Law	Parental Notice[2,9]
Illinois	Minor May Consent[7]	Minor May Consent[5]	No Law
Indiana	No Law	No Law	Parental Consent
Iowa	No Law	No Law	Parental Notice[6]
Kansas	No Law	Minor May Consent[5,10]	Parental Notice
Kentucky	Minor May Consent[4]	Minor May Consent[1,4]	Parental Consent
Louisiana	No Law	No Law	Parental Consent
Maine	Minor May Consent[7]	No Law	Minor May Consent[11]
Maryland	Minor May Consent[4]	Minor May Consent[4]	Parental Notice[12]
Massachusetts	No Law	Minor May Consent[1]	Parental Consent
Michigan	No Law	Minor May Consent[4]	Parental Consent
Minnesota	No Law	Minor May Consent[4]	Parental Notice[2]
Mississippi	Minor May Consent	Minor May Consent[5]	Minor May Consent[2]

Table 3 (*continued*)

State or Jurisdiction	Contraceptive Services	Prenatal Care	Abortion Services
Missouri	No Law	Minor May Consent[1 4 5]	Parental Consent
Montana	Minor May Consent[4]	Minor May Consent[4 5]	Parental Notice
Nebraska	No Law	No Law	Parental Notice
Nevada	No Law	No Law	No Law
New Hampshire	No Law	No Law	No Law
New Jersey	No Law	Minor May Consent[4 5]	No Law
New Mexico	Minor May Consent	No Law	No Law
New York	Minor May Consent	Minor May Consent	No Law
North Carolina	Minor May Consent	Minor May Consent[1]	Parental Consent[6]
North Dakota	Minor May Consent	No Law	Parental Consent[2]
Ohio	No Law	No Law	Parental Notice[13]
Oklahoma	Minor May Consent[4 14]	No Law[1 4]	No Law
Oregon	Minor May Consent[4]	Minor May Consent	No Law
Pennsylvania	No Law	Minor May Consent[2]	Parental Consent
Rhode Island	No Law	No Law	Parental Consent
South Carolina	No Law[15]	No Law[15]	Parental Consent[6]
South Dakota	No Law	No Law	Parental Notice
Tennessee	Minor May Consent	No Law	No Law
Texas	No Law	Minor May Consent[1 4 5]	No Law
Utah	No Law	No Law	Parental Notice[2 9]
Vermont	No Law	No Law	No Law
Virginia	Minor May Consent	No Law	Parental Notice
Washington	No Law	No Law	No Law
West Virginia	No Law	No Law	Parental Notice[16]
Wisconsin	No Law	No Law	Parental Consent[6]
Wyoming	Minor May Consent	No Law	Parental Consent

Notes:

1. Excludes abortion.
2. Involvement of both parents is required in most cases.
3. Minor must be age 12 or older.
4. A doctor may notify the parents.

5. Includes surgery.

6. Notice or consent may be given to or by a grandparent, or, alternatively, in Delaware to a licensed mental health professional, or in Wisconsin, by another adult relative over age 25.

7. Minor may consent if she has a child or if a doctor believes she would suffer a "probable" health hazard if services are not provided; in Florida and Illinois, also if the minor is pregnant; in Illinois, also if referred by a doctor, member of the clergy or a Planned Parenthood clinic.

8. Minor must be at least age 14.

9. Does not include a judicial bypass procedure.

10. Minor over the age of 16 may consent to general medical care if a parent is "not immediately available."

11. Minor may be counseled by a physician or counselor in lieu of obtaining parental consent or court authorization.

12. The law has no judicial bypass procedure. However, a physician may waive notification if the minor does not live with a parent, if the physician determines that the minor is mature enough to give informed consent, or if the physician believes that notification may lead to physical or emotional abuse of the minor or would otherwise be contrary to her best interests; or if reasonable efforts to give notice were unsuccessful.

13. A stepparent, grandparent or sibling over age 21 may be notified if the minor files an affidavit stating that she fears physical, sexual or severe emotional abuse from a parent.

14. A minor may consent if she has ever been pregnant in the past.

15. Any minor age 16 and older may consent to any health services other than operations. Health services may be rendered to minors of any age without parental consent when the provider believes that the services are needed.

16. Notice or the judicial bypass procedure can be waived if a second physician determines that the minor is mature enough to give consent or that notice would not be in her best interests.

Source: The Alan Guttmacher Institute, "Teenager's Right to Consent to Reproductive Health Care," *Issues in Brief,* 1997.

125

authorized and federally funded, at least in part. Planned Parenthood clinics obtain operating money through Title X.

Title X–funded clinics provide their services regardless of age or marital status. They consider a teen's financial resources separate from the resources of the parents, so a young person can easily qualify.

Young women are especially dependent on Title X–funded clinics for contraceptives; four out of ten teens who are in need of birth control services turn to them.[1] For a teen who wouldn't use birth control if she had to talk to a parent first, a confidential visit to a family planning clinic can literally prevent a pregnancy.

Are the services of Title X–funded clinics always confidential?

Yes. Courts have overturned state laws requiring federally funded family planning clinics to notify a parent when a young woman receives a prescription for contraceptives. These clinics must maintain client confidentiality as a matter of law. Even so, a teen who goes to a family planning clinic should ask a staffperson about its confidentiality policies.

Teen access to family planning clinics recently came under attack in Congress and in certain state legislatures. In 1997 the U.S. House of Representatives narrowly defeated a provision requiring Title X–funded clinics to give five-day advance notice to parents before providing prescription contraceptives to a minor. That same year a number of state legislatures tried to prohibit state family planning funds from being used for contraceptives for minors. Attempts were also made to limit the ability of minors to obtain prescriptions for sexually transmitted diseases, or STDs.

These legislative attempts will continue in the years to come, even though they run contrary to trends in the past three decades expanding teens' legal authority to make decisions about their bodies.

Does a teen have a right to be sterilized without parental consent?

Few states actually have laws addressing this issue. When state law is silent, written consent would undoubtedly be required, even if state law expressly permits teens to obtain prescription contraceptives. In fact, the laws of many states *exclude* sterilization of a minor from the list of medical services that don't require parental consent.

In many states, parents can't sterilize a mentally competent minor over the minor's stated objection. But in any event, finding a physician willing to perform a sterilization on a minor would be extremely difficult.

See Chapter Ten, "Your Right to Be Healthy and Safe from Abuse," for more about situations in which young people can arrange for their own medical care.

Would an older teen be entitled to federal funding for a sterilization?

No. Although public funds can be used to perform sterilizations on adults in some cases, none are available for persons under age 21.

Does a young person have a right to sex education classes in public school?

No, even though many states now require them above a certain grade level. When sex education is included in the curriculum, parents sometimes argue that public schools violate their constitutional right to control their child's religious upbringing. Although parents have never won these cases in court, most states allow parents to stop a child from attending sex education classes if the requirements of the class can be fulfilled in some other meaningful way.

ABORTION RIGHTS

Are abortions legal?

Abortions have been legal in the United States since 1973, when the Supreme Court decided the famous and controversial case of *Roe v. Wade*.

The Supreme Court ruled in *Roe v. Wade* that the decision to have an abortion is another type of private decision that the Constitution protects from *excessive* government interference. *Roe v. Wade* stated that before a fetus is able to survive outside the womb—before a fetus is "viable"— a woman has a constitutional right to choose an abortion. Viability is estimated to occur 12 to 13 weeks after conception.

But states can pass laws restricting the abortion of a viable fetus in certain cases. With respect to the second 12 weeks of pregnancy—the second trimester—states may restrict abortions in cases in which the procedure is likely to endanger the woman's life or health. In the third trimester, states may legally forbid abortions. These restrictions don't interfere with a woman's constitutional right to privacy.

Does a teenage woman have a legal right to an abortion?

Yes. Although *Roe v. Wade* dealt with an adult woman's right to have an abortion, later Supreme Court decisions have stated that this right extends to teens. This special privacy right applies to all women—adult or teenager, married or single.

Can a teen legally obtain an abortion without parental consent?

According to the Supreme Court, a state may require a minor to obtain parental consent or give advance parental notice for an abortion. Thirty states explicitly require either parental notice or consent. Only two states and the District of Columbia actually have laws confirming a minor's right to consent to a confidential abortion.

But importantly, the Supreme Court has also ruled (as early as 1979) that states must have a *judicial bypass procedure* to protect a minor's privacy rights in abortion matters. As a matter of constitutional law, a teenage woman must be able to petition a family court to order that parental notice or consent be avoided, or "bypassed."

Specific court procedures must be followed to effect a judicial bypass for an abortion. The minor and her assigned attorney or counselor must meet with a family court judge, who determines whether the minor understands the consequences of her decision as well as the alternatives to an abortion. Some factors that a judge would consider are the young woman's emotional and intellectual development, her outside interests, and her life experiences. If the judge believes that the minor is sufficiently mature to make her own decision, he or she will issue an order permitting parental consent to be bypassed. Once this happens, the minor can give the required medical consent on her own.

A confidential abortion is also possible in cases in which the judge *doesn't* believe the minor is mature enough to make an informed decision. In these situations the judge can order that parental notice be bypassed if a confidential abortion is clearly in the minor's best interests. It may be, for example, that the minor would face possible physical abuse if she raises the abortion issue with her parents. In such cases the court would give the consent.

The bypass petition must move through the court swiftly. By virtue of this overall procedure, a young woman's constitutional right to privacy is protected. Her identity remains anonymous, and the court's involvement remains confidential.

Note, however, that fourteen states, including Ohio, Pennsylvania, and

Wisconsin, do impose a preabortion waiting period. In these states a woman who has received state-funded abortion counseling must wait up to 24 hours before going ahead with her abortion.

See Table 3 for additional information on American teens' abortion rights.

Must a pregnant woman obtain the consent of her sex partner to obtain an abortion?

No—otherwise her constitutional right to privacy in the area of reproductive rights would be violated. This rule of course applies to teens as well as adults. If consent from the sex partner were required, the Supreme Court's ruling in *Roe v. Wade* would have little meaning. Nor does a woman need to check with her sex partner before using contraceptives.

Can a young woman's parents legally force her to have an abortion if she doesn't want to?

No, and neither can the state. All women have a constitutional right to decide about having children without excessive interference from anyone.

If a teen can't afford an abortion, is she entitled to one at public expense?

It's not likely. Federal legislation forbids the use of public money such as Medicaid funds for abortions except in situations of rape or incest, or if the mother's life is in danger.[2] (Medicaid is a joint federal/state program, administered by each state, that provides health care to poor people.) Also, the Supreme Court has confirmed that neither the federal government nor the states are required to fund abortions, even if they fund pregnancy-related services.

Vocal critics argue that these laws simply make abortions unavailable to the poor. It is true that these laws make legal, confidential abortions impossible for a great many teens.

SEXUALLY TRANSMITTED DISEASES

Does a minor have a right to counseling and treatment without parental consent for sexually transmitted diseases such as herpes, gonorrhea, syphilis, and human immunodeficiency virus/acquired immunodeficiency syndrome (HIV/AIDS)?

Yes. Even though doctors usually are required by law to obtain parental consent before treating young people, every state makes an exception for sexually transmitted diseases, or STDs. Laws permitting minors to consent to treatment for STDs appear to cover treatment for HIV/AIDS. Even so, 18 states expressly authorize a minor to consent privately to HIV/AIDS treatment.

Minors can usually obtain these services at very low cost or no cost at Title X–funded clinics.

RAPE

What is rape?

Rape occurs when a person is forced against his or her will to participate in a sexual activity. Rape is the severest form of sexual assault.

In some states the legal definition of rape is any forced contact of a man's penis with a woman's vagina. In others, rape includes forced oral and anal sex and also includes forcing objects into sexual openings of a person's body. Rape is a very serious crime of aggression, but many rapists go unpunished.

Can a man also be raped?

Yes, under the legal definition of rape in many states.

Is rape on the increase in this country?

That's a tough question, because rape was rarely reported to the authorities in years past. It is certain, however, that rape is a crime of epidemic proportions. Ponder the following statistics. An estimated 106,600 rapes occurred in the United States in 1991—equivalent to 292 rapes each day. From 1972 to 1991 the number of reported rapes increased by 128 percent.[3] Tragically, an estimated 13 percent of the women in this country have been victims of at least one completed rape, and 39 percent have been raped more than once.

Teens are both victims and perpetrators. A recent survey found that a majority of rapes occur when the victim is under 11 years old, and 32 percent occur between the ages of 11 and 17. In 1994, an estimated 6,000 juveniles were arrested for rape in the United States. Of the total, 38 percent were under age 15, and 43 percent were between the ages of 16 and 17.[4]

A rapist isn't likely to be a stranger. Only 22 percent of rape victims are assaulted by someone they've never seen before. Nine percent are raped by husbands or ex-husbands, 11 percent by fathers or stepfathers, 10 percent by boyfriends or ex-boyfriends, 16 percent by other relatives, and 29 percent by other nonrelatives such as friends and neighbors.[5]

Must a rape victim forcibly resist the aggressor for rape to occur?

No, particularly if resisting the rapist might place the rape victim in even greater danger. In fact, this is almost always the case.

What is "date rape"?

It is forced sexual activity that takes place in a social situation or between a dating couple. Date rape carries the same legal consequences as rape occurring in a nonsocial setting.

Date rapists aren't likely to label themselves as rapists, as certain male attitudes suggest. In a recent survey, 61 percent of the men questioned said that "it would be exciting to use force to subdue a woman." Sixty-three percent said, "I get excited when a woman struggles over sex," and 83 percent said that "some women look like they're just asking to be raped." This doesn't mean that most dating men are closet rapists, but it does mean that inappropriate aggression may indeed play a role in a man's idea of acceptable sexual behavior.

Can a woman be legally raped or sexually assaulted by her date if she has "led him on"?

Yes. Even if a woman has encouraged her date by her aggressive sexual behavior (or even her *passive* sexual behavior), she shouldn't let him invade her sexual comfort zone. This would be true even if she is drunk or stoned, or very seductively dressed. It would also be true if the two have been petting heavily. The woman should leave if her partner becomes just too rough and aggressive. It really could degenerate into a rape scene.

Is rape difficult to prove?

Not necessarily. "Competent" evidence of rape, attempted rape, or actual or attempted sexual assault might include bruises, scratches, and injury to bodily openings. It might also include the presence of a weapon, the man's semen, and of course the victim's description of the encounter. The prosecuting attorney would consider any and all information in deciding whether to charge the aggressor.

Some state laws distinguish between "simple rape" and "aggravated rape." With simple rape there is no obvious injury and usually little evidence of struggle. Simple rape can be more difficult to prove than aggravated rape, and fewer people are charged with it. Jurors often believe that with simple rape a female victim is partly to blame, even if her account of the incident is highly incriminating.

What is statutory rape?

Statutory rape occurs when a man has sexual intercourse with a minor who is below a certain age. In every state a woman under that age is, by law, unable to legally consent to sex, even though she may have *in fact* consented, either expressly or by implication. If the young woman is below the legal age, the man is said to have committed a rape.

Statutory rape is also a crime. The age that a minor can legally consent to sex is between 14 and 18 years, depending on the state. Because this type of rape is solely the creation of a state law or "statute," it is called "statutory" rape.

To be charged with statutory rape, does the man involved have to be above a certain age?

In many states, yes. It usually is between the ages of 15 and 18, depending on state law.

Does this mean that if a teenage couple has sex, the man can be charged with statutory rape?

In some states, yes.

Why isn't the woman also charged with statutory rape? Isn't the law unfair if it only punishes the male partner?

Statutory rape laws that punish only the man aren't considered unfair and aren't unconstitutional. Courts have ruled that states have a legitimate interest in preventing young women from becoming pregnant or contracting sexually transmitted diseases—and from being "taken advantage of."

Is it statutory rape for a woman over age 18 to have sexual intercourse with a young man under, say, age 14?

Not usually. Courts have ruled that women who have sexual intercourse at a very young age are at much greater risk than young teenage men. A teenage woman might become pregnant or have to go through an abortion. These experiences can be traumatic for many women, but particularly young teens.

NOTES

1. J. J. Frost, "Family Planning Clinic Services in the United States, 1994," *Family Planning Perspectives* 28, 98 (1996).

2. About 16,000 women have abortions as a result of rape or incest each year. *Facts in Brief: Abortion in the United States*, The Alan Guttmacher Institute, 1993, p. 1. But only one in 100 rapists is sentenced to more than one year in prison. Report of the Majority Staff of the Senate Judiciary Committee, *The Response to Rape: Detours on the Road to Equal Justice.* May 1993.

3. Federal Bureau of Investigation, United States Department of Justice, *Crime in the United States, 1991*, August 30, 1992, pp. 14, 17, 24, 58, Table 1. Index of Crimes, United States, 1972–1991.

4. National Victim Center and the Crime Victims Research and Treatment Center, *Rape in America: A Report to the Nation*, April 23, 1992:1–16.

5. Ibid.

FOR FURTHER READING

Sex Issues and Sexual Rights

Basso, Michael J. *The Underground Guide to Teenage Sexuality*. Minneapolis: Fairview Press, 1997.

Mitchell, Carolyn B. *The Planned Parenthood Women's Health Encyclopedia*. New York: Crown Publishers, 1996.

Moglia, Ronald Filiberti, and John Knowles, eds. *All about Sex: A Family Resource on Sex and Sexuality.* New York: Three Rivers Press, 1997.

Pasquale, Samuel A., and Jennifer Cadoff. *The Birth Control Book: A Complete Guide to Your Contraceptive Options.* New York: Ballantine Books, 1996.

Roberson, Mitch, ed. *Getting It On: A Condom Reader.* New York: Soho Press, Inc., 1999.

Abortion

Andryszewski, Tricia. *Abortion: Rights, Options, and Choices.* Brookfield, CT: Millbrook Press, Inc., 1996.

Rosenblatt, Roger. *Life Itself: Abortion in the American Mind.* New York: Random House, Inc., 1992.

Rape and Date Rape

Anderson, Laurie Halse. *Speak.* New York: Farrar, Straus & Giroux, 1999.

Bode, Janet. *The Voices of Rape: Healing the Hurt.* New York: Dell Publishing Company, Inc., 1992.

Brownmiller, Susan. *Against Our Will: Men, Women and Rape.* New York: Ballantine Publishers, 1993.

Levy, Barrie, and Patricia Occhiuzzo Giggans. *What Parents Need to Know about Dating Violence.* Seattle: Seal Press, 1995.

Scarce, Michael. *Male on Male Rape: The Hidden Toll of Stigma and Shame.* New York: Insight Books, 1997.

Warshaw, Robin. *I Never Called It Rape: The Ms. Report on Recognizing, Fighting, and Surviving Date and Acquaintance Rape.* New York: Harper Perennial Library, 1994.

Wiseman, Rosalind. *Defending Ourselves: A Guide to Prevention, Self-Defense, and Recovery from Rape.* New York: Noonday Press, 1995.

Sexually Transmitted Diseases

Ford, Michael Thomas. *100 Questions and Answers about AIDS: A Guide for Young People.* New York: Macmillan Publishers, 1993.

Johnson, Earvin "Magic." *What You Can Do to Avoid AIDS.* New York: Times Books, 1993.

Nevid, Jeffrey A. *Choices: Sex in the Age of STDs.* 2nd ed. Needham Heights, MA: Allyn & Bacon, 1997.

Nevid, Jeffrey A. *201 Things You Should Know about AIDS and Other Sexually Transmitted Diseases.* Needham Heights, MA: Allyn & Bacon, 1997.

OTHER INFORMATION SOURCES

Organizations

Alan Guttmacher Institute
120 Wall Street
New York, NY 10005
(212) 248-1111
E-mail: info@agi-usa.org
Home page: www.agi-usa.org

National Campaign to Prevent Teen Pregnancy (NCPTP)
2100 M Street NW
Washington, DC 20037
(202) 261-5655
Home page: www.teenpregnancy.org

National Organization on Adolescent Pregnancy, Parenting and Prevention
(NOAPPP)
2401 Pennsylvania Avenue, Ste. 350
Washington, DC 20037
(202) 293-8370
E-mail: noappp@noappp.org
Home page: www.noappp.org

Planned Parenthood Federation of America
810 Seventh Avenue
New York, NY 10019
(212) 541-7800
E-mail: communications@ppfa.org
Home page: www.plannedparenthood.org

Rape Abuse & Incest National Network (RAINN)
635-B Pennsylvania Avenue SE
Washington, DC 20003
(800) 656-HOPE
E-mail: rainnmail@aol.com
Home page: www.rainn.org

Online Sources

Planned Parenthood for Teens
Home page: www.teenwire.com

The Safer Sex Page
Home page: www.safersex.org

Sex, Etc. (online magazine for teens)
Home page: www.sxetc.org

Hotlines

AAA Abortion Helpline
(888) 41-WOMAN

Alcohol, Drug and Pregnancy Helpline
(800) 638–2229

America's Pregnancy Helpline
(888) 4-OPTIONS

Birthright
(800) 550–4900

Centers for Disease Control National AIDS Hotline
(800) 342-AIDS

Centers for Disease Control National STD Hotline
(800) 227–8922

Gay and Lesbian National Hotline
(888) THE-GLNH

National Teen AIDS Hotline
(800) 234-TEEN

Rape, Abuse & Incest National Network (RAINN)
(800) 656-HOPE

— 9 —

Marrying and Having Children

PARENTAL CONSENT FOR MARRIAGE

At what age can a young person marry without parental consent?
At the age of majority, which in most states is age 18. The minimum age for marrying *with* parental consent is age 16 in most states, although exceptions do apply. For a marriage to be legal, both marriage partners must be old enough to marry or must have obtained the required consent. See Table 4 for ages at which minors can legally marry in the 50 states and the District of Columbia, and see Chapter Three, "At Home," for more about legal rights at the age of majority.

Early marriages tend to be unstable. Studies show that the earlier a woman marries, the greater the chance she has of divorcing or separating within five years. Women who marry as teens are twice as likely to separate as those who marry after age 22. Furthermore, most couples who marry before age 21 experience financial problems, have children before they can afford to adequately support them, and struggle to finish school.

What happens if a minor marries without the required parental consent?
Some states say there is no marriage. Others take the position that the marriage can be set aside in court but is valid until this happens.

Table 4
Minimum Age for Marriage, with Consent(a), for Minors Under Age 18, by State,
1999

State or Jurisdiction	Age of Majority	Males	Females
Alabama	19	14(b,c)	14(b,c)
Alaska	18	16(d)	16(d)
Arizona	18	16(d)	16(d)
Arkansas	18	16(d,e)	16(d,e)
California	18	(f)	(f)
Colorado	19	16(d)	16(d)
Connecticut	18	16(d)	16(d)
Delaware	18	18(e)	16(e)
Florida	18	16(b,e)	16(b,e)
Georgia	18	16(e)	16(e)
Hawaii	18	15(d)	15(d)
Idaho	18	16(d)	16(d)
Illinois	18	16(g)	16(g)
Indiana	18	17(e)	17(e)
Iowa	18	(f)	(f)
Indiana	18	17(e)	17(e)
Kansas	18	(f)	(f)
Kentucky	18	(f)	(f)
Louisiana	18	18(d)	18(d)
Maine	18	16(d)	16(d)
Maryland	18	16(e,h)	16(e,h)
Massachusetts	18	14(i)	12(i)
Michigan	18	16	16
Minnesota	18	16(d)	16(d)
Mississippi	21	(f,i)	(f,i)
Missouri	18	15(j)	15(j)
Montana	18	16(d)	16(d)
Nebraska	19	17	17
Nevada	18	16(d)	16(d)
New Hampshire	18	14(i)	13(i)
New Jersey	18	16(d,e)	16(d,e)
New Mexico	18(k)	16(e,j)	16(e,j)
New York	21	16(i)	16(i)
North Carolina	18	16(e)	16(e)
North Dakota	18	16	16
Ohio	18	16(d,e)	18(d,e)
Oklahoma	18	16(d,e)	16(d,e)
Oregon	18	17(l)	17(l)
Pennsylvania	18	16(j)	16(j)
Rhode Island	18	18(j)	16(j)
South Carolina	18	16(e)	16(e)
South Dakota	18	16(e)	16(e)

Table 4 (*continued*)

State or Jurisdiction	Age of Majority	Males	Females
Tennessee	18	16(j)	16(j)
Texas	18	14(i)	14(i)
Utah	18	14(b)	14(b)
Vermont	18	14(d)	14(d)
Virginia	18	16(b,e)	16(b,e)
Washington	18	17(j)	17(j)
West Virginia	18	18(e)	18(e)
Wisconsin	18	16(c)	16(c)
Wyoming	18	16(j)	16(j)
Washington, D.C.	21	16(b)	16(b)
Puerto Rico	21(m)	18(d)	16(d)

Note: Generally, the age of majority is the age at which an individual has legal control over his or her own actions and business (e.g., the ability to contract) except as otherwise provided by statute. In many states the age of majority is arrived at upon marriage if the minimum legal marrying age is lower than the prescribed age of majority.

a. With parental consent. The minimum age for marrying without consent is 18 years in all states except Mississippi, where the minimum age is 21.

b. Parental consent is not required if the minor was previously married.

c. Other statutory requirements apply.

d. Younger persons may marry with parental consent and/or the permission of a judge. In Connecticut and Puerto Rico, judicial approval is required.

e. Younger persons may obtain a license in case of pregnancy or the birth of a child.

f. No age limits.

g. Judicial consent may be given when parents refuse to consent.

h. If under 16, proof of age and the consent of parents in person are required. If a parent is ill, an affidavit by the incapacitated parent and a physician's affidavit to that effect are required.

i. Parental consent and/or permission of a judge are required. In Texas, if below the age of consent, the minors need both parental consent and the permission of a judge.

j. Younger persons may obtain a license in special circumstances.

k. Minors can be emancipated by a valid marriage or by court issuance.

l. If a party has no parent residing within the state, and one party has residence within the state for six months, no permission is required.

m. Either age 21 or when the minor is self-supporting through marriage.

Source: Copyright 1998 The Council of State Governments. Reprinted with permission from *The Book of States.*

If teens who are too young to marry in their home state are married in a state where they are old enough to marry without parental consent, is the marriage legal?

The marriage is usually legal in the state where it was performed. As to the legality of the marriage at home, some states rely on the rule that if a marriage is legal where it was performed, it is legal everywhere.

Others refuse to honor an out-of-state marriage that wouldn't have been legal if performed in-state.

In one case a 15-year-old New York woman married a 20-year-old Virginia resident in Georgia. They separated a few years later. The woman sued to have the marriage set aside or "annulled" in New York. The court said the marriage was valid in Georgia, and it recognized the marriage under the laws of New York because it didn't involve polygamy (having more than one wife).

If a teen marriage is illegal, does it automatically become legal if the couple is still together when both partners have reached the age of majority?

In most states, yes.

OTHER TEEN MARRIAGE ISSUES

Does marriage emancipate a minor?

Yes. When minors are emancipated, their parents no longer have any legal power over them and are no longer required to support them. For more about emancipation see Chapter Five, "On Your Own."

Are interracial marriages legal?

Yes. A law restricting marriage between members of different races would be a clear violation of the federal Constitution.

The Supreme Court first ruled on this issue as late as 1966. Two residents of Virginia, a black woman and a white man, were married in Washington, D.C., in 1958. When they moved back to Virginia in the same year they were charged with violating Virginia's ban on interracial marriages. The couple pleaded guilty to the charges and were sentenced to one year in jail, although the judge suspended their sentences on the condition that they leave Virginia and not return for 25 years. On appeal, the Supreme Court declared Virginia's ban on interracial marriages unconstitutional.

Can a married teen legally buy alcoholic beverages if the drinking age in a particular state is 21?

No. State laws prohibiting the sale of alcoholic beverages to persons under age 21 apply to everyone.

Can a married couple be prohibited from obtaining public welfare benefits because they happen to be teens?
No, provided they are truly independent of their parents.

Can the parents of a married teen carry the teen on their car insurance policy?
Only if the auto that the teen drives is owned by the parents and is garaged at their residence. Insurance companies have special rules relating to coverage for married children of policyholders. A sales agent for the insurance company should be consulted when this issue comes up.

THE RIGHTS OF TEENAGE PARENTS

Do teenage parents always have the right to make independent decisions about raising their children?
Yes, except when a family court decides that they really can't handle such decisions. The parent-child relationship is protected by the federal Constitution, and states may not excessively interfere with the way parents raise their children. This right extends to teenage parents and their offspring. For example, a state may not require a couple to abandon custody of a child just because one or both have not reached the age of majority.

As with adult parents, a child can be removed from a teenage parent's home only if the child has been neglected, mistreated, abused, or abandoned, and *then* only after a full due process hearing. For more about these and related matters, including due process, see Chapter Ten, "Your Right to Be Healthy and Safe from Abuse."

In 1996, about 3,915,000 children were born in the United States. Of this figure, about 494,300 were born to women between the ages of 15 and 19, and about 383,050 of these women were single mothers. This is unfortunate because both parent and child suffer. It is encouraging to note, however, that the teen birth rate has been declining in recent years.[1]

What legal responsibilities do teenagers have as parents?
The same responsibilities as adult parents. In every state, teenage parents must provide their offspring with adequate care, nurturing, education and support. These responsibilities exist regardless of whether the child is born outside marriage, and they continue to exist until the child reaches the age of majority, even if a court forbids a parent to visit his or her child.

Can teenage parents consent to medical care for their child?

Yes, and furthermore, no state requires the involvement of a teen's parents in such matters.

Does a teen have legal rights with respect to a child born outside marriage?

Yes. The Constitution gives parents of all ages the right of custody over their minor children. This right always includes children born outside of marriage and children of teenage parents.

When the parents of a child born outside of marriage are involved in a dispute over child custody, will a family court always award custody to the mother?

No. Courts in certain states still regard the mother as the natural guardian of a minor child, particularly a very young child. (This is called the "maternal preference.") But a mother's right to custody of a child born outside of marriage is far from absolute—it will yield to the child's best interests.

As a practical matter, family courts are most likely to award custody to the parent who has been *caring for* the child since that parent knows the child best. If the parents are unmarried teens, the mother almost always is the caregiver, because teenage fathers rarely live with their children. What this means is that unless a teenage father can convince a court that the mother can't take care of the child *and* that he can, the mother will usually be awarded custody.

Even so, a teenage father who wants to take day-to-day responsibility for his child can certainly seek to obtain custody. In a disputed case, if a family court determines that awarding custody to the father is in the child's best interests, it may make such an award, even if the parents have never lived as a couple under the same roof.

Can custody of a child ever be changed?

Family courts hesitate to modify custody arrangements once they have been established. To do so, the circumstances in the child's home must have changed dramatically, and the court must be convinced that a new home clearly would be in the child's best interests. If this can be shown, the court might award custody to the child's father, a grandparent, or another relative.

As discussed in Chapters Three and Ten, every state has the power to remove neglected, mistreated, or abandoned children from their homes, either temporarily or permanently. Matters such as these are handled in child protection proceedings in family court.

If a teenage mother has physical custody of a child born outside of marriage, is the father legally entitled to visit the child?

Yes, unless the family court believes that contact with the child isn't in the child's best interests. A teenage father has the right to be involved with his offspring unless he has been proved unfit or has forfeited his parental rights.

Can a teenage mother voluntarily place her child for adoption?

Yes. The consent of both parents is necessary in order to place a child for adoption, except in cases in which a parent's rights have already been terminated under state law. The consents must be in writing, and they can only be given after the birth of the child.

In a few states, such as Minnesota, if a birth parent is below age 18, his or her parents (or legal guardian) must also consent. However, the underage birth parent is entitled to the advise of an attorney, a member of the clergy, or a physician before executing the consent form.

Of course, if either parent's legal rights have already been terminated under state law, that parent's consent isn't required.

Can a teenage father stop the mother from placing their child for adoption?

The simple answer would be yes, because the father can withhold consent. But in fact, the answer is a bit more complicated. If the father can't be found or hasn't provided for the child financially, most states don't require his consent. Some require the father's consent only if his "paternity" has been established.

In an increasing number of states, a man who believes he many have fathered a certain child can establish his right to be notified of any and all adoption hearings relating to that child. He can, in other words, "register" for notice of the hearings—whether or not the birth mother has named him on the birth certificate as the child's father. The registration can occur any time prior to the birth of the child, but in most states, must occur no later than 30 days after the child's birth. If the birth mother decides to voluntarily relinquish her parental rights, the adoption agency and the family court must notify the registrant.

Some legal scholars believe that a state law which fails to require notification to the father is an unconstitutional denial of "due process of law." For more about due process see Chapter Two.

Can parental rights ever be terminated without a court hearing?

No. Terminating parental rights without a full due process hearing in family court would be a clear violation of the Constitution.

FINANCIAL HELP FOR YOUNG FAMILIES

Do teenage parents have the right to receive financial assistance at public expense?

Public financial assistance isn't a constitutional right. Even so, the federal government and state and local governments provide assistance to families in need. A family who meets the financial qualifications for assistance can't be turned down just because one or both parents is under age 18.

For many years the largest public assistance program for parents was Aid to Families with Dependent Children, or AFDC. But Congress abolished AFDC in 1996 and replaced it with the Personal Responsibility and Work Opportunity Reconciliation Act of 1996. This legislation, popularly known as the "Welfare Reform Act," requires each state to establish a welfare plan meeting broad federal guidelines and gives each state a grant of money to assist in its implementation and operation.[2]

Like AFDC, the Welfare Reform Act assists needy families when one parent lives elsewhere or is incapacitated. It compensates families—very modestly—for the support that the missing or incapacitated parent would otherwise contribute.

But the new legislation differs from AFDC in important ways. Amid great controversy, Congress crafted it to help prevent public assistance from devolving into a way of life. First, a family can only receive federal assistance for five years. Second, by the year 2012 at least 50 percent of all families on assistance must have an adult working at least 30 hours per week. Third, assistance may now come in the form of vouchers or services instead of money. With these changes, welfare is no longer an "entitlement." In fact, the new program is often described as a "welfare-to-work" program.

Moreover, the Welfare Reform Act specifically targets teen parents. Now, to obtain public assistance, a minor with a child must live either at home or in an adult setting. Furthermore, the minor must go back to high school or attend a training program as soon as his or her child is 12 weeks old.

How does a family qualify for assistance under the Welfare Reform Act?

The basic eligibility requirements carry over from AFDC. First, there must be a needy, dependent child in the house. A child is "needy" if the household's income and other resources are below a certain dollar amount. Second, one of the parents must have passed away, left home, or become incapacitated. If a family qualifies, it is almost automatically covered by Medicaid as well. (Medicaid is a joint federal/state program which provides medical care to the indigent. In 1996 about 36 million individuals participated in Medicaid programs in the 50 states and the District of Columbia.)

Persons on public assistance receive regular visits from an assigned caseworker. If the recipient refuses to allow the caseworker in the home, benefits can be terminated. Recipients must help caseworkers to establish the paternity of any child born outside of marriage and must cooperate to obtain support from the absent parent. Usually this means providing the other parent's name and address unless giving such information would place the welfare recipient in obvious danger.

Many of America's teens and children live in poverty. In 1996 the official poverty level in the United States was $16,036 for a family of four. In that year, eight percent of all children in the United States lived in families with incomes at *one-half* the poverty level—$8,018. Furthermore, 31 percent of all children lived in four-person families with incomes at 150 percent of the poverty level—$24,054. Studies show that there are fewer middle income families in recent years and more wealthy families. This means that the income gap between the rich and poor is growing.[3]

To find out where to apply for assistance under the Welfare Reform Act and other programs, visit your county welfare or "economic security" office.

Can a minor qualify for food stamps?

If a teenage parent qualifies for public assistance because he or she has physical custody of a child, both parent and child will probably qualify for a federal or local food plan as well. By far the largest food plan is the federal Food Stamp Program.

Food stamps traditionally took the form of coupons. They were issued to the head of the household to purchase food items at grocery stores, but not in restaurants. These days many states are replacing the food coupons with electronic accounts. Instead of receiving a coupon book, a program participant receives a food stamp card worth a certain dollar amount. When the participant presents the card to the grocery store cashier, his or her account is electronically "debited" to reflect the value of the purchase.

In 1995, almost ten percent of the population—about 26 million individuals—participated in the federal food stamp program. Each participant received an average monthly benefit of $71. The benefit amount is based on a so-called "thrifty food plan," which is a low-cost food budget.

Besides the Food Stamp Program, a special federal program called the WIC program provides low-income pregnant women and their children with extra food such as eggs, milk, infant formula, fruit juice, cereal, and cheese. The WIC program covers needy children to age four. Also, nonprofit elementary and secondary schools and child-care institutions receive government funds to serve milk, well-balanced meals and snacks to students and preschool children.

For couples with no children, about 7.5 percent receive some form of public assistance. For couples who have at least one child, the figure increases to about ten percent. However, for single mothers, the percentage of participants skyrockets to 49 percent. About one in four persons who participates in a public assistance program is under age 18.[4]

NOTES

1. U. S. National Center for Health Statistics, *Vital Statistics of the United States* (1997).

2. Sometimes states don't adequately fund their assistance programs. In 1997, the Supreme Court heard the case of *Blessing v. Freestone*, in which citizens entitled to child support services sued the State of Arizona for funding shortfalls in its welfare system. The claimants based their lawsuit on a federal civil rights statute. Although the case was sent back or "remanded" to the Federal Court of Appeals for further consideration, the decision did not rule out future civil rights lawsuits to correct welfare program deficiencies.

3. Federal Interagency Forum on Child and Family Statistics, *America's Children* (1998).

4. *Statistical Abstract of the United States* (1997).

FOR FURTHER READING

In General

American Bar Association Guide to Family Law. New York: Times Books, 1996.

Guggenheim, Martin, et al. *The Rights of Families: The Authoritative Guide to the Rights of Family Members Today (ACLU)*. Carbondale: Southern Illinois University Press, 1996.

Couples

Gertz, Frederick. *Legal Affairs. Essential Advice for Same Sex Couples.* New York: Henry Holt and Company, Inc., 1998.

Lindsay, Jeanne Warren. *Teenage Couples: Coping with Reality.* Buena Park, CA: Morning Glory Press, 1995.

Lindsay, Jeanne Warren. *Teenage Couples' Expectations and Reality: Teen Views on Living Together, Roles, Work, Jealousy and Partner Abuse.* Buena Park, CA: Morning Glory Press, 1996.

Luker, Kristin. *Dubious Conceptions: The Politics of Teenage Pregnancy.* Cambridge, MA: Harvard University Press, 1996.

Pogamy, Susan Browning. *Sex Smart: 501 Reasons to Hold Off on Sex.* Minneapolis: Fairview Press, 1998.

Roleff, Tamara L., and Mary E. Williams. *Marriage and Divorce.* San Diego: Greenhaven Press, 1997.

Parenting

Beyer, Kay, and Ruth C. Rosen. *Coping with Teen Parenting.* New York: Rosen Publishing Group, Inc., 1995.

Granville, Karen, and Leslie Peterson. *Teenage Fathers.* New York: Julian Messner, 1993.

Horn, Wade F., and Jeffrey Rosenberg. *The New Father Book.* Des Moines: Better Homes and Gardens Books, 1998.

Mattes, Jean. *Single Mothers by Choice.* New York: Times Books, 1994.

Sifferman, Kelly Ann. *Adoption: A Legal Guide for Birth and Adoptive Parents.* Broomall, PA: Chelsea House Publishers, 1994.

Simpson, Carolyn. *Coping with Teenage Motherhood.* Center City, MN: Hazelden Press, 1998.

Terkel, Susan Neibung. *Understanding Child Custody.* New York: Franklin Watts, Inc., 1991.

Poverty

Davis, Bertha. *Poverty in America: What We Do about It.* New York: Franklin Watts, Inc., 1991.

Hershkoff, Helen, and Stephen Loffredo. *The Rights of the Poor (ACLU).* Carbondale: Southern Illinois University Press, 1997.

Mulroy, Elizabeth A. *The New Uprooted: Single Mothers in Urban Life.* Westport, CT: Auburn House, 1995.

OTHER INFORMATION SOURCES

Organizations

Friends First
Box 356
Longmont, CO 80502
(800) 909–WAIT
E-mail: info@friendsfirst.org
Home page: www.friendsfirst.org

National Center for Fathering
Box 413888
Kansas City, MO 64141
(800) 593–DADS
E-mail: dads@fathers.com
Home page: www.fathers.com

The National Parenting Center (TNPC)
22801 Ventura Boulevard, Ste. 110
Woodland Hills, CA 91367
(800) 753–6667
E-mail: ParentCtr@tnpc.com
Home page: www.tnpc.com

Online Sources

Teen Advice Online
Home page: www.teenadviceonline.org

Hotlines

Youth Crisis Hotline
(800) 448–4663

— 10 —

Your Right to Be Healthy and Safe from Abuse

ABUSE AND NEGLECT

What is child abuse?

The definition varies somewhat from state to state, but basically it is described as any physical, sexual, mental, or emotional injury to a minor that is caused by a parent or any other individual. Child abuse always includes child sexual molestation.

From a legal standpoint, the abuser doesn't need to have intended to cause harm for child abuse to occur. An abusive act performed "intentionally, knowingly, recklessly, or with criminal negligence" can be child abuse.

By definition, how serious does the abuse actually need to be?

Serious physical injuries are certainly child abuse, but beatings, whippings, and severe spankings may constitute child abuse even if no cuts or bruises result.

Consider the following remarks by a well-known legal authority:

We do not take very good care of many of the children in America. All too often, children are tortured, brutalized, kidnapped (often by their own parents), forced into sexual bondage, burned with cigarettes, scalded with boiling water, made to have sex with one parent while the other watches, physically mutilated, forced to ingest large amounts of laxatives and other "punishment medicines," secreted in isolated rooms, chained to the toilet, made to drink urine, abandoned, sold off to others for drug money, left alone for days on end, born with drug addictions, victimized by incest, molested, raped, beaten unmercifully, thrown against walls, sodomized, shaken so severely that they are injured, poisoned, dressed in filthy lice-infested clothing, starved to the point of emaciation and death, cut, pushed down stairs, dropped on their heads, photographed naked for inclusion in pornographic magazines, and murdered. . . . [P]arents and guardians take the sadness, loneliness, and hopelessness of their own lives out on their children simply because they are there, and because they will not or cannot fight back.[1]

Here are some grim facts about child abuse in the United States.

1. An estimated 2.81 million cases of child abuse, child sexual abuse, and child neglect occurred in 1993.
2. The number of children suffering serious injuries from child abuse nearly quadrupled between 1989 and 1993, from 141,700 to 565,000.
3. Abused and neglected youth often suffer drops in IQ and an increase in learning disabilities, depression, and drug use.
4. Parental abuse of alcohol and other drugs is a major factor contributing to child abuse and early childhood death. Each year, nearly 12 million minors are affected in some way by the substance abuse of their parents.
5. At least three children die every day as a result of abuse and neglect.[2]

How does child neglect differ from child abuse?
Child neglect is defined somewhat less precisely than child abuse. Usually it is described as a lapse of care by a parent or other responsible person. Child neglect occurs when parents don't provide for a minor's basic survival needs. The most obvious example is the failure of a parent to provide a child with adequate food, clothing, shelter, or supervision.

The laws of many states limit state intervention in neglect cases to situations in which the parents are able to provide for a minor but refuse to do so. Certain states limit state action to situations in which the parents knowingly refuse to accept public assistance for a minor.

How are child abuse and child neglect cases reported?
The easiest way to report a suspected case is to call the police or the state or local child protection agency. See Table 5. Crisis intervention

Table 5
State Child Protection Offices

Call the office in your state to report cases of abuse or neglect. Someone will tell you whom to contact locally.

ALABAMA
Bureau of Family & Children Services
Department of Human Resources
50 North Ripley Street
Montgomery, AL 36130
Phone: (334) 242–9500

ALASKA
Division of Family & Youth Services
Box 110630
Juneau, AK 99811
Phone: (907) 465–3191

ARIZONA
Children, Youth & Families
Department of Economic Security
1789 West Jefferson, Room 750A
Phoenix, AZ 85005
Phone: (602) 542–3598

ARKANSAS
Children & Family Services
Department of Human Services
Box 1437
Little Rock, AR 72203
Phone: (501) 682–8772

CALIFORNIA
Children & Family Services Division
Department of Social Services
744 P Street, MS 17–18
Sacramento, CA 95814
Phone: (916) 657–2614

COLORADO
Child Welfare Program
Department of Human Services
1575 Sherman Street, 2nd Floor
Denver, CO 80203
Phone: (303) 866–3672

CONNECTICUT
Department of Children & Families
505 Hudson Street
Hartford, CT 06106
Phone: (860) 550–6300

DELAWARE
Department of Services for Children,
    Youth & Families
1825 Faulkland Road
Wilmington, DE 19805
Phone: (302) 633–2500

DISTRICT OF COLUMBIA
Children & Youth Services
Building 1
2700 M.L. King, Jr. Avenue, SE
Washington, DC 20032
Phone: (202) 727–5947

FLORIDA
Family Safety & Preservation
Department of Children & Family
1317 Winewood Boulevard, Building 8
Tallahassee, FL 32399
Phone: (850) 488–8762

GEORGIA
Department of Juvenile Justice
2 Peachtree Street, 5th Floor
Atlanta, GA 30303
Phone: (404) 657–2410

HAWAII
Child Protective Services
Department of Human Services
810 Richards Street, Suite 400
Honolulu, HI 96813
Phone: (808) 586–5667

IDAHO
Children's Services
Department of Health & Welfare
450 West State Street
Box 83720
Boise, ID 83720–0036
Phone: (208) 334–5700

ILLINOIS
Department of Children & Family Services
406 East Monroe Street
Springfield, IL 62701
Phone: (217) 785–2509

Table 5 (*continued*)

INDIANA
Division of Families & Children
Family & Social Services Administration
IGC-South, Room W392
Indianapolis, IN 46204
Phone: (317) 232–4705

IOWA
Adult, Children & Family Services
Hoover State Office Building
1305 East Walnut
Des Moines, IA 50319
Phone: (515) 281–5521

KANSAS
Children & Family Services
Social & Rehabilitation Services
300 SW Oakley, West Hall
Topeka, KS 66606
Phone: (785) 296–4653

KENTUCKY
Division of Family Services
Department for Social Services
2775 East Main Street
Frankfort, KY 40301
Phone: (502) 564–6852

LOUISIANA
Department of Social Services
Box 3776
Baton Rouge, LA 70821
Phone: (504) 342–0286

MAINE
Child & Family Services
Department of Human Services
11 State House Station
Augusta, ME 04333
Phone: (207) 287–5060

MARYLAND
Governor's Office of Children
   Youth & Families
Executive Department
301 West Preston Street, 15th Floor
Baltimore, MD 21201
Phone: (410) 767–4092

MASSACHUSETTS
Executive Office of Health & Human Serv-
   ices
Department of Youth Services
24–43 Wormwood Street, Suite 400
Boston, MA 02210
Phone: (617) 727–7575

MICHIGAN
Office of Delinquency Services
Family Independence Agency
235 South Grand Avenue
Lansing, MI 48909
Phone: (517) 335–6158

MINNESOTA
Family & Children Services Division
Department of Human Services
444 Lafayette Road
Saint Paul, MN 55155
Phone: (619) 296–2487

MISSISSIPPI
Division of Family & Children's Services
Box 352
Jackson, MS 39205
Phone: (601) 359–4555

MISSOURI
Children's Services
Division of Family Services
Department of Social Services
615 Howerton Court
Box 88
Jefferson City, MO 65103
Phone: (573) 751–2882

MONTANA
Child & Family Services Division
Department of Public Health &
   Human Services
1400 Broadway, Room C114
Helena, MT 59620
Phone: (406) 444–5900

NEBRASKA
Protection & Safety Division
Department of Health & Human Services
Box 95044

Table 5 (*continued*)

Lincoln, NE 68509
Phone: (402) 471–9308

NEVADA
Division of Child & Family Services
711 East Fifth Street
Carson City, NV 89701
Phone: (702) 687–5982

NEW HAMPSHIRE
Office of Family Services
Division of Children, Youth & Families
6 Hazen Drive
Concord, NH 03301
Phone: (603) 271–4714

NEW JERSEY
Division of Family Development
Department of Human Services
Quakerbridge Road
Box 716
Trenton, NJ 08625
Phone: (609) 588–2401

NEW MEXICO
Family Preservation Unit
PERA Building, Room 254
Box 5160
Santa Fe, NM 87502
Phone: (505) 827–8400

NEW YORK
Office of Children & Family Services
52 Washington Street
Rensselaer, NY 12144
Phone: (518) 473–8437

NORTH CAROLINA
Department of Health & Human Services
325 North Salisbury Street
Raleigh, NC 27603
Phone: (919) 733–3055

NORTH DAKOTA
Children & Family Services
Department of Human Services
600 East. Boulevard Ave., 3rd Floor
Bismarck, ND 58505
Phone: (701) 328–2316

OHIO
Family & Children's Service Division
Department of Human Services
65 East State Street
Columbus, OH 43215
Phone: (614) 466–1213

OKLAHOMA
Health & Human Services
Department of Human Services
Box 25352
Oklahoma City, OK 73125
Phone: (405) 521–2778

OREGON
Commission on Children & Families
530 Center Street, NE, Suite 300
Salem, OR 97310
Phone: (503) 373–1283

PENNSYLVANIA
Children, Youth & Families
Department of Public Welfare
Box 2675
Harrisburg, PA 17105
Phone: (717) 787–4756

RHODE ISLAND
Department of Children, Youth & Families
610 Mount Pleasant Avenue
Providence, RI 02908
Phone: (401) 457–4750

SOUTH CAROLINA
Child Protective & Preventative Services
Department of Social Services
Box 1520
Columbia, SC 29202
Phone: (803) 734–5670

SOUTH DAKOTA
Child Protective Services Division
Department of Social Services
Kneip Building
700 Governors Drive
Pierre, SD 57501
Phone: (605) 773–3227

Table 5 (*continued*)

TEXAS
Department of Protective & Regulatory
 Services
Mail Code E–654
701 West 51st Street
Austin, TX 78751
Phone: (512) 438–4778

UTAH
Division of Child & Family Services
Department of Human Services
120 N. 200 West, Room 225
Salt Lake City, UT 84103
Phone: (801) 538–3993

VERMONT
Department of Social & Rehabilitation
 Services
103 South Main Street
Waterbury, VT 05671
Phone: (802) 241–2101

VIRGINIA
Department of Social Services
Theater Row West Building
730 East Broad Street
Richmond, VA 23219
Phone: (804) 692–1901

WASHINGTON
Children & Family Services Division
Department of Social & Health Services
Box 45710
Olympia, WA 98504
Phone: (360) 902–7910

WEST VIRGINIA
Office of Maternal & Child Health
Bureau for Public Health
Department of Health & Human Resources
1411 Virginia Street, East
Charleston, WV 25301
Phone: (304) 588–5388

WISCONSIN
Division of Children & Family Services
Health & Family Services
1 West Wilson, Room 465
Box 7851
Madison, WI 53707
Phone: (608) 266–3036

WYOMING
Department of Family Services
Hathaway Building, 3rd Floor
2300 Capitol Avenue
Cheyenne, WY 82002
Phone: (307) 777–6948

groups and medical clinics such as Planned Parenthood can also be called. They have reporting information at their fingertips.

In addition, most communities have 24-hour child abuse and child neglect telephone hotlines (sometimes called "helplines"). The numbers to call are usually listed in the front of the local phone book. Important hotline numbers, including national child abuse hotlines, are listed in Table 6. Calls to hotlines are always confidential.

If a young person is being abused by a parent, a housekeeper, a co-worker, a date, a neighbor, a parent's boyfriend or girlfriend, a brother or sister—*anyone*—the young person or anyone else may report it. The abuser doesn't have to be a parent for the state to be concerned about stopping it and preventing it from happening again.

Table 6
National Toll-free Hotline Numbers

ABUSE
Parents Anonymous
(800) 352–0386 (California)
(800) 421–0353 (elsewhere)

National Child Abuse Hotline
(800) 4–A–CHILD

DRUG ABUSE
National Institute on Drug Abuse
(800) 662–HELP

National Cocaine Hotline
(800) COCAINE

ALCOHOLISM
National Council on Alcoholism and Drug
Dependence Hotline
(800) 622–2255

Mothers Against Drunk Driving (MADD)
(800) 438–6233

CIVIL RIGHTS
Civil Rights Complaint Hotline
(800) 368–1019

HEALTH CARE
National Health Information Center
Department of Health & Human Services

(301) 565–4167 (Maryland)
(800) 336–4797 (elsewhere)

SEXUALLY TRANSMITTED
DISEASES (STDs)
National STD Hotline
(800) 227–8922

CDC National AIDS Hotline
U.S. Public Health Service
(800) 342–2437
SIDA (Spanish line) (800) 344–7432

PREGNANCY
Pro-Choice
Abortion Hotline
(800) 770–9100

Right-to-Life
Birthright, Inc.
(800) 848–LOVE

RUNAWAYS
National Runaway Switchboard
(800) 621–4000
TTY (hearing impaired) (800) 621–0394
www.nrscrisesline.org

Runaway Hotline
(800) 231–6946

Can a minor report an abusing parent?

Anyone can make a report. For the sake of the victim, the abuser, and the abuser's family, all physical and sexual abuse cases should be reported, as should all neglect cases. The more detailed the report, the more quickly the child protection agency is likely to respond.

Are reports of abuse to child protection services offices confidential?

Always.

Can one parent report the other parent?

Yes.

If a person fails to report a case of child abuse or child neglect, has he or she broken the law?

In some situations, yes. In the past, only doctors and nurses were "mandatory reporters." But now the list includes teachers, psychologists, psychotherapists, dentists, and other health care providers because these individuals are often the first to see evidence of the abuse. In most states, social workers, day care employees, the police, and judges are also mandatory reporters, and in some states *everyone* is required to report. Even so, few individuals are ever prosecuted for failing to report a child abuse incident. This fact probably contributes to even greater underreporting.

Is a minor ever a mandatory reporter?

As a practical matter, no.

Can a person get in trouble for making a child abuse report if no abuse actually occurred?

No. Every state provides legal immunity for mandatory reporters who make a child abuse report in good faith. This means that if a mandatory reporter makes a report of suspected abuse or neglect, and if the investigators finally determine that no abuse or neglect occurred, the reporter can't be taken to court for slander or libel. In many states this rule also applies to voluntary or "nonmandatory" reporters.

The questions and answers that follow assume that the suspected abuser is a parent. However, for a child protective agency to act, the abuser or neglectful person needn't be a parent. He or she can be a teacher, housekeeper, relative, sibling, or any other person.

How does a child protection agency act on a report of abuse or neglect?

A "child protection team" of professionals goes to work. If the problem is in the home, the agency conducts a home investigation. At least one social worker will visit the child's residence, often unannounced. He or she will interview the parents, the child, other suspected abusers, and often neighbors and friends. Frequently the social worker will also interview the child's teachers and health care providers.

The child protection team might also include mental health experts, nurses, and attorneys.

If evidence of abuse or neglect turns up, the lawyer for the child protective agency may file a "petition" in state family court for authority to take custody of the minor or protect the minor in some other way. Filing a petition officially begins the case, which is a "civil action" as opposed to a "criminal action." In most states these cases are called "child protection proceedings."

For more about the difference between civil and criminal actions see Chapter Seventeen, "Taking Matters to Court."

Does the investigation procedure differ in an emergency situation?

Yes. If the young person appears to be in serious danger and there's no time for a home study or even a preliminary hearing in court, the child can be removed immediately. (This can also occur in cases of child abandonment.) But the family court must hold a hearing as soon as possible after the removal in order to decide exactly how to proceed. If it turns out that removing the child wasn't needed, the child must be returned home promptly.

Is a petition filed in family court after every investigation?

No. A petition won't be filed if the investigation doesn't reveal evidence of abuse or neglect. But even if such evidence exists, the agency may decide against filing a petition if the parents agree to participate in parenting classes, counseling, or some other suggested rehabilitation program. Meanwhile a social worker from the child protective agency will make periodic visits to the family to make certain the home situation is stable. If the parents don't make an effort to attend the special classes, counseling, or rehab program, the agency may decide to go ahead and file the petition.

Does the minor remain at home during the investigation?

It depends on the circumstances. If the abuse or neglect appears especially serious or if allowing the minor to stay home is likely to be a bad idea for some other reason, the judge may order the minor to stay with a relative or perhaps a family friend. Other possibilities are placing the minor in temporary foster care or with a volunteer family. (Foster care is discussed at the end of this chapter.)

What actually happens in a family court hearing?

Investigators, social workers, and medical witnesses present their evidence to the family court judge. These individuals might be cross-examined by the parents' attorney, who will attempt to protect their interests and their reputation as parents. Documents, medical records, and studies might be offered, and the judge often asks additional questions. Usually no one is in the courtroom except the judge, the witnesses, social workers, relatives, and persons with a stake in the outcome.

Will the minor testify at the hearing?

It depends upon his or her age and maturity, and upon the nature of the case. Small children seldom testify, but teens often do.

Although the minor is usually the key witness at an abuse or neglect hearing, minors often find court intimidating. There's never anything to be afraid of. But even so, many minors fear their testimony will infuriate their parents, and sometimes it does. For this reason, family court judges sometimes permit a minor's testimony to be taken outside the courtroom and away from the parents. Testimony might be videotaped or tape-recorded, or taken inside the judge's office.

Can a minor be required to testify?

Yes, if the judge determines that the minor is "competent" to do so. See Chapter Seventeen for additional information about the testimony of minors.

Will the court always remove a minor from the home in a proven abuse or neglect situation?

No. If the problem isn't expected to continue and allowing the minor to stay at home appears to be the preferred arrangement, a family court won't authorize removal. Instead, a social worker will monitor the family and try to help them better understand their problems. In-home counseling often is an enormous help to troubled families.

If parents are suspected of abuse or neglect, will a lawyer be appointed to represent their interests if they can't afford one?

Yes, in both civil and criminal cases. Although parents don't have a constitutional right to a lawyer in child protection proceedings, most states now authorize court-appointed counsel to assist poor parents.

Is the minor entitled to a court-appointed lawyer as well?

Yes, although in some states the minor's representative doesn't need to be a licensed attorney. That lay person is often called a guardian *ad litem.*

In fact, a subtle difference exists between the roles of the lawyer and the guardian *ad litem.* A lawyer represents the minor; a guardian *ad litem* represents the best interests of the minor. Occasionally these interests conflict, as in cases in which a minor with legal counsel insists on remaining with a parent in a troubled, unsafe home. When this occurs, the judge must decide what is best for the young person.

Will the minor's lawyer and the parents' lawyer always be different people?

Yes, because the parents' position in the case might be contrary to the child's. They might, for example, claim that neither has ever laid a hand on the child, despite the child's obvious cuts and bruises. For this reason, family courts almost always appoint a lawyer or guardian *ad litem* to represent the minor.

Who pays for the minor's lawyer?

Usually the state.

Does the family court go after the abuser?

No. A family court's basic purpose is to protect a minor from abuse or neglect. But as this is being arranged, the state prosecuting attorney may decide to charge the suspected party with criminal abuse or neglect, or perhaps even "battery" or attempted homicide. (Battery is any touching of another person without first obtaining the consent of the person who is legally allowed to give it.)

An important factor in the prosecutor's decision is this: he or she knows that *criminal* abuse and neglect are harder to prove than *civil* abuse and neglect. For a person to be convicted on criminal charges, the prosecutor must prove "beyond a reasonable doubt" that the person committed the act. But for a family court to intervene, the facts of the case only have to show it was "more likely than not" that abuse or neglect occurred. If the prosecutor doesn't believe the state's "burden of proof" can be met, he or she won't file criminal charges, and the case will only go to family court.

In addition, the criminal system can be slow to act. But civil or family courts are usually "at the ready" and are also more likely to help other family members.

Criminal abuse trials are discussed in detail in the next section.

SEXUAL ABUSE

How does the law define sexual abuse?

Sexual abuse is any forced or required sexual contact. The sexual contact includes any attempted or actual penetration of a minor's vagina or anus, and also oral sex. Additionally, it includes an adult's handling of a minor's genitals, or a request for a minor to handle an adult's genitals.

Sexual abuse doesn't have to involve actual physical contact. When no contact occurs the abuse is sometimes called "child exploitation." It is sexual exploitation for a minor to be forced or required to look at an adult's genitals or forced or required to undress in front of another. It is also sexual abuse for an adult to require a minor to submit sexually to a third person.

Sexual abuse often begins when a child is quite young and often progresses from fondling to intercourse. Sometimes child sexual abuse leads to other forms of abuse or exploitation such as child pornography.

Is sexual abuse always a crime?

Yes. Persons who sexually abuse or sexually molest minors or adults can be charged with criminal sexual abuse. Most states impose a maximum of between 10 and 20 years imprisonment for sexual intercourse with a child. When the victim is an adolescent, the maximum sentence for forced sex usually is ten years. Some states provide lesser penalties.

Some experts believe that criminal prosecution in child sexual abuse cases can cause more emotional damage to a minor than the abuse itself. Even so, a criminal prosecution is a symbol that society protects minors and that their rights and welfare are respected.[3]

Can a parent be criminally charged with child sexual abuse?

Anyone can be charged with child sexual abuse, including a parent.

If a parent is charged with suspected child sexual abuse, can the other parent also be charged?

In certain cases, yes. Usually it depends on whether the nonparticipating parent knew that the child was being sexually abused but didn't do anything to stop it.

What are conditions known as "battered child syndrome" and "sexually abused child syndrome"?

These conditions exist when medical examinations establish that the minor has been either physically or sexually abused, but no clear link exists between an adult's misconduct and the minor's physical or psychological state. A parent or other adult can be charged with child abuse in connection with these conditions.

Proving these offenses require the state prosecuting attorney to prove that only the person charged was undoubtedly responsible for the abuse. Often the syndrome isn't identified until the child has died or lapsed into a critical physical or psychological state.

"Maternal deprivation syndrome" is also a form of child abuse and involves a similar type of proof.

Can a teen be charged with criminal sexual abuse for having sex with another teen?

Here it depends on whether the sex is forced. An obvious example of teen sexual abuse would be date rape. For more about teens and sex see Chapter Eight, "Your Sexual Life."

How can a sexually abused minor obtain immediate help?

By contacting the state child protection agency or the police. Child sexual abuse is a form of child abuse, so the state child protective agency can always intervene. As in physical abuse and neglect cases, it can act in an emergency, then bring a child protection proceeding after intervening. At a later date the state prosecuting attorney will decide whether to criminally prosecute the suspected abuser.

What would a criminal abuse or neglect trial be like?

In all honesty, it wouldn't be fun. Prior to trial the minor would be required to repeat the details of the incident to several different police officers, doctors, social workers, counselors, and the suspect's attorney. The trial would probably be open to the public. The minor might be required to take the stand, and there would be plenty of legal jargon used during the investigation and trial that the minor wouldn't comprehend.

No civil hearing or criminal trial on a physical or sexual abuse matter is pleasant for the individuals involved. The law can require or "subpoena" key persons to participate. Even so, the social workers, counselors, lawyers, and others involved are always extremely caring and supportive of the minor.

Are physical and sexual abuse tough to prove in court?

Not necessarily. Child abuse used to be difficult to prove because courts didn't trust the testimony of minors, even if the minor was a teen and the only witness to the abuse. But these days a minor's testimony is permitted and often required in both civil and criminal physical and sexual abuse cases, except when the minor is a young child.

A special issue in criminal sexual abuse cases is "hearsay," which is a person's statement about what someone else said. Hearsay statements usually aren't permitted in court to prove a point. In an abuse case, the rule against hearsay could prevent an individual such as a school nurse from stating what the minor confided about the sexual abuse. Instead, the court would require the minor to testify on his or her own.[4] This can be a major obstacle if the minor is afraid to testify.

The hearsay rule is often relaxed in child sexual abuse and rape cases, and also in custody cases, but only if the minor's hearsay statements appear particularly reliable. Courts have treated "excited utterances" and "spontaneous declarations" of young people as reliable testimony on this theory. In a 1988 custody case in Connecticut, a psychologist was permitted to testify that a minor had spontaneously claimed that her father caused her genital injuries. The court admitted the child's declarations as reliable testimony even though they were hearsay. The father's visitation rights were drastically restricted as a result.

On the other hand, in a 1987 Georgia case a mother wasn't permitted to testify about words spoken by her son in his sleep regarding a certain act of anal sex by another person. Not surprisingly, the court ruled that her testimony was unreliable hearsay.

Testimony by a minor in court is discussed earlier in this chapter and also in Chapter Seventeen.

MEDICAL CARE

If parents don't provide a minor child with adequate medical care, what can happen?

The state child protection agency can intervene, because failing to provide medical care to a minor is a form of child neglect. The state can also intervene if parents remove their child from a doctor's care before treatment is complete.

Family courts consider both the seriousness of the problem and the risks and benefits of treatment in determining whether to order medical help. They also consider whether the child wants to go through with the procedure.

Does a minor's life need to be in danger before a family court will order treatment?

No, but sometimes it is difficult to predict whether treatment will actually be ordered.

Courts don't hesitate to issue orders for blood transfusions and other accepted procedures, despite parental objections. Vaccination cases fall into this category. In 1993, a Missouri court ordered the vaccination of a child (and also ruled that child neglect had occurred) after it found that the parents had knowingly failed to have him vaccinated during a measles outbreak. In that case the court ruled that the scientific basis for vaccinating children for measles was well established. It also ruled that the parents' opposition to vaccines was not based on their personal religious beliefs.

On the other hand, a Pennsylvania court earlier refused to order a spinal operation for a young boy because neither he nor his parents wanted to go through with it—even though his condition was quite serious. But in 1972 an Iowa court approved simple tonsillectomies for three siblings over the religious objections of the parents.

Can parents prevent a minor child from receiving medical treatment for religious reasons, even if the minor wants it?

Yes, but only if the refusal to obtain treatment doesn't seriously endanger the minor's health or otherwise amount to neglect. Cases like this raise a freedom of religion issue under the First Amendment, so courts usually hesitate to order treatment unless the minor's condition is very serious. Even if medical treatment is ordered, courts are reluctant to remove children from their homes or from the physical custody of their parents. But removal will be ordered if abuse, neglect, or abandonment is shown to exist.

For more about First Amendment rights including the First Amendment's Free Exercise Clause, see Chapter Two, "At School."

Can a minor arrange for his or her own medical care?

As a rule, minors can't enter into agreements for medical care or provide consent for their own treatment. But two exceptions exist. First, a minor can legally consent to needed treatment if the parents refuse. Second, mature, married, pregnant, and "emancipated" minors and those who are parents or runaways can give consent to routine treatment.[5] (Emancipation gives a minor most of the privileges and responsibilities of adulthood, as Chapter Five explains.) In addition, most states have laws permitting minors to consent to confidential treatment for alcoholism, drug abuse, and sexually transmitted diseases (STDs) including human immunodeficiency virus/acquired immunodeficiency syndrome (HIV/AIDS).[6]

If a minor arranges for his or her own medical care, who is financially responsible?

Often the minor pays because he or she wants to keep the treatment confidential. Even so, medical "necessaries" are the legal responsibility of the parents even if they don't contract for them, and even if they don't have a close relationship with their minor child.

Wouldn't a doctor still hesitate to treat a minor absent parental consent?

In most cases, yes, Although the exceptions discussed earlier mean that a doctor can't be sued for battery if he or she treats a minor without parental consent, many won't take the risk.

What should a teen do if he or she needs medical care and the parents won't cooperate?

Call the state child protection agency, or a teacher, minister, relative, or adult friend. The addresses and phone numbers of child protective agencies in each state are listed in Table 4.

Can a minor sign up for publicly funded medical care such as Medicaid if he or she doesn't live at home?

In most states it depends on whether the minor is still under the control of his or her parents or whether the minor is emancipated.

In a 1977 case, New York's highest court decided that because a teenage woman had emancipated herself, she could legally apply for publicly funded medical services. The young woman had left home to avoid her father's control. The state medical welfare agency argued that it shouldn't have to pay for her care because her father had enough income to support her and hadn't thrown her out of the house. The New York court ruled that the woman's "implied" emancipation relieved her father of his parental responsibilities. She was therefore entitled to public medical assistance.

OTHER ISSUES RELATING TO ABUSE AND NEGLECT

Can a minor be taken from the custody of a parent because the parent is "living with someone"?

Not for that reason alone. A California appeals court ruled as early as 1967 that a mother wasn't unfit to parent just because she and her children were living with a man she wasn't married to. The judge's decision, rendered against the county agency seeking custody of the woman's two children, said that the woman and her boyfriend were "satisfying the children's need for family love, security and physical well-being." The decision noted that "many homes, however blessed by marital vows, fall short of an ideal environment for children." Courts across the country have reached similar conclusions in similar cases.

Can a minor be taken from the custody of his or her parents because their home is dirty and messy?

Again, not for that reason alone. A home that strikes someone as dirty or messy doesn't necessarily indicate that the parents are neglectful—some parents just place more importance on a clean house than others. However, a home that truly constitutes a health hazard could be the basis for neglect proceedings.

Can a minor be taken from the custody of his or her parents because one of them has been convicted of a crime?

The fact that a parent has been convicted of a serious crime can be grounds for child protection proceedings in some states. So can a parent's habitual drug or alcohol use.

Can a state take custody of a minor because a parent in the home is gay or lesbian?

In most states a custodial parent's homosexuality can't support a claim of child neglect in and of itself. But family courts will consider a parent's active sexual conduct when deciding whether the parent is fit to raise children. To learn about situations in which parental rights can be terminated altogether see Chapter Three, "At Home."

MENTAL HEALTH ISSUES

Can a teen see a psychiatrist or psychologist without parental consent?

Although at least half of the states and the District of Columbia now permit minors to consent to confidential outpatient mental health treatment, it is very difficult for a young person to obtain mental health counseling without parental approval. Many public and private mental health agencies refuse to meet with a teen more than once without notice to a parent. Psychiatrists and psychologists in private practice rarely confront this issue because teens usually can't afford to see them.

A local mental health association is the best place to contact for information about confidential mental health counseling and treatment.

Can parents admit a minor to a mental hospital without the minor's consent?

Parents have the legal power to consent to a minor's mental health treatment in a private hospital.

Can parents admit a minor child to a public mental hospital without a court hearing?

According to a 1979 Supreme Court case, a full due process hearing isn't required. However, some sort of court review must take place to determine whether admitting the minor is necessary or whether the parents are simply shoving a difficult minor aside. Usually these reviews are conducted by a doctor who hasn't treated the minor in the past. For information about the meaning of due process see Chapter Two.

FOSTER CARE

What is foster care?

It is a state-sponsored living arrangement for young people whose parents are unable to provide proper care and nurturing. In foster care, "foster parents" take minors into their homes and are responsible for their day-to-day care and supervision. Foster care is meant to last for a limited period, although sometimes foster care arrangements last many months, and sometimes years.

A foster child usually is placed in a foster home at the direction of a family court. However, parents can place a child in a foster home voluntarily. The state agency authorized to place children in foster care retains legal custody over the foster child, licenses foster homes, and supervises the foster parents.

Can a teen be a foster "child"?

Yes.

Why might a family court judge order a minor into foster care?

The reason might be that the parents have abused, neglected, or abandoned the child, or that one parent is in prison. It might be that the family is having severe financial difficulties or that a parent is experiencing poor health or emotional problems. There are dozens of reasons for placing young people in foster care.

Do minors in foster care have any legal rights?

Young people in foster homes always have the right to receive adequate care, including food, clothing, shelter, education, and medical treatment, all at state expense. In addition, foster children with special needs are legally entitled to receive special medical or psychiatric care and also rehabilitation training.

Foster children also have the right to be protected from abuse and neglect at the hands of their foster parents. If a young person is abused while in foster care, the state must remove the child. In most states a foster child (assisted by an adult) can go to court to recover money damages against the foster care agency for its failure to supervise the foster parents properly. For more about recovering damages in court see Chapter Seventeen, "Taking Matters to Court."

Do minors in need of foster care have a right to choose their foster parents?

No. The decision is made by the state foster care agency. But many agencies actively seek out relatives who might be willing to serve as foster parents.

Do the natural parents retain any authority over a child in foster care?

In most states, yes. Although the family court transfers legal custody to the foster care agency, it often permits the natural parents to continue to make major decisions relating to their child, including decisions about the child's medical care, schooling, and religion.

Do foster children have a legal right to see their natural parents while in foster care?

In most cases, yes, and the parents usually have a right to see their child. There is a strong belief that foster children need to maintain contact with their parents; as a result, foster care agencies now authorize regular visits by the parents, except in extreme cases.

Do foster children have a legal right to be reunited with their families after being in a foster home?

Yes. Federal law requires that states develop case plans to reunite foster children with their natural families as soon as possible, provided it is in the child's best interests. States must determine within 18 months of placement whether the child should be returned home, placed for adoption, or put in a more permanent foster home. This law was passed after studies proved that children were remaining in foster care either too long or for no good reason.

Can foster parents legally prevent a foster child from being returned to his or her natural parents?

The laws of some states now permit foster parents to challenge a foster child's return to his or her natural parents. Usually the foster parents may object to a foster child's removal only if the child has been with them for a long time—3 to 18 months, depending on the state.

Do foster parents have a legal right to adopt a foster child?

In many states, yes, but only if the parental rights of the natural parents have been terminated. Although foster parents used to be forbidden to adopt foster children, in recent years such adoptions have gained favor with legislatures, courts, and child protective agencies.

Can a minor adopt his or her foster parents?

No, but if foster parents want to adopt a foster child, many states require the child's consent to the adoption if the child has reached a certain age. The age of consent falls between ages 10 and 14, again depending on the state.

For a discussion of whether a minor can divorce his or her parents in favor of foster parents or others, see Chapter Seven.

Do foster parents receive payment for taking a foster child?

In most cases, yes. The state makes regular payments to foster parents to assist with the cost of care.

NOTES

1. Donald T. Kramer, *The Legal Rights of Children*, 2nd ed. (Colorado Springs: Shepard's/McGraw-Hill, 1994).

2. U.S. Department of Health and Human Services, *Children Today* (1992) 21:2.

3. David Finkelhor, *Sexually Victimized Children* (New York: The Free Press, 1979).

4. The hearsay rule protects the criminal suspect's constitutional right to confront his or her accuser and the constitutional right to cross-examine.

5. More than 500,000 young people run away annually. Unfortunately, consent by minors in many medical and clinical settings, particularly for runaways, often is not accepted. Council on Scientific Affairs, "Health Care Needs of Homeless and Runaway Youths," *Journal of the American Medical Association* (1989) 262:1358–1361.

6. Few patient populations are more vulnerable than runaway adolescents. Sexual abuse and physical victimization, substance abuse, pregnancy, and

HIV/AIDS leave runaways in serious need of good medical care and psychological support. *New York Times* (October 8, 1989): A1. Runaway teens are at very high risk for contacting HIV/AIDS, as 5.3 percent of runaways in New York City and 8.2 percent of those in San Francisco are HIV infected, through either sexual activity or intravenous drug use. R. L. Stricof et al., "HIV Seroprevalence in a Facility for Runaway and Homeless Adolescents," *American Journal of Public Health* (1991) 181:50–53; "Prevalence of Sexually Transmitted Diseases (STDs) and HIV in a Homeless Youth Medical Clinic in San Francisco," *Abstracts of the Sixth International Conference on AIDS*, Abstract 231, San Francisco, June 23, 1990.

FOR FURTHER READING

In General

Goldentyer, Debra. *Family Violence*. Orlando: FL: Raintree/Steck Vaughn Company, 1995.

Mariani, Cliff, and Patricia Sokolich. *Domestic Violence Survival Guide*. Flushing, NY: Looseleaf Law Publications, 1996.

Morey, Ann-Janine. *What Happened to Christopher: An American Family's Story of Shaken Baby Syndrome*. Carbondale: Southern Illinois University Press, 1998.

Parton, Nigel. *Governing the Family: Child Care, Child Protection and the State*. New York: St. Martin's Press, 1991.

Scales, Cynthia. *Potato Chips for Breakfast: The True Story of Growing Up in an Alcoholic Family*. New York: Bantam Books, 1990.

Legal Issues

Clement, Mary. *The Juvenile Justice System: Law and Process*. Woburn, MA: Butterworth-Heinemann, 1996.

Guggenheim, Martin. *The Rights of Families: The Authoritative ACLU Guide to the Rights of Family Members Today*. Carbondale: Southern Illinois University Press, 1996.

Hibner, John, and Jill Wolfron. *Somebody Else's Children: The Courts, the Kids, and the Struggle to Save America's Troubled Families*. New York: Crown Publishers, 1998.

Wallace, Harvey. *Family Violence: Legal, Medical, and Social Perspectives*. Needham Heights, MA: Allyn & Bacon, 1998.

Sexual Abuse

Dziech, Billie Wright, et al. *On Trial: America's Courts and Their Treatment of Sexually Abused Children*. Boston: Beacon Press, 1991.

Reinert, Dale Robert. *Sexual Abuse and Incest*. Springfield, NJ: Enslow Publishers, Inc., 1997.

Medical Care

Isler, Charlotte. *The Watts Teen Health Dictionary*. New York: Franklin Watts, Inc., 1996.

Mental Health Care

Cohen, Daniel, and Susan Cohen. *Teenage Stress*. New York: Dell Publishing Company, Inc., 1992.

Newman, Susan. *Don't Be Sad: A Teenage Guide to Handling Stress, Anxiety, and Depression*. New York: Julian Messner, 1992.

Foster Care

Bartholet, Elizabeth. *Nobody's Children: Abuse and Neglect, Foster Drift, and the Adoption Alternative*. Boston: Beacon Press, 1999.

Glatz, Janet Clayton. *Fostering or Adopting the Troubled Child: A Guide for Parents and Professionals*. Brunswick, ME: Audenreed Press, 1998.

Falke, Joseph. *Living in a Foster Home*. New York: Crown Publishers, 1995.

OTHER INFORMATION SOURCES

Organizations

American Red Cross
1621 North Kent Street
Arlington, VA 20009
(703) 248–4222
E-mail: info@usa.redcross.org
Home Page: www.redcross.org

Med Help International
Box 188
63000 North Wickham Road
Melbourne, FL 32940
(407) 733–0069
E-mail: staff@medhelp.org
Home page: //medhlp.netusa.net

National Clearinghouse for Child Abuse and Neglect Information
330 C Street SW
Washington, DC 20447
(800) 394–3366
E-mail: nccanch@calib.com
Home page: www.calib.com/nccanch

National Foster Parent Association (NFPA)
Box 81
Alpha, OH 45301
(800) 557–5238
E-mail: nfpa@donet.com
Home page: www.nfpainc.org

Rape Abuse & Incest National Network (RAINN)
635-B Pennsylvania Avenue SE
Washington, DC 20003
(800) 656-HOPE
E-mail: rainnmail@aol.com
Home page: www.rainn.org

Online Sources

Child Abuse Prevention Network
Home page: www.child.cornell.edu

Hotlines

National Domestic Violence Hotline
(800) 799–SAFE
(800) 787–3224 (TTY)

Rape Abuse & Incest National Network (RAINN)
(800) 656–HOPE

(800) THERAPIST
www.1-800-therapist.com

Alcohol and Drugs

THE LEGAL DRINKING AGE

At what age can young people legally buy alcoholic beverages?
In most states it is age 21. Many states lowered the legal drinking age to 18 in the early 1970s when the legal age for voting in national elections was lowered from 21 to 18. But in recent years many of the same states have changed the drinking age back to 21, mainly because of concerns over teens who drink and drive.

Businesses may not sell alcohol to underage persons; this is why teens and young adults often are "carded" when they attempt to buy it.

At what age can a person legally possess or consume alcohol?
The same age at which a minor can legally buy it.

Does this mean that possessing alcohol when under the legal age is a crime?
Yes, although it is a misdemeanor. When a minor purchases, possesses, or consumes alcohol, he or she commits a delinquent act. In most states the case will go to juvenile court.

Can a minor legally drink alcohol at home?
In some states drinking at home isn't illegal if the minor has parental permission, although in recent years many states have repealed this twist in their drinking laws.

But even if young people can legally drink at home, they can't legally give alcohol to others. In other words, teens who can't legally buy alcohol can't have parties for other underage drinkers. In a 1989 New Jersey case, a 19-year-old, home for Christmas, threw a "kegger" at his parents' house when they weren't around. About 150 young people came. Many were 16 or 17 years old, and most of them were drinking when the police arrived. The underage host was charged with distributing alcohol to minors. If the host had been over age 21, the charge would have been the same.

If a minor marries or is legally emancipated, is he or she still subject to state laws prohibiting persons under a particular age from purchasing and drinking alcohol?

Yes. Everyone is subject to state laws regulating the purchase and consumption of alcohol, regardless of marital or legal status.

If a minor is caught drinking under age or buying alcohol with false or altered ID, what can happen?

In most states the minor will be arrested, sent to juvenile court, and placed on probation.

If a minor legally purchases alcohol across the state line and brings it into a state that prohibits the possession or consumption of alcohol until age 21, has the minor broken the law?

Yes. State laws regulating the sale, possession, and consumption of alcohol apply to everyone within the state's borders, regardless of where the alcohol was purchased and regardless of whether it was purchased legally.

Can minors work in bars?

Not usually. Most states prohibit minors from working in lounges, bars, night clubs, restaurants, and other establishments serving alcoholic beverages. However, some states and cities permit minors to bus tables in restaurants that serve alcohol.

DRINKING AND DRIVING

Is drunk driving a crime?

The police can arrest a person for committing the crime of driving under the influence of alcohol, or DUI. This offense is also known as driving while intoxicated, or DWI.

America's DUI statistics are deplorable. In 1996 a total of 1,467,000 arrests were made for DUI offenses, and in the same year, 17,126 alcohol-related traffic deaths occurred. An estimated 40 percent of all traffic fatalities involve alcohol in some way.[1]

If a person hasn't been drinking, he or she has a .016 percent chance of being involved in an accident while driving. But if a person has been drinking, his or her chance of being in an accident increases to .045 percent. Problem drinkers cause a disproportionate number of accidents.

In a 1997 survey, an estimated 20.5 percent of young people between ages 12 and 17 said they drank alcohol at some point in the month immediately preceding the survey. (See Table 7.) An estimated 8.3 percent of these drinkers said they were binge drinkers, and an estimated 3.1 percent admitted to being heavy alcohol users. The only good news is that the survey percentages have fallen steadily since 1979.[2]

Drunk driving arrests usually are "warrantless" because drunk drivers are an immediate danger to passengers, other drivers, and pedestrians. For more about arrests and warrants see Chapter Twelve, "Teens and Crime."

On the other hand, the police don't arrest someone who commits a minor traffic offense such as exceeding the speed limit, parking illegally, or driving at night with one headlight. They simply issue a citation, which requires the offender to either pay a fine or appear in court.

How do the police know when a driver is intoxicated?

First, police officers are trained to recognize physical signs of inebriation in a driver or other individual. Among these indicators are slurred speech, alcohol breath, a flushed face, failing to comprehend the officer's questions, staggering when exiting a vehicle, and leaning on the vehicle for support.

Second, an officer can tell by the way a person drives that something isn't right. Intoxication is suggested when a driver swerves or weaves in and out of traffic, turns with an extra-wide radius, follows too closely,

Table 7
Percentage of Respondents Reporting Alcohol Use in the Past Month—1996 and 1997

Survey Year Numbers Reporting	1979 (7,224)	1988 (8,814)	1997 (24,505)
Alcohol Use			
Ages 12 to 17	49.6[2]	33.4[2]	20.5
Ages 18 to 25	75.1[2]	64.6	58.4
"Binge" Alcohol Use[1]			
Ages 12 to 17	---	15.1[3]	8.3
Ages 18 to 25	---	28.2	28.0
Heavy Alcohol Use[1]			
Ages 12 to 17	---	4.0	3.1
Ages 18 to 25	---	11.1	11.1

Notes: Estimates for 1979 through 1993 may differ from estimates for these survey years published in other National Household Survey on Drug Abuse (NHSDA) reports. The estimates shown here for 1979 have been adjusted to improve their comparability with estimates based on the new version of the NHSDA instrument that was fielded in 1994 and subsequent NHSDAs. In this table, respondents who had a missing response to the item, "in the past 30 days, or how many days did you have five or more drinks on the same occasion?" were excluded from the analysis.

--- Estimate not available.

1. "Binge" alcohol use is defined as drinking five or more drinks on the same occasion on at least one day in the past 30 days. By "occasion" is meant at the same time or within a couple of hours of each other. Heavy alcohol use is defined as drinking five or more drinks on the same occasion on each of five or more days in the past 30 days; all heavy alcohol users are also "binge" alcohol users.

2. The difference between this estimate and the 1997 estimate is statistically significant at the .05 level.

3. The difference between this estimate and the 1997 estimate is statistically significant at the .01 level.

Source: Office of Applied Studies, Substance Abuse and Mental Health Services Administration, *National Household Survey on Drug Abuse, 1979–1997.*

stops unnecessarily, accelerates or decelerates too quickly, or drives without headlights at night.

Third, the police are able to put a DUI suspect through certain "field sobriety tests" after a stop. They might ask a suspect to attempt to walk steadily along a straight line, recite the ABCs, stand on one leg, or perform other basic actions requiring balance and coordination. A bad performance suggests intoxication and will usually result in the suspect's arrest.

Fourth, a driver is said to be intoxicated if his or her blood alcohol content, or BAC, is at or above 0.10 percent. A person with a BAC of 0.10 percent has 0.10 grams of alcohol per 100 milliliters of blood. A chemical test establishes an individual's BAC. With a "breathalyzer test" the DUI suspect is required to blow deeply into a breathalyzer machine, or "drunkometer." Usually the test is administered at the police station—to both adults and teens.

Studies show that most people are unable to operate a car properly when their BAC is 0.10 percent. On any weekend night, an estimated 10 percent of all drivers have a BAC of 0.10 percent or greater. Indiana was the first state to have the wisdom to pass drunk driving laws; in 1937, it established a 0.10 percent BAC limit. Although its limit remains at 0.10 percent, a number of states including Illinois, Massachusetts, North Carolina, and California have lowered their BAC limit to 0.08 percent.

In every state a DUI suspect gives implied consent to be chemical-tested. This includes minors. The suspect doesn't have the right to consult an attorney before taking a chemical test. If he or she requests one, the police won't wait for the attorney to appear before running the tests.

Is a minor always subject to the same BAC limit as an adult?

No. In recent years at least 35 states have adopted "zero-tolerance" policies toward intoxicated teen drivers. Their legislatures have established lower BAC limits for persons under age 21—usually 0.02 percent. States with zero-tolerance policies report a 15 percent decline in traffic fatalities for young drivers.

What is the purpose of a "penlight test" or "horizontal gaze nystagmus test" at the arrest scene?

This maneuver estimates the angle at which a DUI suspect's eye begins to jerk about or "oscillate." ("Nystagmus" is a medical term for eye oscillation.) To perform the test, the police officer requires the suspect to follow the beam from a penlight at close range, straight ahead, and then from right to left. If the suspect's eye begins to jerk before 45 degrees off the center, a BAC of over 0.05 percent is suggested. Although the results of this field test are usually inadmissible as evidence, the test is commonly used.

What happens if a DUI suspect refuses to take the field sobriety tests or the breathalyzer test?

With respect to the field sobriety tests, the police officer must determine whether to make an arrest—although probably his or her decision will already have been made, based on personally observing the suspect. Again, for further information about arrests and the probable cause requirement see Chapter Twelve, "Teens and Crime."

A different rule applies with respect to the breathalyzer test and other chemical tests such as blood or urine tests. In most states a DUI suspect's license or learner's permit is instantly suspended if the test is refused. Moreover, the suspension usually "sticks" regardless of whether the suspect is later found guilty. The length of the suspension can be up to 12 months.

Can a person be convicted of DUI if his or her BAC is less than 0.10 (or is less than the applicable limit)?

In most states, yes assuming there is other reliable evidence of drunkenness such as slurred speech, stumbling, or alcohol breath.

Could a driver ever be sober, and thus innocent of a DUI offense, even though his or her BAC is above the legal limit?

In theory, perhaps, but seldom in reality. In recent years, 48 states have made driving with excess BAC a "per se" offense. This means that a driver with a BAC at or over the legal limit always breaks the law, no matter how well his or her body may tolerate alcohol.

Loosely translated from Latin, the term "per se" means "that's just the way it is."

If a minor is arrested for drunk driving, does the case go to adult court?

No, it goes to juvenile court.

If a minor accused of DUI can't afford a lawyer to fight the charge, will the court appoint one?

Yes, particularly if the offense is punishable by residential treatment. A DUI suspect should always be represented by an attorney.

Can a person be jailed for a DUI conviction?

Yes. This often happens to adults. In most states, however, an adult's first DUI conviction usually involves a stiff fine, a license suspension, mandatory attendance at a DUI rehabilitation course, and probation for up to three years.

For a second offense, an adult will often go to jail. Furthermore, his or her vehicle might be impounded, a community service obligation might also be imposed, and attendance at a series of Alcoholics Anonymous meetings might be ordered. For a minor, the consequences are similar, although confinement in an institution is uncommon unless the minor is a "recidivist"—a repeat offender.

Driving a moped and riding a bicycle while intoxicated are also punishable offenses. You can't legally ride a horse while while intoxicated either.

Is it against the law to have open alcoholic beverages in a car, even if none of the passengers is drinking or drunk?

Absolutely. These days just about everyone knows about statewide "open container" laws.

Can the police stop cars at random to determine whether the driver is legally intoxicated?

Not usually. As a rule, a car stop is allowed only if the officer has a good reason to believe the driver is committing a traffic offense or some other criminal act. For example, a driver can only be pulled over if the officer sees the car speeding or drifting in and out of a lane of traffic. If the officer believes the driver is intoxicated after asking some questions, observing the driver's movements, and perhaps detecting alcohol on his or her breath, an arrest can be made on the theory of probable cause.

Are drunk driving roadblocks legal?

Sometimes, even though the police can't otherwise stop drivers who don't appear to be breaking the law. Many believe "sobriety checkpoints" violate the search and seizure protections of the Fourth Amendment for this reason.

In 1985, roadblocks in New Hampshire were declared illegal because 175 DUI arrests were made in a six-month period using traditional police methods, but during the same period only 18 drivers were arrested for DUI out of 1,680 cars stopped at 47 roadblocks. Other courts have ruled that drunk driving roadblocks are legal if they don't delay the driver too long and the police officers are well supervised in the field.

ILLEGAL DRUGS

Which drugs are illegal?

At last count, dozens. The laws of each state list the drugs that are always illegal within its borders, regardless of whether the drug is possessed, purchased, or sold. Each state also lists the drugs that are illegal unless prescribed by a physician. In addition, federal law prohibits the possession, purchase, and sale of many types of drugs. State and federal laws usually refer to illegal drugs as "controlled substances"; the older term is "contraband."

Strictly speaking, "drugs" are substances used for the diagnosis, cure, treatment, and prevention of a disease or physical or mental condition. "Narcotics" are substances that dull the senses and become addictive after steady use. "Inhalants" are narcotics, and their use as narcotics is illegal. When inhaled, they rob the body of oxygen and can cause brain damage. Spray paint, hair spray, paint thinner, and bug killers are the commonest types (see Table 8).

Most states group drugs and narcotics into categories established under the federal Uniform Controlled Substances Act. They are categorized according to their potential for harm in contrast to their possible medical benefits. For example, "Schedule I" drugs have no beneficial medical use; they are always harmful. Heroin and LSD are Schedule I drugs. Schedule II drugs include cocaine, opium, and amphetamines. Because Schedule I drugs have no beneficial use, the penalty for possessing and selling any of them is the severest.

Is possessing a controlled substance always a crime?

In fact, no. State and federal laws only prohibit persons from "knowingly or intentionally" possessing illegal drugs. Being innocently in possession of a controlled substance usually isn't sufficient to support a

Table 8
Percentage of Respondents Reporting Drug Use in the Past Month—1996 and 1997

Age Group in Years	12 to 17		18 to 25	
Survey Year	**1996**	**1997**	**1996**	**1997**
Numbers Reporting	**(4,366)**	**(6,239)**	**(4,538)**	**(7,844)**
Any Illicit Drug Use[1]	15.6%	14.7%	9.0%*	1.4%
Marijuana/Hashish	13.2	12.8	7.1*	9.4
Cocaine	2.0**	1.2	0.6	1.0
Crack	0.6	0.4	0.2	0.4
Inhalants	1.0	1.0	1.7	2.0
Hallucinogens	2.3	2.5	2.0	1.9
PCP	0.1	0.1	0.2	0.1
Heroin	0.4**	0.1	0.2	0.2
Nonmedical use of any therapeutic[2]	2.9	2.4	1.9	2.1
Stimulants	0.6	0.7	0.5	0.6
Sedatives	0.3	0.2	0.2	0.1
Tranquilizers	0.9	0.1	0.2**	0.5
Analgesics	2.0	1.3	1.5	1.3
Any illicit drug other than marijuana	6.3	5.4	4.6	5.2

*The difference between this estimate and the 1997 estimate is statistically significant at the .05 level.

**The difference between this estimate and the 1997 estimate is statistically significant at the .05 level.

1. Any illicit drug indicates use at least once of marijuana or hashish, cocaine including crack, inhalants, hallucinogens (including PCP and LSD), heroin, or any prescription-type psychotherapeutic drug used nonmedically. Any illicit drug other than marijuana indicates use at least once of any of these listed drugs, regardless of marijuana use; marijuana users who have also used any of the other listed drugs are included.

2. Nonmedical use of any prescription-type stimulant, sedative, tranquilizer, or analgesic; does not include over-the-counter drugs.

Source: Office of Applied Studies, Substance Abuse and Mental Health Services Administration. *National Household Survey on Drug Abuse*, 1979–1997.

criminal conviction. For example, if a person receives a package in the mail that contains drugs, the person can only be convicted of illegal possession if it is shown that he or she knew the drugs would be delivered and intended to take possession of them.

Of course, it isn't illegal for a person to possess certain drugs if they have been prescribed by a doctor for that same person's illness or injury.

Is *purchasing* a controlled substance a different offense from *possessing* a controlled substance?

Yes. A suspect can be charged with both acts in connection with a single incident.

Selling controlled substances and manufacturing them are also criminal acts. An adult who is convicted of either offense can receive a prison sentence of up to 15 years and be fined as much as $25,000.

Is *giving* drugs to another person a criminal act?

Yes. The "sale" of a controlled substance includes giving a drug to someone. It's not necessary to receive something in exchange. This means that cash doesn't have to change hands for a drug sale to occur.

Does the seriousness of a drug offense depend on the quantity of drugs the suspect possesses or sells?

Yes. Possessing a small quantity of marijuana is usually a misdemeanor, but possessing large amounts of any illegal drug is a felony. When someone is caught with a cache of controlled substances, most criminal courts presume that the individual intended to sell them. To beat a "trafficking" charge, the suspect's lawyer must present strong evidence to overcome or "rebut" the court's presumption. But even if the trafficking charge is successfully rebutted, the suspect might still face a charge of illegal possession.

Obviously, trafficking in large quantities of drugs or narcotics is a serious offense, particularly if the substances cross state lines.

Can the police personally search a minor for drugs?

The police can search anyone who is under arrest. Furthermore, they can stop and frisk anyone for drugs and narcotics, and also weapons.[3]

If a minor is arrested for a drug offense, does the case go to juvenile court?

In most cases, yes. If the minor's parents can't afford an attorney to represent their child, the minor has a right to be assigned one at public expense.

Juvenile courts in the United States handled 159,100 drug cases in 1995.[4] The juvenile justice system is explained in Chapter Twelve.

If the police find drugs on a minor, will the drugs always be used as evidence?

Not if the police search is illegal, in which case the drug evidence would be "suppressed." Without this evidence, a finding of delinquency probably wouldn't occur.

Rules relating to personal searches are discussed in Chapter Twelve, "Teens and Crime."

How do juvenile courts handle drug cases?

Cases involving the possession, purchase, or sale of drugs are often easier to prove than other criminal offenses because the "elements" of the offense are straightforward. As a result, guilty pleas are common in juvenile court, and formal hearings on drug charges are infrequent.

This makes a minor's sentencing the focus of the case. As explained in Chapter Twelve, juvenile delinquents are entitled to "treatment" after being convicted because the legal philosophy behind juvenile courts is to rehabilitate rather than punish.

If a minor is found guilty of a drug offense, what is likely to happen next?

For a first offense, a minor will probably be required to attend rehabilitation classes and be subject to random drug testing. If and when the minor follows through with the program, the juvenile court will close the case. If the minor fails to complete it, the court won't hesitate to order detention, probation, or both, and the minor's driving privileges will almost certainly be suspended.

In a drug-related offense, does a minor ever go to adult court?

Yes. If the offense involved a particularly large quantity of drugs, if the minor's "accomplices" were adults, or if the minor has been convicted of a drug offense in the past, in many states an adult court will take jurisdiction.

Can school officials personally search a minor for drugs? Can they search a minor's locker, desk, gym bag, or purse?
Yes.

Can the police come onto school property to arrest a minor for possessing or selling drugs?
Yes, provided the police have "probable cause" for the arrest. Possessing or selling drugs on school grounds is a criminal act.

Drug possession on campus also violates school rules and usually results in long-term suspension or expulsion, whether or not the student is arrested.

Important rules about school searches are discussed in Chapter Two, "At School."

Can a minor obtain drug treatment without parental consent?
In most states, yes. For more about situations in which a minor may legally consent to medical care see Chapter Ten, "Your Right to Be Healthy and Safe from Abuse."

NOTES

1. National Highway Traffic Safety Administration, *Selected Highway Statistics and Charts*, annual.

2. Office of Applied Studies, Substance Abuse and Mental Health Services Administration, *National Household Survey on Drug Abuse*, 1979–1997.

3. In another 1997 survey, an estimated 23.7 percent of young persons between the ages of 12 and 17 reported that they had used drugs at least once. Of these individuals, 18.8 percent said they had used drugs in the past year, and 11.4 percent said they had used drugs in the month immediately before the survey. Marijuana and hashish were used most widely. Office of Applied Studies, Substance Abuse and Mental Health Services Administration, *National Household Survey on Drug Abuse*, 1997.

4. United States National Center for Juvenile Justice, *Juvenile Court Statistics*, annual, Pittsburgh, PA.

FOR FURTHER READING

Alcohol

Cohen, Daniel, and Susan Cohen. *A Six-Pack and a Fake ID: Teens Look at the Drinking Question.* New York: Dell Publishing Company, Inc., 1992.

Grosshandler, Janet. *Coping with Drinking and Driving.* New York: Rosen Publishing Group, Inc., 1997.

Jacobs, James B. *Drunk Driving: An American Dilemma.* Chicago: University of Chicago Press, 1989.

Land, Alan R. *Alcohol: Teenage Drinking.* Broomall, PA: Chelsea House Publishers, 1992.

Lewis, John F. *Drug and Alcohol Abuse in Schools: A Practical Guide for Administrators and Educators for Combatting Drug and Alcohol Abuse.* 2nd ed. Dayton, OH: Education Law Association, 1992.

Milhorn, Thomas, Jr. *Drug and Alcohol Abuse: The Authoritative Guide for Parents, Teachers, and Counselors.* New York: Plenum Publishing Corp., 1994.

Drugs

Currie, Elliott. *Dope and Troubled Portraits of Delinquent Youths.* New York: Pantheon Books, 1992.

Grosshandler, Janet. *Drugs and Driving.* New York: Rosen Publishing Group, Inc., 1997.

Schaler, Jeffrey A., ed. *Drugs: Should We Legalize, Decriminalize or Deregulate?* Amherst, NY: Prometheus Books, 1998.

Taylor, Clark. *The House That Crack Built.* Chicago: Chronicle Books, 1992.

OTHER INFORMATION SOURCES

Organizations

Al-Anon & Al-Ateen
1600 Corporate Landing Parkway
Virginia Beach, VA 23454
(888) 4AL–ANON
E-mail: SWO@al-anon.org
Home page: www.al-anon.alateen.org

Cocaine Anonymous
Box 2000
Los Angeles, CA 90049
(800) 347–8998
E-mail: cawso@ca.org
Home page: www.ca.org

Mothers Against Drunk Driving (MADD)
Box 541688
Dallas, TX 75354
(800) GET–MADD
E-mail: info@madd.org
Home page: www.madd.org

Narcotics Anonymous
Box 9999
Van Nuys, CA 91409
(818) 773–9999
E-mail: info@na.org
Home page: www.na.org

National Council on Alcoholism and Drug Dependence
12 West Twenty-first Street
New York, NY 10010
(212) 645–1690
Hotline: (800) NCA–CALL
E-mail: national@ncadd.org
Home page: www.ncadd.org

Students Against Driving Drunk, Inc. (SADD)
(also, Students Against Destructive Decisions, Inc.)
Box 800
Marlborough, MA 01752
(508) 481–3568
Home page: www.saddonline.com

— 12 —

Teens and Crime

ARRESTS

What exactly is an arrest?

It is an action in which a police officer takes away a person's freedom in some significant way. A person can be arrested when an officer has a good reason to believe the person has committed a crime or is in the process of committing one.

A police officer doesn't have to say "you're under arrest" for an arrest to occur—a command such as "Stand still" or "Come along" usually is enough. A good test for an arrest is whether the suspect realizes or should realize that he or she isn't free to walk away.

If a person isn't sure whether he or she has been arrested, it is always appropriate to ask the officer, "Am I under arrest?"

Can minors be arrested?

Yes, although strictly speaking, minors aren't "arrested." They are "taken into custody." This distinction in the law emphasizes the fact that the juvenile court system exists to protect and rehabilitate minors rather than punish them. In this chapter, however, the terms "arrested" and "taken into custody" mean the same. "Minor" and "juvenile" also mean the same. Many terms in this chapter are defined in the Glossary at the back of the book.

What can adults be arrested for?

Adults can be arrested if they commit or are suspected of committing "felonies" or "misdemeanors," the two broad categories of crimes. Felonies are more serious than misdemeanors. Joyriding, for example, is a misdemeanor, but stealing a car without any intent to return it is a felony. As a rule, felonies are punishable by at least one year in prison.

What can minors be arrested for?

For almost all the same reasons as adults. In addition, minors who need supervision, special care, or medical treatment or who are runaways can also be arrested.

Whom do the police represent?

They represent the state or a political subdivision within a state, such as a city or county. States grant authority to their political subdivisions to enforce state laws and pass laws of their own. Police officers have the job of enforcing the law, and one of their most important enforcement tools is the power to arrest.

What makes a particular act a crime?

An act is a crime only if a public law says it is. If an act isn't prohibited by a federal, state, or local law, the police can't arrest for it, and the prosecuting attorney can't bring criminal charges against a person suspected of committing it.

Do the police have to be absolutely certain that a person committed a crime before he or she can be arrested?

No. To arrest an adult, a police officer only needs to have "probable cause" to believe that a crime was committed and that a particular individual committed it. This is a requirement based on the Fourth Amendment of the Constitution.

To understand probable cause, consider the following scenario. Two men are exchanging money on the street, and one has a brother who is a known drug dealer. With only this information, a police officer observing the transaction can't arrest either of them for attempting a drug deal. The evidence isn't sufficient to establish probable cause to conclude that the pair are trafficking in illegal substances—they could be exchanging money for a perfectly legal reason.

Is an arrest warrant needed to arrest a person? What really is a warrant?

A warrant is a court order authorizing an arrest or a police search. Without a warrant, an arrest or search would be a violation of a citizen's privacy rights under the Fourth Amendment. "Warrantless" arrests and searches are legal only if they fall under one of the few exceptions to the Fourth Amendment's warrant rule.

To obtain a search warrant from the court, a police officer must be able to detail, in writing, the person, place, or things to be searched. The officer's request to a judge—usually a signed "affidavit"—must be based on probable cause that the item to be searched for is where the officer says it is.

However, an arrest warrant isn't needed if the officer believes he or she must detain the suspect on the spot. This exception to the warrant rule makes sense and is considered fair: if the officer needed to make a trip for a warrant, the suspect would undoubtedly vanish in the meantime.

Are innocent people arrested?

It does happen. When the police need to think fast, they sometimes make both reasonable and unreasonable mistakes.

If an arrest wasn't required, the officer may release the "arrestee" on the spot. Otherwise, the subject may be released at the station or upon his or her initial appearance in court.

Does probable cause apply when minors are arrested?

Yes. If, for example, a police officer observes a minor fumbling with a packet of white powder and overhears the minor tell a third person that it contains cocaine, the officer would have probable cause to believe a crime has occurred. The crime would be possession of a controlled substance.

If the officer observes the parties entering into negotiations for the sale and purchase of the cocaine, he or she now has probable cause to believe that the illegal sale of a controlled substance is occurring.

Can the police legally detain a person short of an arrest?

Yes. The police can make three kinds of "stops." The first is a basic type of police-citizen contact. It takes the form of a request for information or identification and allows a police officer to sniff out a potential problem. No force can be used, and the officer doesn't legally restrict the subject's personal freedom in any major way.

The second type is a brief stop to investigate a suspicious situation and ask probing questions. Such a stop is called a "Terry stop," after the landmark Supreme Court case of *Terry v. Ohio*. For a Terry stop to be legal, the police officer must have "reasonable suspicion" to believe that a crime has been committed or is about to be committed. Reasonable suspicion requires less suspicion than probable cause.

The third type of stop is a full-scale arrest requiring probable cause and also the *Miranda* warnings.

The difference between a Terry stop and an arrest is important. Consider the following case. In 1990, police in Arizona stopped an unarmed, passive minor. They patted him down for weapons, gripped him by the arm, and made him sit in the back of a squad car. He was in the car for 20 minutes, during which time the police questioned him extensively. Never was the youth told he was free to leave.

During the questioning the minor admitted he had fled from a van that the police were following in connection with a theft. An appeals court ruled that the nature and length of the stop made it an arrest and not a Terry stop. Furthermore, it was an illegal arrest because the police lacked probable cause to detain the minor for more than a brief period. As a result, his confession could not be used.

THE *MIRANDA* WARNINGS

What actually happens when a person is arrested?

To begin with, a police officer confronts an individual and asks some questions about a particular incident. Then the officer will request the person's name and address and ask to see some identification. It is always best to cooperate on these preliminary matters.

If the officer has probable cause to believe the person being questioned has committed a crime, he or she will state that the suspect is under arrest and then recite the suspect's "*Miranda* rights." That is, the officer will advise the suspect of the following:

1. that the suspect may legally refuse to answer any police questions;

2. that the suspect may call a lawyer or be assigned one at public expense;

3. that the suspect may stop answering police questions at any time, or wait until a lawyer arrives before answering any additional questions; and

4. that anything the suspect says may be used by the state prosecuting attorney to establish the suspect's guilt.

Miranda v. Arizona, a famous Supreme Court case, established that every criminal suspect has these rights—hence the term "*Miranda* rights." A police officer's recitation of a suspect's *Miranda* rights is referred to all over the country as the "*Miranda* warnings."

Are minors entitled to the *Miranda* warnings?

Yes. In fact, in many states the *Miranda* warnings *must* be given to an arrested minor, without exception, before any questions leading to a possible confession can be asked.

What happens if a police officer doesn't recite the *Miranda* warnings at the time of an arrest?

The law treats any statements made by the suspect as having been made in violation of his or her Fifth Amendment right to remain silent. The statements are deemed involuntary and are therefore illegal, even though the suspect may actually have made them willingly. When statements such as these are illegal under the law, they may not be used as evidence to convict a suspect of a crime. This rule of evidence is known as the "exclusionary rule."

Is the exclusionary rule fair?

Let's just say that inquiring minds—including police officers, practicing attorneys, judges, and law professors—have pondered this question for years. In late 1999 the Supreme Court agreed to entertain an appeal regarding the *Miranda* warnings and the exclusionary rule. This came as no sudden surprise. Many believe the exclusionary rule has often been too broadly applied, that the Supreme Court's decision to hear the appeal is long overdue, and that the Court was possibly waiting for the best case upon which to base new constitutional guidelines.

What happens if a suspect decides to confess to a crime after being "Mirandized"?

The confession can be used to convict. The suspect is presumed to have knowingly given up, or "waived," the right to remain silent.

Once a person waives the right to remain silent, can he or she withdraw the waiver and refuse to answer any more questions?

Yes. At any point, a criminal suspect may decide to quit talking—and may at that point also request a lawyer.

If a person receives the *Miranda* warnings and later confesses to a crime, will the confession always be treated as voluntary?

No. A court can also declare a confession illegal if it was given when the suspect was under too much pressure from the police during questioning, even if the *Miranda* warnings were recited.

Is a police officer required to recite the *Miranda* warnings in connection with casual questioning?

No. Neither probable cause nor reasonable suspicion is required for an officer to ask questions about a particular event, and the officer needn't recite the *Miranda* warnings before asking them. (See the discussion about police stops in "Searches and Seizures" in this chapter.) But if probable cause develops during the questioning, the officer must recite the *Miranda* warnings before continuing.

In a recent case similar to the Terry stop case, a teen's conviction for sexual abuse was reversed after an appeals court ruled that he had been arrested without receiving the *Miranda* warnings. A police officer went to the teen's house and asked him to step outside for a chat. After two hours of questioning, the youth admitted to the offense.

Then he asked if he was under arrest. The officer said he wasn't. The appeals court disagreed, stating he was under arrest as soon as he was required to step outside. Because the officer failed to recite the *Miranda* warnings at that moment, the prosecuting attorney couldn't use the youth's damaging admissions against him.

WHEN MINORS ARE ARRESTED

What should a minor do if he or she is taken to the police station after an arrest?

First, if an officer again asks the minor to state his or her name and address, the minor should comply promptly. Second, the minor should ask to telephone a parent, guardian, or other adult.

Third, the minor should refrain from answering questions or volunteering information until an adult arrives, even if the minor fully understood the *Miranda* warnings. Police stations are particularly intimidating. For this reason, many states limit all police questioning of minors during a "custodial arrest" until a parent or other adult is on hand, especially if the police are likely to press for a confession.

Does a minor have a legal right to call his or her parents after being taken into custody?

Yes, although it's important to know that in some states the police aren't legally required to advise minors of this right.

Can a minor forfeit or "waive" his or her Fifth Amendment right to remain silent and proceed to talk?

Yes, but the law makes it difficult. If an adult waives the right to remain silent and then confesses to a crime, the waiver is presumed valid. But if a minor chooses to confess, the prosecuting attorney must prove that the minor's waiver was truly voluntary. This shifting of the "burden of proof" occurs because minors are considered particularly vulnerable to police pressure, especially at the police station, and therefore less likely to remain silent.

The legality of a minor's waiver depends on a variety of factors, including the minor's age, maturity, and past involvement with the police. It may also depend on whether the minor's parents or lawyer were present when the waiver and confession were made.

Consider a recent New Mexico waiver case in which a 17-year-old's juvenile court conviction for firing a deadly weapon was upheld as voluntary. Two police officers were called to investigate gunshots. When they approached the car of a young suspect to ask some questions, one of the officers spotted some beer and a rifle on the car seat. The suspect immediately stated, without pressure from either officer, that he had fired a shot into a residence.

As the other officer prepared to recite the *Miranda* warnings, the young man said he had fired a shot but didn't know if he'd hit anything. The second officer said, "Stop, let me read you your rights," but the suspect said he knew what his rights were. Under these circumstances, the court ruled that the youth's admission was voluntary. This meant it could legally be used as evidence against him in juvenile court.

If a minor calls his or her parents but confesses before they arrive, is the confession valid?

It depends on whether the confession was the result of legal police questioning. Once a minor asks to talk to a parent, a lawyer, or another adult, the police must stop asking questions. If they continue and the minor confesses, the confession is treated as involuntary and is therefore illegal. But if, without additional questioning or pressure, the minor either spontaneously confesses or waives his right to remain silent and confesses "knowingly, voluntarily, and intelligently," the confession is probably legal.

It is always best to remain silent after a custodial arrest. Researchers note that *truly* knowing, voluntary, and intelligent waivers of First Amendment rights by juveniles in custody, alone and without an attorney, are rare indeed.[1]

SEARCHES AND SEIZURES

Once the *Miranda* warnings are recited, are the police permitted to search their suspect?

Yes. The search is called a "search incident to an arrest." The police will always question their suspect both during and after a search incident to an arrest unless the suspect has exercised his or her Fifth Amendment right to remain silent.

Can a minor be searched?
Yes.

What is a search warrant? Does a search incident to an arrest require a search warrant?

A search warrant is a court order authorizing a search of a person, place (such as a bedroom or locker), or object (such as a purse or backpack). A request to the court for a search warrant must be based upon "probable cause" that specific items actually will turn up and must clearly describe the person, place, or object to be searched.

Under the Constitution, every search requires a warrant. Warrantless searches are legal only if they fall under one of the few legal exceptions to the warrant requirement. One of these exceptions is the arrest warrant, discussed previously in this chapter. A search incident to an arrest can also be conducted without a warrant. Another type of warrantless search is one required in an emergency, such as a car search.

Why isn't a search warrant required for a search incident to an arrest?

For this simple reason: If an officer needs a search warrant before making an on-the-spot search of a suspect or his or her surroundings, evidence of a crime could be hidden or disposed of while the officer was in court obtaining the warrant.

Are police searches ever illegal?

Yes. If a personal search, including a search incident to an arrest, is made without full probable cause, the search is illegal. It is again important to note that the "fruits" of an illegal search can't be used to convict a suspect in court.

Locker searches at school are governed by different, somewhat looser rules. For information about searches on school grounds see Chapter Two, "At School."

Do special rules apply to car searches?

Yes. If a car is involved in an incident for which an arrest is made, certain areas of the car can be searched immediately and without a warrant. The police can search any bags and containers within the suspect's reach inside the car, and also the glove compartment. The trunk usually can't be searched until the police obtain a warrant, although to prevent the contents of the trunk from being removed, they may seize or "impound" the car until a warrant is obtained.

Note, however, that "vehicle seizure laws" have been widely criticized in recent years as unconstitutional in the manner in which they are applied. Changes in this legal area are likely to occur in the not-too-distant future.

What is a "stop-and-frisk" search?

A "stop-and-frisk" is a limited personal search that a police officer may conduct if he or she thinks a dangerous situation exists. The purpose of stop-and-frisks, or "pat-downs," is to search for weapons.

Reasonable cause to believe that danger is lurking, and not full probable cause, is needed for a stop-and-frisk. If the police detect a hard object such as a weapon during a stop-and-frisk, they can then arrest the suspect, recite the *Miranda* warnings, and proceed with a full personal search.

In 1993, the Supreme Court ruled that if the police detect something that "feels like drugs" during a stop-and-frisk, they can make an arrest and then fully search their suspect.

Can minors be subjected to stop-and-frisk searches?
Yes.

Can a minor consent to an otherwise unlawful personal search?
It depends. Like a minor's waiver of the right to remain silent, the legality of the consent depends on the minor's age, maturity, and past contacts with the police. Courts tend to rule that a minor can't legally consent to a search that would be illegal (because conducted without a warrant or conducted in connection with an unlawful arrest) except for the consent.

Do the police need a search warrant to enter a minor's home or bedroom to conduct a search?
Yes. Furthermore, an officer can seize additional criminal evidence once inside, but only if it is in "plain view." This is none other than the "plain view exception" to the Fourth Amendment warrant rule.

Consider the following example: A police officer obtains a warrant to search a minor's closet for illegal drugs. He notices drug paraphernalia on the minor's bed. He can seize these items also, without an additional search warrant.

Applying the plain view exception, a California court in 1993 upheld an officer's warrantless search of a carport after a group of juveniles were seen flagging down motorists from the carport and selling them drugs. A warrantless search of a trash can also be legal, particularly if it isn't right up against the suspect's house. Here, courts reason that the suspect doesn't have an expectation of privacy in items already thrown away.

Can parents consent to a warrantless police search of a teen's bedroom or car?
Courts in some states have ruled that parents legally control their minor children's property, so they have the power to forfeit a child's right

to be free from warrantless searches. Other states take the position that parents who have no involvement in a suspected criminal act can't consent to a warrantless search of a child's private space.

In yet other states, whether a parent can legally consent to a warrantless search of a minor's room or other property depends on whether the minor should be able to expect an extra level of privacy with respect to the area to be searched. In these states, parents can lawfully permit the police to look at items on a child's desk or chest of drawers, but a closet or purse can't be searched without a warrant. If the police find illegal drugs inside a closet or purse, they can't be used as evidence against the minor.

INTAKE

What happens to a criminal suspect at the police station?

Unless the suspect has exercised his or her right to remain silent, the police will ask more questions. Their purpose will usually be to obtain a confession and discover the names of any accomplices.

The police have the power to detain a suspect even if they don't yet have enough evidence for criminal charges. When they do have sufficient evidence, they will "book" the suspect. (Sometimes the police let suspects go in simple misdemeanor cases, especially if the "misdemeanant" didn't injure anyone.)

If the police book a minor, will the case always end up in juvenile court?

No. After booking, the police and one or more juvenile probation officers (and possibly a social worker) meet to discuss how the case should be handled. This stage is called "intake." The intake participants may decide to place the minor on probation, send the minor to counseling, dismiss the case altogether, or determine that the minor should be charged with a delinquent act.

Intake officials consider many factors in deciding how to handle a case, including the seriousness of the offense, the minor's age, school record, home life, and previous delinquent acts. "Attitude" is also a consideration. A young person's attitude is usually conveyed by his or her actions or language at intake, but it can also be shown by clothing, and even hairstyle.

Does the minor participate in the intake meeting?

Yes. Intake officials always interview the minor, although the minor does have the right to remain silent. The parents also participate.

Can a minor be represented by a lawyer at intake?

In many cases the minor won't yet have a lawyer. But in any event, a lawyer normally doesn't participate because the purpose of intake is to decide whether to handle the minor's case outside juvenile court— without judges and lawyers. But a lawyer can always advise what kinds of information the minor should reveal at intake and what to keep quiet about.

What is diversion?

It is a special way of handling a minor's case outside the juvenile court system. Under a diversion program, intake officials may decide to "divert" a minor to a private agency that arranges for special services such as counseling, rehabilitation, or foster care. The agency might also assist the minor in finding a job or adjusting better at home or in school.

Diversion programs operate with the consent of the juvenile court, the prosecuting attorney, and the court's probation officials. Their success depends on the minor's voluntary participation because the agencies co-ordinating them don't have any real enforcement power. This sometimes reduces their success.

Across the country, about 50 percent of all cases against minors are removed from the juvenile courts at intake.

If the intake officials determine that a minor should be charged with a delinquent act, when are formal charges made?

At the minor's "advisory hearing," which is usually the minor's first encounter with the juvenile court judge. At this hearing, which is short, the judge state the charges, explains that the minor has the right to a lawyer, and asks the minor how he or she wants to plead. In addition, a trial date is set.

In some states the advisory hearing is called the "initial appearance."

Does a minor have a right to a lawyer in juvenile court?

Yes, at every stage—and the court is legally required to advise the minor of this fact. If the parents can't afford a lawyer, the state will provide one at public expense.

Is a minor always free to plead not guilty?

Yes. A plea of not guilty means there will be a trial, or "formal hearing."

Is a minor always free to plead guilty?

Yes. In fact, a minor's lawyer often recommends that he or she do so in return for a lighter sentence. But a juvenile court won't accept a guilty plea unless the minor fully understands its consequences, including the fact that there won't be a formal hearing to present evidence.

Guilty pleas are common in juvenile court.

PRETRIAL DETENTION

If a minor isn't diverted out of juvenile court at intake, is detention next?

It can be, although "pretrial detention" is the exception rather than the rule. Usually the police release the minor to a parent or relative pending the formal hearing. But if the minor is dangerous, likely to leave the state, or in need of special protection from his or her family, a judge may order detention. Pretrial detention may be in a juvenile facility, a foster home, or shelter care.

In most states a minor can't be held in pretrial detention for more than 72 hours without a detention hearing, and in some states the time limit is 24 hours. Detention without an immediate hearing often occurs if the minor is picked up over the weekend. The hearing usually takes place at the same time as the advisory hearing.

Detention of juveniles prior to the formal hearing is one of the thorniest issues in juvenile law. Critics argue that the juvenile is being punished before the court determines guilt or innocence. Their point is worth considering.

Is there a minimum age for pretrial detention?

Detention below a specified age is prohibited in about 15 states. The minimum age varies from New York, which prohibits detention below age 10, to Illinois, which prohibits detention below age 16.

Can a minor be represented by a lawyer at his or her pretrial detention hearing?

Yes. The constitutional right to be represented by a lawyer in criminal cases applies to minors in all juvenile court hearings.

Does a minor have any legal rights while in detention?

Yes. The juvenile "detainee" has a right to be free of all special restrictions—except, of course, the right to leave. This means he or she has a right to adequate clothing, bedding, sanitary conditions, educational facilities, and medical care, and also access to a library.

Is a detention facility the same as a jail?

No. Only adults go to jail. Minors cannot legally be incarcerated with adults. Physical and sexual abuse of juveniles illegally detained in adult jails isn't uncommon.

In a 1974 Kentucky case a 16-year-old was taken into custody for a curfew violation. The police refused to allow him to call his parents, and he was immediately detained in an adult jail, although under Kentucky law he should have been released. The boy remained in jail for five days.

A federal appeals court stepped in, ruling that by refusing to permit the boy to call a parent, and by keeping him in an adult jail before trial, the police inflicted "cruel and unusual punishment" on him in violation of the Constitution.

Past research shows that the suicide rate for minors detained in adult jails is nearly eight times that of minors detained in juvenile facilities.[2]

JUVENILE COURT HEARINGS

What types of cases do juvenile courts handle?

They handle criminal offenses committed by minors. In every state these offenses are called "delinquent acts." Sometimes juvenile court is referred to as family court or children's court.

Juvenile court is always separate from adult court. A minor's age at the time of his or her offense determines which court receives the case. In most states the age limit is 18, although in some states, including New York, juvenile court jurisdiction only extends to minors through age 16.

What is a "juvenile delinquent"?

A juvenile delinquent is a young person, usually under age 18, who is proved to have broken a criminal law.

In some states a minor who is charged with murder, rape, kidnapping, or other serious crime can be tried in adult court. If convicted of one of these offenses in adult court, the minor will be a "criminal" rather than a "juvenile delinquent."

How does a minor's case actually get to the juvenile court judge?

If the juvenile court's intake process doesn't divert the minor out of the system, the prosecuting attorney files a "petition" against the minor. This formal document describes the specific charges against the juvenile and the facts supporting them.

How does a minor discover the contents of the petition?

The minor and his or her parents are entitled to a copy of it. In some states if the petition doesn't clearly spell out the possible consequences of a finding of guilt, a juvenile court conviction on the charges can be "reversed."

If a minor doesn't plead guilty to a delinquency charge, can he or she present witnesses and evidence at the formal hearing?

Yes, usually through his or her lawyer. These are constitutional rights, guaranteed by the Due Process Clause of the Fourteenth Amendment. Minors also have the constitutional right to question or "cross-examine" those who testify against them. For more about court procedure including cross-examination see Chapter Seventeen, "Taking Matters to Court."

Can a juvenile suspect handle his or her formal hearing without a lawyer?

Yes, but as in waiving the right to remain silent, the minor must have a keen understanding of the consequences of waiving the right to a lawyer. For a juvenile court judge to accept such a waiver, the minor must fully comprehend the charges and also the possible punishment. In addition, he or she must understand that a lawyer will be assigned free of charge if his or her parents can't afford one. Finally, the minor must understand the difficulties involved in going ahead without a lawyer, especially the challenges involved in presenting evidence.

Some juvenile courts prohibit a minor from waiving the right to a lawyer unless one has already been involved in the case and has explained to the minor the consequences of the waiver.

Do minors have a right to a jury at a formal hearing?

Not usually. Under the Constitution, the right to a jury trial applies only to adults. But some states, including Alaska, Colorado, Michigan, Texas, Wyoming, and New Mexico, do allow jury trials in juvenile court.

Can a minor choose to remain silent during the formal hearing?

Yes. Minors can't be required to testify against themselves.

Can a minor insist on taking the stand in his or her own defense?

No one can prevent a minor from testifying. But taking the stand can hurt rather than help a minor's case, since it gives the prosecuting attorney a chance to "cross-examine." In other words, it gives the state an opportunity to probe the minor about his or her earlier "direct" testimony. The perils of cross-examination are the reason why lawyers often advise both criminal defendants and minors charged with delinquent acts not to testify at all.

Can a minor be convicted in juvenile court on a confession alone?

It depends on the state. In most, a minor's out-of-court confession is insufficient to convict unless it is supported by additional "hard" evidence, because a minor is considered more likely than an adult to give a false confession. In some states, a minor's confession is sufficient if supported by the testimony of another person involved in the crime. In others, even an accomplice's testimony isn't enough to convict. Rather, the confession must be supported by the testimony of an independent, innocent witness.

What must the state prove in order to convict a minor of a delinquent act?

It must prove the minor's guilt "beyond a reasonable doubt." This is the state's burden of proof.

Proving guilt beyond a reasonable doubt is the burden of proof required in all criminal cases, including juvenile court cases. This is a higher burden than in a noncriminal or "civil" case—which means that convicting a minor in a juvenile court trial can sometimes be difficult. For more about burden of proof see Chapter Seventeen, "Taking Matters to Court."

What happens if the minor is found guilty?

He or she is then considered a juvenile delinquent. At that point the judge has a right to sentence the minor.

The term "disposition" is used instead of "sentence" in juvenile court. A judge's disposition may include community service, restitution for property damage, probation, treatment such as counseling or therapy, or participation in a chemical dependency program. Dispositions and disposition hearings are discussed later in this chapter.

Can a minor claim insanity as a defense to a delinquent act?

In some states, yes. In others, the insanity defense has no bearing on whether the minor is guilty of a delinquent act; it is only important in deciding how to handle the minor's case after the court has declared the minor a delinquent.

Proving the insanity defense is complicated and difficult. To establish insanity under the Constitution, it must be shown that the offender was insane when the offense was committed and couldn't have understood the nature of the act because of the insanity. In cases in which the offender actually understood what he or she was doing, it must be shown that insanity prevented the defendant from realizing the act was wrong.

Can a minor appeal a juvenile court conviction?

There is no federal constitutional right to appeal any court decision. However, state constitutions or state laws guarantee this right to both adults and minors.

If a minor has the right to appeal a determination of delinquency, does the minor have the right to a lawyer free of charge for the appeal?

Yes.

MINORS IN ADULT COURT

Can a minor be tried as an adult?

Yes. Every state permits minors above a certain age to be tried in adult court for a handful of serious offenses. In Connecticut, for example, a minor can be transferred to adult court if he or she is charged with murder, rape, or another serious felony *and* has committed a serious felony in the past. To try a minor as an adult in Illinois, the minor must be at least age 13, the offense must be very serious, and the juvenile court judge must have determined that it wouldn't be in the best interests of either the minor or the community to try the case in juvenile court.

In most states a minor can be transferred to adult court between the ages of 14 and 16, provided the minor has committed an offense such as murder or attempted murder, aggravated robbery, arson, burglary, and sometimes possession of explosives and killing by auto if under the influence of drugs. (The types of offenses vary from state to state.) About 15 states set the age at 16 for any crime and age 14 for a short list of particularly serious crimes. A few permit transfer to adult court for certain offenses regardless of age.

To determine the circumstances under which a minor in a given state can be tried as an adult, check the state's criminal laws at any public library. A reference librarian can provide needed assistance. For more about how to find the law, see Chapter Eighteen.

Who finally decides if a minor should be tried as an adult?

Usually it is a juvenile court judge, although in some states an adult court judge decides.

The laws in this area are changing. In response to the growing number of minors committing serious crimes such as murder, some states have revoked the power of the juvenile court to decide the transfer issue. This means that with respect to certain serious offenses, either the case goes directly to adult court, or the *prosecutor* decides which court will hear it. When juvenile cases go to adult court, punishment replaces treatment as the driving force behind the case, as the next section explains.

But in fact, minors are sometimes better off being tried as adults. Certain protections apply in adult court that don't apply in juvenile court, including stricter rules of evidence. Furthermore, because criminal juries are more sympathetic to young criminals, they are often less likely to convict. They know a conviction means the minor may end up in a hopeless prison situation for many years.

Cases regarding the removal of minors to adult court are often appealed, simply because so many more minors are committing serious offenses. Between 1985 and 1994, juvenile arrests increased 150 percent for murder, 57 percent for robbery, and 97 percent for aggravated assault.[3] Furthermore, between 1985 and 1993, juveniles transferred to adult court increased 41 percent to 11,800. Ninety-six percent were males, and 12 percent were 15 years old or younger.[4]

What factors are important in determining whether a minor actually goes to adult court?

In addition to the nature of the offense and the age requirement, important factors are the maturity of the minor, whether he or she has previously committed serious offenses, amount of evidence supporting the charges, whether any accomplices are adults, and whether the minor is likely to respond to discipline or treatment from the juvenile court.

If the prosecuting attorney wants a transfer to adult court, is the minor entitled to a hearing on the issue?

Yes—due process of law requires it.

If the prosecuting attorney seeks an adult court trial, he or she must establish the factors described. But if state law requires that cases involving particularly serious offenses *originate* in adult court, the burden is on the minor's attorney to prove to the adult court judge that adult court is inappropriate—that juvenile court is the best "forum" for the case. In other words, the burden of proof shifts to the minor's attorney.

If a minor is tried in adult court, will he or she go to an adult prison if sentenced to a prison term?

In most circumstances, yes.

Adult prisons aren't nice places. Research indicates that minors in adult institutions are 500 percent more likely to be sexually assaulted than minors in a juvenile facility, 200 percent more likely to be beaten by staff, and 50 percent more likely to be attacked with a weapon.[5]

Can a minor be sentenced to death in adult court?

The answer to this question isn't clear. To date, sentencing a minor to death hasn't been found to constitute "cruel and unusual punishment" in violation of the federal Constitution. However, some state constitutions or laws forbid capital punishment for minors.

As of the end of 1997, 14 persons under the age of 20 were on death row.[6]

SENTENCING

How are juvenile delinquents sentenced?

Sentencing occurs by the juvenile court judge at a "disposition hearing."

Juvenile court dispositions have historically focused on rehabilitation and treatment rather than punishment, and this distinguishes them from sentencings in adult court. In every state the juvenile court's stated goal is to act "in the best interests of the child" and to correct the underlying reasons for the delinquency.

When is the disposition hearing?

Usually within two months of the formal hearing. This time lapse occurs because a court worker must gather together the juvenile's school, medical, work, and other records. Based on this information and also the court record, the court worker tailors a "social history report." The judge's decision rests heavily on the findings and recommendations in this key document. Psychological testing or counseling may also occur.

Where does the delinquent stay in the meantime?

Usually at home, although if the minor needs special supervision, the court can order secure detention or place the minor in a foster home.

Is the minor entitled to have a lawyer at the disposition hearing?

In most states, yes. But in fact, the prosecuting attorney, the minor's attorney, and a social worker often work out the specific terms of the disposition and the judge simply reviews it and agrees. This means the disposition hearing can be quite short.

What type of treatment or rehabilitation might a delinquent receive?

Because the judge must order the least restrictive alternative, in-home detention and probation are common for lesser offenses. For more serious cases, the delinquent is placed in a foster home, a supervised group home, or a nonsecure treatment facility. A nonsecure treatment facility is somewhat like a group home—an institutional-type setting without the regimentation of a secure institution.

Sometimes secure treatment facilities for delinquents are called "training schools," "industrial schools," or "juvenile correction facilities." These days, many aren't unlike prisons. School instruction is given in them, however, and delinquents who are sentenced to them have a right to be personally safe.

When a minor is institutionalized, an important goal is to reunite the minor with his or her family as soon as possible.

Can a minor be required to pay a fine or perform community service for a delinquent act?

Yes, and the juvenile court can also require a minor to repair property he or she has damaged. This is called "restitution." Some of these measures are part of today's more punishment-oriented approach to treating juvenile delinquents and are also part of the growing concern for the rights of crime victims.

However, a minor can't be convicted in juvenile court just because he or she can't pay a fine. In a recent case a minor who stole a baseball cap, a knife, and a wrench was convicted in juvenile court of petty theft. The judge would have dropped the case if the youth had been able to come up with $62.50 to pay restitution. The appeals court set aside the boy's sentence, ruling that a minor can't be convicted simply because he or she is poor, or "indigent."

Does a delinquent ever leave court without receiving any form of treatment or punishment?

Yes, if the judge believes this course of action is appropriate.

Can a minor be sentenced to death in juvenile court?

No. But if a minor is transferred to adult court and tried for a capital offense, the death penalty is possible in most states. As previously stated, the Supreme Court has ruled that sentencing a minor to death isn't necessarily cruel and unusual punishment in violation of the federal Constitution.

PROBATION

What is probation?

It is a type of disposition in which the delinquent stays under court supervision but isn't sent to an institution or foster home. In fact, because the judge is required to order the "least restrictive alternative," a delinquent on probation usually stays at home or with a relative.

Probation always restricts the delinquent's personal freedom. Contacts with a probation officer take place on a regular basis, by phone and in person. There may be a strict curfew. The delinquent may have to maintain good grades in school and must remain a law-abiding citizen. If the offense involved a car, a driver's license may be suspended. In addition, the delinquent may be required to enroll in a local treatment program for drugs, alcohol, or a behavioral problem.

Also, the juvenile court may prohibit the delinquent from possessing weapons, associating with gang members, and wearing gang clothing and symbols. It can also forbid a delinquent to associate with persons not approved by a parent or probation officer.

Sometimes the terms of probation can be particularly "creative." A juvenile court in Florida recently ordered a youth to obey his mother's lawful demands, including the demand that he join a youth group at church. He appealed, arguing that the court's order violated his religious rights under the First Amendment.

The appeals court upheld the order, finding that the youth's mother had a legal right to direct his activities in this instance. It reasoned that some church youth programs are often social rather than religious. Since the court had no information as to whether the program was either religious or secular, it said it would be premature to rule that ordering the youth into the program violated his religious rights.

The modern tendency is to directly involve the parents in the probation process. For example, a parent may be required to attend and complete parenting classes. If the parent doesn't bother to take the classes, the juvenile court can hold the parent "in contempt." This means the court may order the parent, under threat of a heavy fine or other punishment, to complete the classes by a certain date.

How long does probation last?

It varies, but many states limit it to two years. In certain states probation can't extend into a delinquent's majority (usually age 18), but in others it can extend up to age 21.

If a juvenile delinquent violates the terms of his or her probation, is there a right to a hearing before probation is revoked?

Yes. Adults have been granted this right by the Supreme Court, and in most states it has been extended to minors. Juvenile delinquents don't have a constitutional right to an attorney at a probation revocation hearing, but again, certain states have made this guarantee.

What must the state prove to revoke probation?

It must prove that the delinquent violated at least one condition of the judge's probation order and that no good reason existed for the violation.

What happens if the judge revokes probation?

He or she has the power to send the delinquent to a treatment facility, group home, or foster home, or to simply place the minor back on probation.

TREATMENT IN AN INSTITUTION

Does an institutionalized delinquent always have a right to treatment?

In theory, yes, As a matter of constitutional law, a delinquent in a treatment facility is entitled to counseling, educational and social services, and treatment for special medical problems. The form of treatment might be classes to correct a behavioral or emotional problem, a learning disability, or a physical impairment.

But as a practical matter, sending a delinquent to secure treatment is often intended as a type of "shock therapy," or "juvenile boot camp." Few would deny that these facilities are dismal. Usually they are overcrowded and understaffed, and the employees rarely have much expertise in counseling or vocational training. Treatment and rehabilitation take a second seat to everyday control and discipline matters.

How long does institutional treatment last?

In most states the judge works with official "length of stay guidelines." This means that the judge's order for treatment will be within a recommended minimum and maximum time period, in light of the particular offense. The delinquent's case is reviewed once he or she has completed the minimum length of stay. If at this point the supervising agency doesn't believe the delinquent is rehabilitated or otherwise ready to leave, more time may be ordered.

Note, however, a modern trend toward institutionalizing delinquents for a minimum number of months for particularly serious offenses, regardless of how much treatment or rehabilitation they need. This is called "specific sentencing" and is another example of today's more punishment-oriented approach to treating delinquents.

In New York, for example, minors age 14 and 15 who have committed serious felonies against elderly victims may be held for six months to one year in a secured facility and kept another six months to one year in residential treatment.

Can the juvenile court give a longer sentence than an adult court could give for exactly the same offense?

In most states, yes. A delinquent can be kept in a treatment facility until the agency supervising the treatment believes the delinquent is ready to leave.

If equal or better treatment can be obtained for the delinquent outside a treatment facility, is he or she entitled to it?

In many states, yes, because most states require their juvenile courts to consider the least restrictive alternative to institutional treatment.

In a 1987 Nevada case, an appeals court set aside a 13-year-old girl's sentence to one year in a treatment facility after she struck a schoolmate. The young woman had never been in juvenile court before, and her church had even suggested its counseling program to the court for her probation. A higher court set aside the girl's sentence, ruling that probation is always proper unless it is against the best interests of either the minor or the state.

Most states will not provide a lawyer to assist a minor in challenging a sentence to a treatment facility.

Are personnel in treatment facilities prohibited from using corporal punishment?

The Constitution prohibits punishment that is excessive to the point of being cruel and unusual, so corporal punishment would appear to be unconstitutional in a juvenile treatment setting. Beatings, solitary confinement for an extended length of time, and the use of unnecessary psychiatric medications have been declared forms of cruel and unusual punishment.

JUVENILE COURT RECORDS

Is a juvenile delinquent a criminal? Does a juvenile delinquent have a "record"?

The answer to both questions is no. A delinquent isn't a criminal because a conviction in juvenile court isn't a criminal conviction.

Are juvenile court records confidential?

In most states, yes. The purpose of keeping juvenile court records confidential is to promote the rehabilitation of young people. Confidentiality keeps the records out of the hands of school officials, government agencies, future employers, and the general public.

Inactive juvenile court files are either sealed, stamped "confidential," or destroyed. If a file is sealed, a judge's written order is required to open it. States that don't destroy juvenile court records usually permit limited inspection of them by the minor, probation officers, any agency caring for the minor, and persons doing scholarly research.

Some states have laws requiring a delinquent's court file to be destroyed or permanently sealed after the delinquent reaches age 23, or after a specified number of years from the date of the conviction. On the other hand, police records relating to a delinquent's actions (such as arrests) are never confidential.

In states in which juvenile court records are confidential, can a delinquent deny that he or she has a record?

Yes. The delinquent can legally deny that delinquency proceedings ever took place.

In 1989 a Louisiana court ruled that a juvenile could not, as a term of his probation, be required to notify his school that he was a delinquent. In many states the juvenile court can legally deny to outsiders that a delinquent (or former delinquent) has any juvenile record at all.

If a minor is a witness in an adult criminal trial, can he or she be required to answer questions about past juvenile court convictions?

Yes. Minors can be cross-examined about past delinquent acts as a way to test their credibility as witnesses, particularly if their delinquent acts were both serious and recent.

Can juvenile court records be used against a former delinquent who is on trial in an adult criminal case?

In most states an adult can't be cross-examined about previous delinquent acts. The reason is that delinquent acts aren't considered crimes and should therefore be off-limits. However, many states permit judges to review juvenile records to help in determining what sentence to give a convicted adult.

Can a judge legally exclude the press or public from a juvenile court hearing?

State courts are inconsistent on this issue. However, for the sake of privacy and fairness, most states exclude the press in at least some circumstances. In 1995 a federal appeals court in Massachusetts agreed that a formal hearing relating to juveniles charged with hate crimes was properly closed to the press. Similar orders have been issued in other jurisdictions.

Whether the media is allowed in the courtroom, if at all, depends on a number of factors. These include the nature of the offense, the surrounding circumstances, the juvenile's age, whether his or her name will be used in the newspaper (especially if the juvenile is quite young), and whether the press has already covered the case to excess.

Can the press be prosecuted for publishing the name of a young person charged with a delinquent act?

No. States violate the First Amendment if they pass laws prohibiting the media from publishing information about trials, whether or not a minor is being tried. If such laws could legally be enforced, newspapers could be prosecuted for publishing truthful information.

In a 1982 case, two Virginia newspapers reported the identity of two high school students who were charged with murdering a classmate. The newspapers were prosecuted under a state law prohibiting the print media from publishing the name of any delinquent without prior authorization from the juvenile court. The Supreme Court overturned the conviction, ruling that laws prohibiting the media from printing information about delinquents violate the First Amendment if the purpose of the law is solely to preserve the minor's anonymity.

NOTES

1. James Grisso, "Juveniles' Waiver of Rights: Legal and Psychological Competence," 3 *Perspectives in Law and Psychology* (B. Sales, ed., 1981).

2. Community Research Forum, *An Assessment of the National Incidence of Juvenile Suicide in Adult Jails, Lockups and Juvenile Detention Centers* (1980).

3. United States Department of Justice, Office of Juvenile Justice and Delinquency Prevention, *Juvenile Offenders and Victims: 1996 Update on Violence.*

4. Ibid.

5. United States Department of Justice, Bureau of Justice Statistics, *Capital Punishment 1997* (1998).

6. Ibid. Of the 3,335 prisoners on death row in the United States in 1997, 1,254 had completed less than 11 years of school.

FOR FURTHER READING

In General

Bergman, Paul, and Sara J. Berman-Bennett. *The Criminal Law Handbook.* Berkeley: Nolo Press, 1997.

Boland, Mary L. *Crime Victim's Guide to Justice.* Naperville, IL: Sourcebooks, Inc., 1997.

Champion, Dean J. *The Juvenile Legal System: Delinquency, Processing, and the Law.* 2nd ed. New York: Prentice Hall, Inc., 1997.

Heilbroner, David. *Rough Justice: Days and Nights of a Young D.A.* New York: Random House, Inc., 1990.

Lewis, Anthony. *Gideon's Trumpet.* New York: Vintage Books, 1989.

Sheidlin, Judy. *Don't Pee on My Leg and Tell Me It's Raining: America's Toughest Family Court Judge Speaks Out.* New York: HarperCollins Publishers, 1997.

Suspects' Rights/The Miranda Warnings

Feld, Barry C. *Justice for Children: The Right to Counsel and the Juvenile Courts.* Boston: Northeastern University Press, 1993.

Wice, Paul B. *Miranda v. Arizona: Suspects' Rights: You Have the Right to Remain Silent.* New York: Franklin Watts, Inc., 1996.

Searches and Seizures

Rossow, Lawrence F., and Jacqueline A. Stefkovich. *Search and Seizure in the Public Schools.* 2nd ed. Dayton, OH: Education Law Association, 1996.

Wetterer, Charles M. *The Fourth Amendment: Search and Seizure.* Springfield, NJ: Enslow Publishers, Inc., 1998.

Probation

Jacobs, Mark D. *Screwing the System and Making It Work: Juvenile Justice in the No-Fault Society.* Chicago: University of Chicago Press, 1990.

Hammer, Hy. *Probation Officer, Parole Officer.* 5th ed. Foster City, CA: IDG Books Worldwide, 1996.

Sentencing/Death Penalty

Burney, Elizabeth. *Sentencing Young People: What Went Wrong with the Criminal Justice Act of 1982.* Brookfield, VT: Ashgate Publishing Company, 1985.

Mello, Michael. *Against the Death Penalty: The Relentless Dissents of Justices Brennan and Marshall.* Boston: Northeastern University Press, 1996.

Mello, Michael A. and David Von Drehle. *Dead Wrong: A Death Row Lawyer Speaks Out against Capital Punishment.* Madison: University of Wisconsin Press, 1999.

OTHER INFORMATION SOURCES

Organizations

American Bar Association
750 North Lake Shore Drive
Chicago, IL 60611
E-mail: info@abanet.org
Home page: www.abanet.org

American Civil Liberties Union
125 Broad Street
New York, NY 10004
(212) 549–2500
E-mail: aclu@aclu.org
Home page: www.aclu.org

Center on Juvenile and Criminal Justice
1622 Folsom Street
San Francisco, CA 94103
(415) 621–5661
E-mail: info@cjcj.org
Home page: www.cjcj.org

National Center for Youth Law
114 Sansome Street, Ste. 900
San Francisco, CA 94104
(415) 543–3307
E-mail: infor@youthlaw.org
Home page: www.youthlaw.org

Teens, Crime, and the Community
1600 K Street NW, Ste. 602
Washington, DC 20006
(202) 293–0088
Home page: www.nationaltcc.org

The Urban Institute
2100 M Street NW
Washington, DC 20037
(202) 833–7200
E-mail: webmaster@ui.urban.org
Home page: www.urban.org

Online Sources

Youth Crime Watch
E-mail: ycwa@ycwa.org
Home page: www.ycwa.org

Age, Race, and Sex Discrimination

AGE DISCRIMINATION

Is age discrimination against minors legal?

In many situations, yes. Society lawfully discriminates against minors on the basis of age every day and in dozens of situations. Young people can't legally drive, vote, go to school, drink, buy tobacco, marry, or hold certain jobs until they reach a certain age. In criminal matters, they don't have the range of constitutional due process rights in juvenile court that exists for adults in adult court.

Discrimination on the basis of minority or "nonage" is in many ways the opposite side of teen rights.

The federal Age Discrimination in Employment Act of 1967, or ADEA, and the Older Workers Benefit Protection Act of 1990 prohibit age discrimination in employment, but only with respect to persons between the ages of 40 and 70. But when federal and state age discrimination laws do apply, they prohibit employers from discriminating because of age with respect to pay, conditions of employment, promotions, and fringe benefits. Age discrimination is often called "ageism."

For more about laws relating to age discrimination in the workplace see Chapter Four, "On the Job."

RACE DISCRIMINATION

> No state shall make or enforce any law which shall . . . deny to any person within its jurisdiction the equal protection of the laws.
>
> —Fourteenth Amendment, U.S. Constitution

Is race discrimination illegal?

Yes, particularly when the discriminatory act is "state-sponsored." In other words, race-based discrimination is illegal when it is the result of an act or law of the federal government, a state or local government, or a government agency.

Since World War II, the Equal Protection Clause of the Fourteenth Amendment of the Constitution (shown above) has been the centerpiece for all of America's anti-discrimination movements. But many federal laws, including Title VII of the Civil Rights Act of 1964, prohibit discrimination as well. Title VII, a product of the Johnson administration, was truly historic, and it remains the most important anti-discrimination legislation ever enacted. Title VII forbids discrimination on the basis of race, gender, age, race, religion, nationality, and color. It requires equal treatment with respect to employment, equal rights with respect to the use and enjoyment of public accommodations and facilities, and equal rights with respect to government benefits and assistance.

What are some examples of illegal race discrimination occurring in the past?

Some laws that the Supreme Court has struck down in this area are:

1. In 1879 it struck down state laws excluding blacks from serving on juries.

2. In 1886 it found illegal discrimination when each of 200 Chinese applicants was denied a permit to operate a laundry in San Francisco even though almost every non-Chinese applicant was granted one.

3. In 1917 it struck down a St. Louis city law prohibiting blacks from living on any city block if at least 50 percent of the residents on the block were white.

4. In 1938 it struck down a scheme in which Missouri provided a state-funded law school for whites but paid for blacks to go to law school out-of-state.

5. In 1954, in the case of *Brown v. Board of Education*, it unanimously rejected the "separate but equal doctrine" in public education. In this decision it ruled

that placing black children in separate schools or classes within a school system deprived all children—blacks as well as whites—of an equal education.

All the above cases violated the Equal Protection Clause. In each a racial minority was illegally denied the "equal protection of the laws."

Brown v. Board of Education is a landmark case, not only because it declared "separate but equal" schemes unconstitutional, but because it began the modern civil rights movement. "Civil rights"—personal liberties to which all American citizens or residents are entitled—was a product of post-Civil War Reconstruction. But these rights were not enforced. Although America had shaken off slavery, every aspect of American society remained segregated on the basis of race, both officially and unofficially.

This situation didn't begin to change until after World War II. In 1950 the Supreme Court ruled that the University of Oklahoma couldn't require its only African-American graduate student to sit in the hall outside class, or inside the classroom but behind a rail labeled "Reserved for Colored." In that same year the Supreme Court overruled Texas legislation creating a law school for blacks in an attempt to prevent racial integration at the University of Texas Law School.

But it was the Supreme Court's decision in *Brown v. Board of Education* that signaled a new era for civil rights—possibly because the ruling in *Brown* affected so many people. Shortly after it was handed down, the modern civil rights movement began to reshape America's thinking on countless issues relating to race and other personal rights. The nation was ready. Many believe that the feminist and gay and lesbian rights movements and even the environmental movement, are rooted in the civil rights concerns addressed in *Brown*.

How did the Supreme Court's rejection of "separate but equal" in *Brown v. Board of Education* affect other race issues?

After *Brown*, the Supreme Court struck down state laws authorizing the separation of races in public parks, restaurants, and bathrooms; at golf courses, beaches, and airports; and in public transportation. In its wake came the federal Equal Pay Act of 1963, the Voting Rights Act of 1965, the Civil Rights Acts of 1967, the Age Discrimination in Employment Act of 1967, the Fair Housing Act of 1968, the Americans with Disabilities Act of 1990, and other important federal enactments—

not to mention countless pieces of state and local civil rights legislation. The *Brown* decision reached every corner of American life. Now, no law or public policy can treat people differently simply because of race or nationality. A white person can't be prohibited from marrying a black person, and the armed services are fully integrated. America's second black justice now sits on the Supreme Court. Never again will any racial or ethnic minority have to go to the back of the bus.

Is it ever legal to have discriminatory laws?

Yes. State and city governments pass them all the time.

Government has the power to treat different categories of people differently. That's what many laws do, so it is true to say that laws can legally discriminate.

For example, a city can legally require all its homeowners to pay a property tax to finance its public schools even though certain homeowners don't have children. Such a law would discriminate against childless homeowners. It would be legal, however, because laws that discriminate for reasons other than race, gender, nationality, religion, age or disability only have to be reasonable. A law to raise money for schools would clearly be that.

But a law that discriminates on the basis of race, gender, nationality, religion, or disability must be more than reasonable. The purpose of such a law must be extremely important, and the law must *precisely* fit the government's purpose. Laws that discriminate on the basis of nationality or race never pass this test.[1]

Can private persons or private businesses discriminate on the basis of race?

If an individual or business is engaged in a government-related function, even remotely, any type of minority-based discrimination is prohibited. Furthermore, states, counties, cities, and Congress have passed laws prohibiting discrimination by private individuals and private businesses in situations that the Constitution may not cover. Clear examples are state and local laws requiring restaurants to seat blacks and other minorities and laws prohibiting private clubs from excluding minorities under their membership policies.

How does student busing relate to race discrimination?

Busing is state-sponsored "desegregation." Busing white children to predominantly black schools and black students to predominantly white schools is a state-sponsored way of correcting racial imbalances and racial injustice.

Busing has almost always been court-ordered, and the practice has always been controversial. These days it is under heavy attack in legislatures, in the courts, and in academia. Busing is criticized as both ineffective and disruptive of the learning process.

Is discrimination against whites illegal?

It can be, because it is another form of race discrimination. *Bakke v. California*, decided in 1978, is the leading case on "reverse discrimination." Here the Supreme Court ruled that public schools can't give special treatment to minorities just because they've been discriminated against in the past.

The *Bakke* case involved a medical school admissions program that set aside 16 of 100 seats for racial and ethnic minorities. One applicant, Alan Bakke, was denied a seat in the freshman class even though he had a better academic record than the average student admitted under the minority program. He was white.

The Supreme Court ruled that the admissions program illegally discriminated against whites and in favor of minorities. The school's interest in having a student body with a variety of races and backgrounds—an interest that the Court praised—didn't justify the existence of the set-aside program. Bakke was admitted because the school couldn't prove he wasn't a victim of reverse discrimination.

What can governments legally do to remedy discrimination occurring in the past?

They can, for example, establish "affirmative action programs," which endeavor to admit or hire a certain percentage of minorities. Under these programs, minorities who are admitted or hired must be at least as qualified as nonminorities who are turned down. However, the use of exact numerical quotas has vanished since the *Bakke* decision.

Would the *Bakke* case apply to young persons applying to college?

Yes, it would. But having said this, note that opposition to all forms of affirmative action grew steadily in the 1990s. In 1997, legal scholars were surprised when an affirmative action case in the Supreme Court—

Table 9
Average Earnings by Educational Attainment, Sex, and Race, 1996

Educational Attainment	Total, both sexes	Total, male	Total, female
Overall	$28,106	$34,705	$20,570
Advanced Degree	61,317	74,405	42,625
Bachelor's degree	38,112	46,702	28,701
Some college or Associate degree	25,181	31,426	18,933
High school graduate	22,154	27,642	16,161
No high school degree	15,011	17,828	10,421

one that was projected to deal a serious blow to the affirmative action cause—abruptly settled.

Shelby Steele, a noted writer on African-American issues, believes that race-based preferences and other types of affirmative action "demean the idea of merit and reinforce racist attitudes." Many critics believe that affirmative action should try to help those on the bottom tiers of America's economic ladder, regardless of race or nationality, instead of focusing on gender or race-based minorities.

Do you think affirmative action works? Do the statistics in Table 9 address the issue of whether this policy has been effective? Do they also speak to issues other than race discrimination?

For more about affirmative action and reverse discrimination see Chapter Four, "On the Job."

Do laws prohibiting discrimination on the basis of race also apply to minorities such as Native Americans, Hispanics, and Asian Americans?

Yes, and they apply irrespective of the age of the minority individual. All of these groups must deal with prejudice. Table 10 shows what America's overall poverty picture looks like.

SEX DISCRIMINATION

Is sex discrimination legal?

It used to be legal, across the board. In 1945 the Supreme Court upheld a state law prohibiting any woman from obtaining a bartender's license

Table 9 (*continued*)

White, both sexes	Black, both sexes	Hispanic, both sexes
$28,844	$21,978	$19,439
61,779	48,731	49,873
38,936	31,955	32,955
25,511	23,628	22,209
22,782	18,722	18,528
15,358	13,110	13,287

Source: Census Bureau, *Current Population Survey*, March 1997 Update.

unless she was the wife or daughter of a man who already had one. This is just one example of past state-sponsored gender discrimination—literally hundreds of instances occurred nationwide.

Laws authorizing or permitting sex discrimination began to fall in the 1970s. In 1975 the Supreme Court ruled unconstitutional a Utah law placing the age of majority at 21 for males but age 18 for females. Utah reasoned that parents should have to support their sons through their college years because a man's education is so important—but because women marry younger, parents should only have to support their daughters to age 18. Similar laws have been struck down.

The Supreme Court has ruled against gender discrimination in other types of cases. Here is a sampling:

1. In 1976 it ruled that Oklahoma couldn't set the legal age for males to buy 3.2 percent beer at age 21 but set it at age 18 for females (3.2 percent beer has less alcohol content than regular beer).

2. In 1979 it struck down a New York law requiring the consent of a child's natural or "birth" mother, but not the birth father, to place a child born outside marriage for adoption.

3. In 1981 it struck down a state law enabling a husband to dispose of property jointly owned with his wife without the wife's consent.

What are some examples of lawful sex or gender gender discrimination?

Women can legally be kept out of combat, and they can be required to wear tops in public places.

Table 10
Percentage of Americans Living in Poverty

	Total Population	Population Living in Poverty	
Whites	222,790,000	24,656,000	(11%)
Blacks	34,333,000	9,694,000	(28%)
Hispanics	30,307,000	8,697,000	(29%)
Native Americans	2,354,000	585,273	(25%)

Source: United States Bureau of the Census; www.census.gov.

Can public high schools legally put men and women on separate high school sports teams?

Sometimes, although it usually depends on whether the sport is a contact sport. For more about gender rules in high school athletic programs see Chapter Two, "At School."

Can a business fire a woman because she becomes pregnant?

Under a 1993 federal law, full-time women employees can now take unpaid pregnancy leave from certain jobs without fear of job loss or demotion. For more about gender issues at work see Chapter Four, "On the Job."

NOTE

1. In fact, on one occasion the Supreme Court *did* uphold a law that discriminated on the basis of a racial class. In *Korematsu v. United States* it let stand a federal law authorizing the creation of relocation or "internment" camps to hold Japanese-Americans during World War II. This decision still nags at the national conscience.

FOR FURTHER READING

In General

Carnes, Jim. *Us and Them: A History of Intolerance in America*. New York: Oxford University Press, 1999.

Cordova, Teresa, ed. *Chicana Voices: Intersections of Class, Race, and Gender*. Austin: University of Texas Press, 1993.

Duvall, Lynn. *Respecting our Differences: A Guide to Getting Along in a Changing World*. Minneapolis: Free Spirit Press, 1994.

Gaskins, Pearl Fuyo. *What Are You? Voices of Mixed-Race Young People*. New York: Henry Holt & Company, Inc., 1999.

Gates, Henry Louis, Jr. *Speaking of Race, Speaking of Sex: Hate Speech, Civil Rights, and Civil Liberties*. New York: New York University Press, 1995.

Hill, Anita, ed. *Race, Gender, and Power in America: The Legacy of the Hill-Thomas Hearings*. New York: Oxford University Press, 1995.

Williams, Juan. *Eyes on the Prize: America's Civil Rights Years, 1954–1965*. New York: Penguin Putnam, 1987.

Wolfson, Nicholas. *Hate Speech, Sex Speech, Free Speech*. Westport, CT: Praeger Publishers, 1997.

Race-Based Discrimination

Angelou, Maya. *I Know Why the Caged Bird Sings*. New York: Random House, Inc., 1970.

Anson, Robert Sam. *Best Intentions: The Education and Death of Edmund Perry*. New York: Random House, Inc., 1987.

Brown, Claude. *Manchild in the Promised Land*. New York: Macmillan Publishers, 1990.

Cleaver, Eldridge. *Soul on Ice*. New York: McGraw Hill Companies, 1968.

McDonald, Laughlin, et al. *The Rights of Racial Minorities (ACLU)*. New York: Puffin Books, 1998.

Parks, Rosa, and Jim Hoskins. *Rosa Parks: My Story*. New York: Dial Press, 1993.

Schwartz, Bernard. *Swann's Way: The School Busing Case and the Supreme Court*. New York: Oxford University Press, 1986.

Steele, Shelby. *A Dream Deferred: The Second Betrayal of Black Freedom in America*. New York: HarperCollins Publishers, 1998.

Steele, Shelby. *The Content of Our Character: A New Vision of Race in America*. New York: Harper Perennial Library, 1991.

Wormser, Richard. *The Rise and Fall of Jim Crow: The African-American Struggle Against Discrimination, 1865–1954*. New York: Franklin Watts, Inc., 1999.

Affirmative Action

Caplan, Lincoln. *Up Against the Law: Affirmative Action and the Supreme Court*. New York: Twentieth Century Fund, 1997.

Curry, George E. *The Affirmative Action Debate*. New York: Addison-Wesley Publishing Company, Inc., 1996.

Jencks, Christopher. *The Black-White Test Score Gap*. Washington, DC: Brookings Institute, 1998.

Sex-Based Discrimination

Cassell, Justine, and Henry Jenkins, eds. *From Barbie to Mortal Kombat*. Cambridge, MA: The MIT Press, 1998.

Gay, Kathlyn. *Rights and Respect: What You Need to Know about Gender Bias and Sexual Harassment*. Brookfield, CT: Millbrook Press, 1995.

Hauser, Barbara. *The Women's Legal Guide: A Comprehensive Guide to Legal Issues Affecting Every Woman*. Golden, CO: Fulcrum Publishing, 1996.

Landau, Elaine. *Sexual Harassment and Teens: A Program for Positive Change*. Minneapolis: Free Spirit Publishing, 1992.

Sack, Steven Michael. *The Working Woman's Legal Survival Guide*. New York: Prentice Hall, Inc., 1998.

Other Minorities

Dietrich, Lisa C. *Chicana Adolescents: Bitches, 'Ho's, and Schoolgirls*. Westport, CT: Praeger Publishers, 1998.

Haines, David W., and Karen E. Rosenblum, eds. *Illegal Immigration in America: A Reference Handbook*. Westport, CT: Greenwood Press, 1997.

Houston, Jeanne Wakatsuki. *Farewell to Manzanar: A True Story of Japanese American Experience during and after the World War II Internment*. New York: Bantam Books, 1983.

Mirande, Alfredo. *Gringo Justice*. South Bend: University of Notre Dame Press, 1990.

Pevar, Stephen L. *The Rights of American Indians and Their Tribes (ACLU)*. New York: Puffin Books, 1997.

Rodriguez, Roberto. *Justice: A Question of Race*. Tempe, AZ: Bilingual Press, 1997.

Utter, Jack. *American Indians: Answers to Today's Questions*. Lake Ann, MI: National Woodlands Publishing Co., 1993.

OTHER INFORMATION SOURCES

Organizations

American Civil Liberties Union
125 Broad Street
New York, NY 10004
(212) 549–2500

E-mail: aclu@aclu.org
Home page: www.aclu.org

National Association for the Advancement of Colored People (NAACP)
1025 Vermont Avenue NW, Ste. 1120
Washington, DC 20005
(202) 638–2269
Home page: www.naacp.org

National Council of La Raza
1119 Nineteenth Street NW, Ste. 1000
Washington, DC 20038
Home page: www.nclr.org

National Organization for Women (NOW)
733 Fifteenth Street NW, 2nd Floor
Washington, DC 20005
(202) 628–8NOW
E-mail: now@now.org
Home page: www.now.org

Native American Rights Fund
1506 Broadway
Denver, CO 80303
(303) 447–8760
E-mail: pereira@narf.org
Home page: www.narf.org

Online Sources

U.S. Department of Justice—Civil Rights Division
Home page: www.usdoj.gov

—14—

Gay and Lesbian Teens

IS IT LEGAL?

Are homosexual acts illegal?

In many states, yes. States and cities may legally enforce laws prohibiting homosexual activities among persons of all ages.

In 1986, the Supreme Court ruled in the case of *Bowers v. Hardwick* that a Georgia statute prohibiting oral and anal sex (or "sodomy") isn't an unconstitutional invasion of privacy when applied to homosexual conduct between adults. This case means that neither consenting adults nor consenting minors have a constitutional right to engage in homosexual acts. It doesn't mean that homosexuality is illegal—it just means that homosexual conduct isn't a privacy right protected by the Constitution.

The *Hardwick* case has been criticized by legal scholars because its reasoning appears contrary to earlier Supreme Court cases upholding the right of privacy in matters relating to sex. Many find it inconsistent with a 1969 Supreme Court case recognizing the right of individuals to view pornography in the privacy of their homes. Others find it inconsistent with *Roe v. Wade*, the 1973 Supreme Court case ruling that the constitutional right to privacy includes a woman's right to have an abortion.

Although states may legally prohibit homosexual acts, a majority of states have revoked laws making private homosexual conduct between consenting adults illegal.

If homosexual conduct between consenting adults isn't illegal under the laws of a certain state, would the same conduct be legal between consenting teens?

No. States that have revoked laws prohibiting homosexual acts between adults haven't gone so far as to legalize such acts between minors.

Can a person who has homosexual relations be convicted of statutory rape?

In some states, yes, although in others, statutory rape can only occur with respect to heterosexual sex.

As discussed in Chapter Eight, "Your Sexual Life," statutory rape occurs when an adult has sex with a minor. It doesn't matter that both parties may have privately agreed to engage in sex. In most states only the older sex partner can be charged.

FAMILY MATTERS

Can parents forbid a minor child to engage in homosexual acts?

Yes, consistent with their right to raise and discipline their children. However, a rule forbidding a minor child to engage in sex, whether the child is gay, lesbian, or straight, isn't always the easiest rule for parents to enforce.

For more about teen and parental rights at home, see Chapter Three.

Can parents throw a minor out of the house because he or she is homosexual?

No. Parents are responsible for the care and nurturing of their minor children, regardless of a child's sexual orientation or sexual activities. Even so, it is estimated that up to 650,000 gay, lesbian, and bisexual youths live on America's streets.

Can parents emancipate a minor just because he or she is gay, lesbian or bisexual?

No—that wouldn't be a sufficient reason. To be emancipated, the minor must be financially independent and able to live safely and in good health on his or her own. For more about emancipation see Chapter Five, "On Your Own."

Can two men legally marry?

No, and neither can two women. Same-sex marriage isn't recognized in any state and is explicitly forbidden in at least 28. This issue is controversial because it boldly challenges time honored notions of marriage and family life.

Gays, lesbians, and straights who advocate marriage between persons of the same sex argue that its prohibition is unconstitutional discrimination. In 1993 the Hawaii supreme court went to far as to rule in *Baehr v. Mike* (formerly *Baehr v. Lewin*) that a "compelling state interest" must exist in order for the state to ban same-sex marriage. However, Hawaii voters later approved a ballot measure to forbid it. In late 1999 the Vermont supreme court ruled in *Baker v. Vermont* that lesbian and gay couples are entitled to all of the same "common benefits and protections" that the law gives to married couples. Proponents of same-sex marriage consider this decision a major victory.

Many cities, including New York, Minneapolis, and the California cities of San Francisco and Santa Cruz, permit two adults of the same sex who are living together to register with the city clerk as "domestic partners." (San Francisco's ordinance has been on the books since 1981.) Registering as a domestic partner allows a gay or lesbian city employee and his or her partner to be covered under the city's group health insurance. In addition, registering makes each partner responsible for the other's basic living expenses as well as his or her own. Brown, Harvard, and Stanford Universities; the Universities of Colorado, Minnesota, Pennsylvania, New Mexico, Wisconsin and Oregon; and other institutions of higher learning extend domestic partnership benefits to both students and staff.

Can a parent who is lesbian or gay obtain custody of a minor child in a divorce?

Lesbian and gay parents can find it difficult to obtain custody of their children when divorcing. As discussed in Chapter Seven, the basis for awarding custody is "the best interests of the child." Many judges believe that awarding custody to a gay or lesbian parent can't in any instance be in the young person's best interests. The National Center for Lesbian Rights notes that only 1 in 100 gays and lesbians gained parental rights through the courts between 1985 and 1995.[1]

Even so, some courts are breaking rank. Divorce courts in at least ten states can no longer lawfully deny custody to a parent simply because of sexual orientation. When such a custody award is made, it is usually to a lesbian mother.

After divorcing, can a gay or lesbian parent be denied the right to visit his or her child?

Not for that reason alone. In order for a court to deny visitation to a gay or lesbian parent, the straight parent would have to persuade the court that such visits would for some proven reason be against the child's best interests. Visitation might be denied, for example, if the homosexual parent and his or her same-sex partner had a habit of kissing or caressing in the minor's presence.

In some states, gay and lesbian parents have been prohibited from keeping a child overnight and have also been prohibited from taking a child to the home the parent shares with a same-sex partner. But courts in other states have permitted these and similar activities.

AT SCHOOL

Can school administrators prevent a gay and lesbian club or support group from meeting on public school property?

Public high school administrators may only prohibit lesbian and gay rights clubs from meeting at school if clear evidence shows that the meetings would either disrupt school discipline or offend the rights of others.

Massachusetts was the first state to officially ban discrimination against gays and lesbians in public schools. Other states have followed suit. The first gay student group for high schoolers was recognized in 1973; the first gay high school was founded in Boston in 1982. As of 1993, more than 100 gay and lesbian clubs existed in high schools across the nation. By now, such clubs and support groups are in high schools in every major U.S. city. However, Utah succeeded in banning gay and lesbian student clubs in 1991.

For more about the constitutional right of free assembly see Chapter Two, "At School."

If school officials can't prevent gay and lesbian teens from organizing at school, what types of school facilities can the club use?

The same facilities that other clubs use, such as meeting rooms, school supplies, access to bulletin boards, and other school benefits and services.

Can schools make gay and lesbian teens stay away from each other at a public school?

No. That would be a clear violation of the constitutional right of free assembly.

In 1981 a federal appeals court in Rhode Island ruled that a public high school couldn't prohibit a male student from taking another male to the senior prom. However, the court based its decision on the First Amendment right of free speech and not the right of free assembly; it ruled that taking a gay man to the prom was a form of symbolic speech.

For more about symbolic speech under the First Amendment see Chapter Two, "At School."

Can schools forbid gay and lesbian teens to display intimate feelings of affection at school?

Yes. It is clearly within the authority of schools to prohibit all students from kissing, embracing, and caressing on school grounds.

What can be done if gay and lesbian teens are harassed by other students at school?

The incident should be reported to school authorities. If the problem persists or if this solution is unwise or even foolish, the best thing to do is discuss the matter with a lawyer associated with a gay or lesbian rights club or a community legal services organization. Legal services attorneys charge little or nothing and are legally required to keep such matters in confidence. The same approach should be followed if a gay or lesbian teen is harassed by a teacher.

An estimated 45 percent of gays and 20 percent of lesbians experience physical or verbal assault in public high schools.[2]

IN PUBLIC

Can a person be discriminated against at work because he or she is gay or lesbian?

Federal law protects racial and ethnic minorities, women, handicapped persons, and the elderly from job discrimination, but not gays and lesbians. However, the federal government is prohibited from firing or demoting a government employee simply because of sexual orientation. A gay or lesbian worker can only be dismissed from federal government work due to sexual orientation if his or her sex-related conduct is inappropriate in light of the job.

The laws of California, Massachusetts, Minnesota, New Jersey, and other states forbid discrimination at work on the basis of sexual orientation. In addition, many communities have laws forbidding such discrimination in restaurants, sports clubs, and with respect to membership in business and professional organizations.

Moreover, many businesses have nondiscrimination policies for gay and lesbian workers. More than half of the Fortune 1000 companies now have them. "Gay-friendly companies" include Apple Computer, Microsoft, Levi Strauss & Company, and Ben & Jerry's.

Can a landlord legally refuse to rent to a gay or lesbian person, or to a gay or lesbian couple?

Yes, unless state or local law forbids discrimination in housing on these grounds. If a nondiscrimination law applies, a landlord may not ask a prospective tenant anything about his or her intimate life. In the absence of a nondiscrimination law, however, a landlord may legally seek out such information and may refuse to rent to anyone—for almost any reason.

The laws of California, Connecticut, Minnesota, and many other states prohibit this type of discrimination, as do the laws of the District of Columbia and many other cities.

Can gays and lesbians join the U.S. armed forces?

Gays and lesbians perceive the duty to serve their country no less than straight people, and they have always been in the U.S. military. Traditionally, whenever a gay man joined up, he was questioned about his sexual orientation. Needless to say, the questions weren't answered truthfully in every case. Certainly, every nonstraight person kept matters of sex a secret from the commanding officer.

As of 1993, however, recruits can't be asked about sexual orientation. Nor can they be questioned about past sexual conduct. This policy, a product of the early Clinton years, is popularly known as the "don't ask, don't tell" policy. Even so, many gays and lesbians claim from personal experience that the military doesn't really want them in their ranks.

NOTES

1. National Museum and Archive of Lesbian and Gay History, *The Gay Almanac* (New York: Berkley Books, 1996).

2. *The Advocate*, April 18, 1995:40.

FOR FURTHER READING

In General

Cohen, Daniel, and Susan Cohen. *When Someone You Know Is Gay*. New York: Dell Publishing Company, Inc., 1992.

Curry, Hayden, et al. *A Legal Guide for Lesbian and Gay Couples*. Berkeley: Nolo Press, 1996.

Flook, Maria. *My Sister Life: The Story of My Sister's Disappearance*. New York: Random House, Inc., 1999.

Hunter, Nan D., Sherryl E. Michaelson, and Thomas B. Stoddard. *The Rights of Lesbians and Gay Men (ACLU)*. Carbondale: Southern Illinois University Press, 1992.

Keen, Lisa, and Suzanne B. Goldberg. *Strangers to the Law: Gay People on Trial*. Ann Arbor: University of Michigan Press, 1998.

Louganis, Greg. *Breaking the Surface*. New York: Random House, 1995.

McIlhaney, Marion. *Sex: What You Don't Know Can Kill You*. Grand Rapids, MI: Baker Book House, 1997.

Monette, Paul. *Borrowed Time*. New York: Avon Books, 1990.

National Museum and Archive of Lesbian and Gay History. *The Gay Almanac*. New York: Berkley Books, 1996.

Scarce, Michael. *Smearing the Queer: Medical Bias in the Health Care of Gay Men*. New York: Harrington Park Press, 1999.

Silver, Diane. *The New Civil War: The Lesbian and Gay Struggle for Civil Rights*. New York: Franklin Watts, Inc., 1997.

Scholinski, Daphne. *The Last Time I Wore a Dress*. New York: Putnam Publishing Group, 1997.

Young, Perry Dean, and Martin Duberman. *Lesbians and Gays and Sports*. Broomall, PA: Chelsea House Publishing, 1994.

OTHER INFORMATION SOURCES

Organizations

American Civil Liberties Union
Gay and Lesbian Rights/AIDS Civil Liberties Project

125 Broad Street
New York, NY 10004
(212) 549–2500
E-mail: aclu@aclu.org
Home page: www.aclu.org

Lambda Legal Defense and Education Fund
120 Wall Street
New York, NY 10005
(212) 809–8585
E-mail: lambdalegal@lambdalegal.org
Home page: www.lambdalegal.org

National Gay and Lesbian Task Force
1700 Kalorama Road NW
Washington, DC 20009
(202) 332–6483
(202) 332–6219 (TTY)
E-mail: ngltf@ngltf.org
Home page: www.ngltf.org

!OutProud! The National Coalition for Gay, Lesbian, Bisexual & Transgender
   Youth
369 Third Street, Ste. B-362
San Rafael, CA 94901
E-mail: info@outproud.org
Home page: www.outproud.org

Parents and Friends of Lesbians and Gays (PFLAG)
1101 Fourteenth Street NW
Washington, DC 20005
(202) 638–4200
E-mail: info@pflag.org
Home page: www.pflag.org

Online Sources

GayLawNet
E-mail: dba@labyrinth.net.au
Home page: www.labyrinth.net.au

Hotlines

Gay and Lesbian National Hotline
(888) THE–GLNH

CDC National AIDS Hotline
(800) 342–AIDS
(800) AIDS–TTY (TTY)

Property Rights and Crimes Against Property

EARNINGS

Are minors legally entitled to keep their personal earnings?

Not necessarily. Because parents are entitled to their children's services, they actually have a legal right to their children's income. This issue is discussed at length in Chapter Three, "At Home."

Do minors legally own the property that their parents provide for them such as clothes, books, bicycles, electronic equipment, and cars?

Not usually. Although parents "give" such property to their children in a definite sense, courts say the parents are the owners. This is because parents have the right to reclaim the property if it is stolen, and they have "standing" to bring a court case against someone if the property is damaged or destroyed.

WHAT CAN A MINOR OWN?

Can teens legally own property?

Yes, despite the fact that they might not have a legal claim to their earnings. They can purchase property, inherit it, and receive it by gift. Property actually and legally owned by a minor belongs to the minor

exclusively, although a minor can also own property "jointly" with someone else. (When a person owns property jointly, at one owner's death
all the property passes to the other joint owner.)

Can a minor have a bank account?

In most states a minor can establish a bank account and make withdrawals without parental consent. But a parent can serve as a "custodian"
for a minor's account. This means a parent's name can appear on the
account along with the minor's, as a sort of money manager. The parent
can make deposits and sign for withdrawals, but only for the minor's
benefit.

In addition, federal law permits parents to serve as custodians for
property they give to a child directly, except when the property is real
estate. (The parent would serve under the authority of the federal Uniform Transfers to Minors Act.) Except for custodian accounts, parents
don't have the automatic right to manage their children's property simply
because of their adult or parental status.

Can a minor legally sell property?

Minors do have the power to "transfer title" to property. But in many
states if a minor sells property—if a minor sells a large item such as a
house or business—the minor may later revoke the sale unless his or her
"property guardian" obtained court approval for the transaction.

What is a property guardian's job?

A property guardian is appointed by a court to manage a minor's
"estate" and serves until discharged. The guardian must manage the estate with a high degree of care and regularly report or "account" to the
court about the estate's status and value. Some transactions that property
guardians enter into, such as selling land and purchasing large invest-
ments, must be preapproved by the court.

Property guardians are sometimes called "conservators" or "guardians
of the estate." As a practical matter, courts only appoint property guardians if the amount of property owned by the minor is worth more than
a few thousand dollars. A property guardian is paid from the property
being managed (subject to court approval) unless the guardian agrees to
do the job for free.

In fact, one or both parents usually are the ones who serve, but a relative, friend, or bank could be appointed instead. (This often happens when a minor inherits property from a deceased parent.) Guardians are also appointed to manage property for adults who, because of illness or old age, are incapable of managing money or property on their own.

Does this mean a minor can't legally sell or trade personal items to friends, or even strangers?

No. Such transactions are really too small to involve a court or guardian.

Do parents have a legal right to use property inherited by a child?

Only if the property was inherited by the child and the parents jointly. Parents are powerless to dispose of a minor's interest in property unless they are the minor's custodian or court-appointed property guardian.

Can a minor require a property guardian to enter into a particular transaction?

No. The property guardian manages the property independently.

Can a minor have a property guardian dismissed?

In certain circumstances. Some states provide that minors age 14 years or older may nominate their own property guardian, although the court must approve the choice. In most states a minor is free to choose a new property guardian at age 14, again subject to court approval.

Might a minor have a legal guardian as well as a property guardian?

Yes, and they can be the same person. For more about legal guardians see Chapter Three, "At Home."

Can a minor retrieve his or her estate from the guardian at the age of majority?

Usually. The court revokes the guardianship at that point unless it believes a good reason exists to keep it in place, such as a person's physical or mental disability.

Can a minor legally give property away?

Yes, but like a minor's sale of property, the gift can be revoked. Again, this only applies to large gifts of property—not birthday presents and such.

WHEN PARENTS DIE

If a parent dies, who inherits his or her property?

It depends on whether the parent died leaving a valid will. Persons above the age of majority may legally decide how their property is to pass at death, and wills are the normal way of directing who gets what. Married people often leave their entire estate to a surviving spouse, although they aren't legally required to. If the "decedent" is a child's second parent to die, the estate often passes to the child and his or her brothers and sisters. This would happen regardless of whether the children are minors.

What happens if a parent dies without a valid will?

The property passes "intestate," which means it passes according to the state's inheritance laws. Under most state "intestacy" laws, if a parent is survived by a spouse and children, the spouse is entitled to one-third to one-half the decedent's estate and the children are entitled to the rest. If there is no surviving spouse, the children share the estate equally. Contrary to popular belief, if someone dies intestate, his or her property isn't forfeited to the government.

Do the courts get involved in the distribution of decedents' estates?

In most cases, yes—particularly when the estate is large.

"Probate" is the legal process for determining the validity of a decedent's will (when one exists), collecting the decedent's property, paying all debts, and distributing the estate to the proper persons. Most states have separate probate courts that supervise the orderly administration of decedents' estates, whether or not the person died with a will.

Can a spouse or child be disinherited?

Yes, but only under a will and not under the laws of intestacy. In some states, if a spouse attempts to disinherit a spouse in a will, the spouse inherits the amount he or she would have inherited had the decedent died intestate.

Can adopted children inherit from their adoptive parents?

Yes. Children of adoptive parents have the same legal rights as children who are related to their parents by blood. In many states adopted children may also inherit from the parents, aunts and uncles, and other relatives of their adoptive parents.

Can adopted children inherit from their natural parents?

In most states an adopted child may not inherit from a natural or "birth" parent if the birth parent dies intestate. This is because the relationship between child and parent no longer exists under the law. But nothing legally prevents a birth parent from leaving property by will to a child who has since been adopted.

Can children born outside of marriage inherit from their parents?

In years past, children born outside of marriage couldn't inherit from their natural *fathers*. Today they may inherit from both parents. To inherit under state intestacy laws, however, the identity of the father may have to be legally established in a "paternity" proceeding in court.

In some states an "illegitimate" child can inherit from his or her father only if the father's identity is established before he dies. Paternity can also be established if the child's parents marry one another or if the father legally declares the child to be his own.

Are stepchildren entitled to inherit from their stepparents?

Only under a will. Intestacy laws don't apply to the relationship of stepparent and stepchild.

If a minor inherits property, can he or she sell it, spend it—do anything with it whatsoever?

No. Again, because minors are legally incapable of managing their own property (except bank accounts), a probate court often will appoint a property guardian to handle their financial affairs. In an inheritance situation, property guardians often are nominated in the decedent's will.

Property guardianships can be complicated and inconvenient, particularly if the minor owns or inherits substantial property. For this reason, parents often create "trusts" during their lifetime to manage property that their children stand to inherit. With a trust, money or property is set aside by one or both parents before death. After they die a "trustee" manages it for the minor and distributes it when the minor becomes an adult. The property never needs to pass through a probate court proceeding.

Although trusts are easy to establish, less costly than guardianships, and subject to little court supervision, a lawyer should draft the trust document. In addition, the trustee should contact a lawyer if problems arise with the trust's management.

WHEN MINORS DIE

Can a minor write a valid will?
No. Only adults can make legally binding wills.

If a person dies before reaching the age of majority, who inherits his or her property?
Because a minor is too young to leave property by will, it must pass intestate, which again means that state law dictates who inherits it. Usually the minor's parents (or the surviving parent) inherit the property. If neither is living, the minor's brothers and sisters inherit it in equal shares.

THE PROPERTY OF OTHERS

Is shoplifting the same as theft? What kind of punishment can a minor receive for shoplifting?
Shoplifting is a form of "larceny," the official term for theft. From a legal standpoint, shoplifting is taking property displayed for sale without paying for it. The mere act of concealing store property inside a coat or purse is shoplifting; this means the shoplifter doesn't need to leave the store to commit the offense.

Teens who are caught shoplifting go to juvenile court. But whether or not the teen is convicted and regardless of whether the court orders probation, the shoplifter is usually required to return the property or make restitution for it.

Is robbery the same as larceny?

Robbery is larceny accompanied by the use of force and is a more serious crime than simple larceny.

Do teens who steal and rob always go to juvenile court?

Usually, although a mature minor can be tried in adult court in some states if charged with "aggravated robbery," which is robbery using a deadly weapon, and for other serious crimes such as arson, kidnapping, rape, murder, and attempted murder.

Chapter Twelve, "Teens and Crime," gives important information about how courts handle young offenders.

TRESPASSING AND PROPERTY DAMAGE

If a store manager asks a teen to leave the business premises, can the teen legally refuse? If the teen refuses, is he or she a trespasser?

A store manager can legally request any customer to leave, but only if the reason for wanting the customer out isn't based on race, color, gender, nationality, religion, or handicap. If the customer refuses, he or she becomes a trespasser and can be arrested.

So trespassing is against the law?

Yes—it is a misdemeanor. A person can be a trespasser if he or she refuses to leave after being asked to, and also if the person wasn't legally on the property in the first place.

If a person causes damage to property or vandalizes it while trespassing, what can the owner do?

Recover money against the trespasser as compensation for the damages because the property damage is a civil "tort." For more about torts and recovering money in court actions see Chapter Seventeen, "Taking Matters to Court."

Legally, what can happen when a minor damages property?

He or she can be sent to juvenile court. Minors can land in juvenile court for throwing rocks through windows, drawing on street signs, defacing bridges and buses, driving across lawns, and breaking through gates and fences. See Chapter Twelve, "Teens and Crime."

Is spray-painting graffiti on walls and buildings illegal?

Defacing property owned by the government (such as a city or state) is a crime. Defacing private property is a crime and also a tort.

Can parents be forced to reimburse a property owner for damage caused by their minor children?

In many cases, yes. They can be held liable in court for the torts of their children, particularly if the parents should have been supervising the child when the damage occurred. This rule applies to legal guardians as well.

FOR FURTHER READING

The American Bar Association Guide to Wills and Estates. New York: Times Books, 1995.

Castleman, Craig. *Getting Up: Subway Graffiti in New York.* Cambridge: The MIT Press, 1984.

Clifford, Denis. *Quick and Legal Will Book.* Berkeley: Nolo Press, 1999.

Dickens, Charles. *Bleak House.* New York: Everyman's Library, 1991.

Jordan, Cora. *Neighbor Law: Fences, Trees, Boundaries, and Noise.* 3rd ed. Berkeley: Nolo Press, 1998.

Leonard, Robin, and Ralph Warner. *Legal Forms for Personal Use: Delegating Authority to Care for Children, Pets and Property.* Nolo eForm Kit at www.nolo.com. Berkeley: Nolo Press, 1998.

Pollot, Mark F. *Grand Theft and Petty Larceny: Property Rights in America.* San Francisco: Pacific Research Institute for Public Policy, 1992.

Warda, Mark. *Neighbor vs. Neighbor.* Naperville, IL: Sourcebooks, Inc., 1999.

OTHER INFORMATION SOURCES

Organizations

National Guardianship Association
1604 North Country Club Road
Tucson, AZ 85716

(520) 881–6561
Home page: www.guardianship.org

Online Sources

Art Crimes (graffiti preservation)
E-mail: winsom@graffiti.org
Home page: www.graffiti.org

Hotlines

Shoplifters Anonymous
(800) 848–9595

— 16 —

Entering into Contracts

THE BASICS

What is a contract?

It is simply an agreement in which one party promises to do something in exchange for another party's promise to do something in return. If one party performs but the other doesn't, the first party can take the second party to court for "breach of contract."

People make contracts all the time, and many are so simple that people don't realize when they've entered into them. A customer contracts with a grocery store when the customer brings his or her selections to the check-out. The nature of their contract is simply this: the store will permit the customer to take the items away if the customer pays the amount shown on the register.

Consider another basic contract. When a person buys an airline ticket, the airline is contracting to take the person to a particular destination. The contract actually is written out—the printed information on the front and back of the plane ticket are the contract terms.

A sophisticated type of contract would be a contract for the sale of land or a contract to buy a car.

Do certain types of contracts need to be in writing?

Yes. By law, contracts that can't be performed in less than one year and contracts for the sale of land must be written. But contracts that don't have to be in writing often are. Written contracts give the parties a permanent and reliable record of their agreement. Sometimes state laws require various types of contracts to be in writing.

How are contracts enforced if one party refuses to perform?

The party who wants the contract performed often takes the other party to court for "breach of contract." If that party loses money as a result of the other's failure to perform, the court can award money or "damages" to the injured party.

Breach of contract actions in civil court are explained in Chapter Seventeen, "Taking Matters to Court."

Do minors have a legal right to enter into contracts?

Yes, and minors can be legally required to perform contracts they enter into. But in every state minors can "avoid" or "disaffirm" contracts, which means they can use the fact of their minority—their "non-age"—to back out of most contracts. In other words, contracts entered into by minors are "voidable."

If a minor enters into a contract, does an adult have to co-sign it or agree to be jointly responsible in order for it to be enforceable?

No, but an adult can certainly agree to do so. Co-signing a contract or agreeing to be jointly responsible means the adult can be required to perform the entire contract (such as paying all the money owed), and not just half of it.

DISAFFIRMING CONTRACTS

Why can minors disaffirm contracts?

The reason given is to protect minors against businesspeople who try to take unfair advantage of them in the marketplace. Many people think the rule allowing minors to disaffirm contracts is outdated and actually unfair for two reasons. First, it can be a hardship on the adults who contract with minors evenhandedly and in good faith. Second, most minors are at home in the marketplace and are usually smart about how it operates.

The rule that minors can avoid contracts doesn't mean, for example, that a minor can agree to buy a computer, take it home, use it, then refuse to pay. It simply means a minor can agree to buy a computer, take it home, then back out of the contract and return it even if the seller doesn't have a return policy. It means the seller must refund the amount paid—although in many states the seller can reduce the refund by the value of any wear and tear.

If the computer has been damaged, many states now require the minor to pay the difference between the original price and its current value. This is called "restitution." Even so, the minor can disaffirm the contract, but adults can't.

Can a minor disaffirm a contract for a car?

It depends on the state. In many, minors can't disaffirm contracts for cars, motorcycles, car insurance, or school loans. Furthermore, minors can't back out of contracts once they reach age 16 in California and a number of other states.

Can an adult disaffirm a contract with a minor?

Not if the minor wants to keep it in force. The contract is "binding" on the adult but not the minor, and the minor can require the adult to complete it.

If an adult agrees to be jointly responsible with a minor on a contract, can the adult disaffirm the contract as well?

No. The adult may be required to perform the contract fully, or pay contract "damages."

NECESSARIES

Are there any types of contracts that can't be disaffirmed by minors?

Yes. Contracts for "necessaries" such as food, clothing, lodging, and medical care can't be disaffirmed, assuming the minor is still dependent on his or her parents. Both the minor and the parents can be legally required to pay the entire bill. And, as stated above, sometimes insurance contracts, school loan agreements, and contracts for certain professional services aren't voidable. For more about emancipation see Chapter Five, "On Your Own."

A proper education often is considered a "necessary," although what constitutes a "proper" education will vary from family to family.

If a minor misrepresents his or her age in order to enter into a contract, can the minor later disaffirm it?
In many states, no. Certain states also prohibit minors from avoiding their contract obligations if they engage in business as an adult.

Does a minor's voidable contract ever become "nonvoidable"?
Yes, at the age of majority.

FOR FURTHER READING

The American Bar Association Guide to Consumer Law: Everything You Need to Know about Buying, Selling, Contracts, and Guarantees. New York: Times Books, 1997.

Smith, Wesley J. *The Smart Consumer: A Legal Guide to Your Rights in the Marketplace.* Washington, DC: HALT: Americans for Legal Reform, 1998.

Ulmer, Mari Privette. *Sign Here: How to Understand any Contract before You Sign.* 2nd ed. Angel Fire, NM: Intrigue Press, 1998.

OTHER INFORMATION SOURCES

Organizations

Public Citizen
1600 Twentieth Street NW
Washington, DC 20009
(202) 588–1000
E-mail: pcmail@citizen.org
Home page: www.citizen.org

Online Sources

Insurance Information Institute
Home page: www.iii.org

— 17 —

Taking Matters to Court

THE VOCABULARY OF A LAWSUIT

What is a lawsuit?

It is a process by which a "plaintiff" takes a "defendant" to court to satisfy a wrong the plaintiff believes the defendant caused.

The legal system has its own vocabulary. Plaintiffs and defendants are "parties" to a lawsuit. Parties don't have to be individuals; they can be businesses, cities, states, the federal government, or a foreign country. A plaintiff's injuries, physical or otherwise, are called "damages." When a plaintiff's relief takes the form of money, the monetary award is called "compensation."

Cases are "civil" in nature when a plaintiff seeks to protect a personal or private right such as property. They are "criminal" in nature when a public entity such as a state or city seeks to protect rights embodied in its public laws.

This chapter is about *civil* cases. For more about the criminal justice system and what happens when young people commit criminal acts see Chapter Twelve, "Teens and Crime."

WHY PEOPLE GO TO COURT

What types of wrongs can a plaintiff seek to recover for?

There are literally dozens, but the main categories are "tort" and "breach of contract."

Most tort and breaches of contract cases aren't based on laws passed by a legislative body. They are based on principles of fairness that have evolved in the American legal system over the years—principles known as the "common law."

What is a tort?

A tort occurs when a party violates a duty owed to another, causing injuries or property damage.

Consider the following example. A man negligently crashes a car into a homeowner's front porch, causing damage. Under tort law, the driver owes a legal duty to the homeowner to drive in a "reasonable" manner. Obviously, the driver didn't adhere to this duty—so he committed a tort.

The homeowner has a "cause of action" against the driver for operating the car negligently and may use the courts to be compensated for the damages. In a civil action to recover for the property damage, the homeowner would be the plaintiff and the driver would be the defendant.

A party must usually have acted either "negligently" or "intentionally" for a tort to occur. To prove negligence in court—to prove that someone breached his or her duty of care toward another—it isn't necessary that the defendant actually have foreseen a danger. It only requires that a reasonably careful or "prudent" person would have foreseen that reckless driving could cause damage and would therefore have avoided the crash.

This is the basic process for analyzing whether someone committed a tort. The Glossary at the end of the book defines many terms relating to civil courts.

What are other examples of torts?

Common torts are negligently failing to repair a car or properly erect a structure, driving a car negligently or recklessly, negligently or intentionally mishandling weapons, negligently treating a patient, negligently or intentionally leaving hidden or even obvious dangers on private property, and manufacturing faulty products. When these and other "tortious" acts cause injury or property damage, the plaintiff has a "cause of action" against the defendant.

Is a tort a crime?

Not necessarily. When a plaintiff sues, he or she rarely does so to obtain satisfaction for a crime, even though an act can be a crime as well as a tort. The plaintiff is generally looking for money.

If the act also is a crime—if the act violates a public law—the state's attorney can prosecute for it. In other words, the state (or one of its legal subdivisions, such as a county) can bring a separate case or "charge" against the defendant. This happens all the time.

What are some examples of torts that are also crimes?

Vandalism, for example. Damaging another's property is against the law even if the damage isn't major. It is also a tort, so the property owner can bring a civil action against the vandal.

Another example is rape. A rapist obviously commits a serious crime, but rapists can also cause severe emotional trauma. The rapist can be sued in civil court for the tort of intentionally inflicting emotional stress on his or her victim, and juries don't hesitate to assign a dollar value to this type of damage.

What is breach of contract?

A breach of contract occurs when a party to an agreement fails to perform according to its terms, thereby causing loss to the other party to the agreement. For example, a person breaches a contract if he or she agrees to sell a motorcycle, accepts full payment from the buyer, but then refuses to deliver it. Here the buyer is the potential plaintiff and the seller is the potential defendant.

For more about contracts see Chapter Sixteen, "Entering into Contracts."

What are some other examples of breach of contract?

Common examples are failing to pay rent or make a mortgage payment, failing to pay a credit card debt, failing to make prompt delivery of an order of manufactured products, and failing to complete construction of a building on schedule.

What forms of relief can courts award in civil actions?

Money is the most common form of relief in both tort and contract cases. But courts can also issue "injunctions," which order a defendant to stop doing something that causes constant harm to the plaintiff.

MINORS AS PLAINTIFFS

Can a minor be a plaintiff?

Yes. A minor can be a plaintiff or a defendant and can sue or be sued for almost all the same reasons as an adult.

But minors lack the legal capacity to file lawsuits on their own, and for this reason an adult files in the minor's behalf. This long-standing rule is meant to protect minors from their own lack of knowledge of the court system and the world at large. The adult representative might be the minor's parent, guardian, or so-called next friend—an individual appointed by the judge to protect the minor's interests.

A teen, for example, could sue a negligent driver for injuries and car damages resulting from an accident. The teen would sue through a parent or next friend. A young person could also be a plaintiff in a lawsuit resulting from another person's carelessness at school or work.

It would be difficult for a minor to sue on his or her own for another basic reason. Hiring a lawyer can be an expensive proposition. Payments to lawyers are discussed later in this chapter.

Can a minor sue his or her parents?

For certain wrongdoings, yes. In the United States, the first lawsuit by a child against a parent took place in 1891. As soon as this happened, states feverishly began passing laws to protect parents *against* lawsuits by their children. In 1905, a Washington court went so far as to prohibit a civil lawsuit by a 15-year-old who had been raped by a parent—it refused to hear the lawsuit out of a concern for family harmony!

Today almost every state permits minors to sue their parents for certain torts. The most common is a suit for personal injuries resulting from a parent's negligent driving. (The child's representative in this type of suit is often an insurance company.) Also, almost every state permits minors to sue one or both parents for personal injuries *intentionally inflicted*. A few permit children to sue for emotional injury caused by bad parenting, but these cases are almost impossible to win.

Can a minor sue an aunt, uncle, grandparent, or other relative?

Yes. These individuals have the same status as unrelated persons.

If a minor's parent is killed by a third party, can the minor sue the killer for money?

Most states have "wrongful death" statutes, which permit certain survivors to sue a person who negligently causes a family member's death. Those who can sue usually are the decedent's spouse and minor children. It doesn't matter whether the death was deliberate or accidental.

Some states limit damages in wrongful death cases to the loss of the deceased parent's services at home and the value of his or her future earnings. This means a dependent child might be able to recover for the estimated dollar value of a deceased mother's services as a parent.

Many states also permit survivors to recover damages for mental anguish endured as a result of a wrongful death. When a court permits recovery for mental anguish, the jury is asked to place a dollar value on the survivors' emotional pain and suffering.

If a child is born with a severe handicap, can the child sue the mother's doctor?

In an increasing number of states, yes. In these cases, called "wrongful life" actions, the child's lawyer argues that the mother could have had an abortion if her doctor had discovered through genetic testing that the child might be severely handicapped. If the child wins the lawsuit, his or her compensation would include expenses for special medical care and pain and suffering to be endured throughout life.

MINORS AS DEFENDANTS

Can a minor be a defendant?

A minor can be sued for torts and sometimes for breach of contract.

Minors who commit torts usually are held to a lower "standard of care" than adults. What this means is that instead of measuring a minor's actions against the level of care of a reasonable adult, courts hold them to a degree of care that a young person of the same age and maturity would be expected to exercise.

Most acts by teen's are measured against a standard of care very close to that of adults.

How does a minor go about defending a case?

Again, the minor has an adult representative, who assists the attorney. The representative must act in the minor's best interests and isn't required to take orders from the minor.

Who pays the damages when a jury decides a minor committed a tort?

In theory, the minor. But minors usually don't have much money— in legal jargon, they are "judgment proof." For this reason, parents often are jointly responsible for the torts of their minor children, particularly in cases in which the minor wasn't properly supervised when the tort occurred.

For example, if a parent left a handgun where anyone could reach it and a minor child managed to wound or even kill someone, the minor and the parents could be sued jointly. They would be "co-defendants." The minor could be sued for negligence and the parents could be sued for negligent supervision. This type of case is definitely on the increase.

LAWYERS

How important is a lawyer?

In most civil cases and in all felony cases a lawyer is critical. Anyone who wants to file a lawsuit in other than a small claims court should consider talking to a lawyer first. A lawyer can determine whether a person has a valid legal claim in tort or contract, whether the person has a decent chance of winning, and whether the estimated damages are worth the effort and expense of going to court.

Does a person need a lawyer to go to court?

No. Individuals can file lawsuits and go to court without legal representation. For better or worse, this happens all the time. Even so, court is exceedingly complex—it befuddles most nonlawyers (and even many lawyers). As a rule, the more complex the case, the more important it is to have legal representation.

Would a lawyer talk privately to a teen about a case the minor wants to file?

A lawyer would undoubtedly urge a minor to bring a parent or other adult along, even for a first office meeting. In addition, a lawyer's availability might depend on whether the minor has any money. Most attorneys charge by the hour, and an hourly rate of $150 isn't at all unusual.

Are lawyers always paid by the hour?

No. Their fees depend on the type of case. For tort actions, the plaintiff's lawyer usually charges a "contingency fee," which means his or her pay is a percentage of the amount recovered from the defendant. Under contingency fee arrangements, the lawyer doesn't get paid *unless* and *until* the plaintiff collects.

A contingency fee is usually one-third of the amount recovered. If the plaintiff loses and the case is appealed, the percentage goes up. In addition to the contingency fee, the plaintiff usually pays filing fees and other standard court charges regardless of the outcome of the case.

In tort actions the *defendant's* lawyer is paid by the hour.

SMALL CLAIMS COURT

What is small claims court?

It is a court that only hears cases in which the damage claim doesn't exceed a certain dollar amount, usually $5,000. Claims for unpaid bills or minor property damage often end up before a small claims court judge.

Small claims courts are in the nature of "people's courts" because the parties rarely use lawyers. Sometimes state law prohibits parties in small claims court from having legal representation at all.

Can a minor take a case to small claims court?

Only if state law permits minors to file lawsuits. Minors lack the legal capacity to file most civil suits on their own.

BRINGING A LAWSUIT

How does a plaintiff begin a civil case?

By filing a "complaint," which is a court document in which a plaintiff explains his or her claim against a defendant and requests a specific type of relief. As a rule, the plaintiff must always set forth enough information in the complaint to put the defendant on notice of the substance of the claim. If there isn't enough information given, the defendant can ask the judge to dismiss the case.

Most courts charge a filing fee to open a case, and the amount depends on the state and also the type of court. The filing fee can be excused if the plaintiff can't afford it.

Can a plaintiff file in any court?

No. Courts have the legal power or "jurisdiction" to hear certain types of cases but not others. A court's jurisdiction depends on several factors, including the residence of the parties, the subject of the case, the damages in dispute, and the legal concepts upon which the plaintiff's claims are based.

There are federal, state, city, municipal, traffic, and tax courts. To find out the appropriate court for a particular case, ask the chief clerk of court at any state or county court.

What is the difference between state court and federal court?

Basically, their respective jurisdictional powers. Federal courts, which are in every state, have jurisdiction over cases in which—

1. the United States government is a party;

2. an issue concerning the federal Constitution or federal statute is raised;

3. the dispute involves more than $50,000 *and* is between two states, a state and citizens of another state, or citizens of different states; or

4. the defendant is charged with a federal crime.

State courts usually deal with civil controversies between a state's residents and property owners, and civil and criminal matters based on state law. County courts and small claims courts are part of the state court system.

Can there be more than one plaintiff in a case?

There can be multiple plaintiffs and multiple defendants.

How does a person find out that he or she is a defendant in a lawsuit?

The person receives a "summons," which proclaims that a case naming that person as a defendant has been filed. The law allows the defendant a reasonable time, 20 to 30 days in most states, to prepare and file his or her "answer."

What should the defendant's answer contain?

It must admit or deny the statements in the complaint, and it may also state why the defendant believes he or she didn't do anything wrong and shouldn't be found responsible.

In a nutshell, the answer is the defendant's "defense" to a complaint.

What happens if the defendant doesn't answer?

A "default" can be entered for the plaintiff. This basically means the plaintiff wins. At that point the plaintiff must present evidence to the judge concerning the damages he or she claims to have suffered. Once the judge calculates the damages (plus lawyer's fees), the plaintiff has an enforceable "judgment" against the defendant in a particular dollar amount.

If the defendant answers, will the case always go to trial?

No. Most lawsuits settle before trial. In the long run, settling a case almost always is less expensive than going to trial, especially if one party's position is weak.

PREPARING A CIVIL CASE

If the parties don't settle their dispute, what happens between the date the answer is filed and the first day of trial?

The parties conduct "discovery," which is the overall process by which they learn more about one another's positions.

Why don't the parties wait until trial to learn more about each other's case?

Because today's court rules encourage parties to share as much as possible about one another's claims and defenses and settle as many issues as they can out of court. Judges only want to hear issues that the parties can't resolve on their own. This philosophy encourages better use of the court's time and, because the lawyer's fees mount up fast once a case goes to trial, always saves money.

Can the defendant ask to see documents in the plaintiff's possession that are likely to damage the plaintiff's case?

Yes, and the plaintiff can obtain damaging documents from the defendant. Prior to trial, a party must produce copies of any documents relating to the case that the other party requests.

Are documents in one party's control ever considered confidential?

Yes. Such items are called "privileged" communications, and they don't have to be turned over to the opposing party. They are protected because they occur in relationships in which honesty and trust are of critical importance. A privileged communication usually takes the form of a personal letter or memorandum, or a medical report.

The attorney-client relationship is a type of privileged relationship—hence, the "attorney-client privilege." A party who claims this privilege may refuse to produce material generated during the course of the relationship, and his or her lawyer *must* refuse. Other examples of privileged relationships are the relationship of husband and wife, the doctor-patient relationship, and the priest-confessor relationship.

Can a party force a person to testify?

Yes. The party would do so by asking the court to "subpoena" the person. A subpoena is a court order directing a particular person to appear as a witness. Often a party requests a subpoena if there is reason to believe the witness won't show up. If the witness ignores the subpoena, the judge declares him or her to be "in contempt of court." If the witness still won't appear, he or she can be fined or even jailed.

TRIALS

How does a trial begin?

Each party presents its "opening statement," which carefully explains what each will attempt to prove during the trial.

What happens after the opening statements?

Each of the plaintiff's witnesses takes the stand and testifies. The plaintiff's lawyer conducts his or her "direct examination" of these witnesses one by one. After the direct examination, the defendant's lawyer has an opportunity to "cross-examine."

What exactly is cross-examination?

Cross-examination occurs when a witness for one party is questioned by the lawyer for the other party. The cross-examiner will always attempt to test the truth or reliability of the witness's direct testimony and will also try to develop additional facts supporting his or her client's position.

What happens after all the plaintiff's witnesses have testified and been cross-examined?

The defendant's lawyer calls the defense witnesses. One by one he or she questions them, and one by one the plaintiff's lawyer cross-examines them.

How does material other than in-court testimony come into evidence?

Each party's lawyer can request that items such as letters, memos, photos, weapons, bills, and results of scientific tests also be considered. The judge rules on the admissibility of each item as it is offered into evidence.

Can a young person testify?

Anyone who can remember significant events or evidence, express them clearly, and understand the duty to tell the truth is "competent" to testify. Minors often are placed on the stand.

In some states, if a minor is 10 years old (12 in other states) or younger, his or her ability to testify isn't taken for granted. If a party to a case believes a minor won't be able to offer reliable testimony, the judge will talk to the minor in private to determine whether he or she can understand questions, respond in court, remember important events, and comprehend the difference between true and false.

When determining a minor's competency to testify, age is often less significant than maturity. Judges have permitted children as young as three years old to testify in open court.

What is an "objection"? Why would a lawyer raise an objection in court?

A lawyer will object when an item of evidence, a question asked by the opposing party's lawyer, or a certain court procedure appears inappropriate. If a lawyer makes an objection, he or she must be ready to explain to the judge why the question, evidence, or procedure is out of line. If the judge agrees, he or she will "sustain" the objection. If the judge disagrees, it will be "overruled."

What happens after all the witnesses testify?

The lawyers present their "closing arguments." Each summarizes his or her client's case and tells the jury why it should decide the case in that party's favor.

What does a jury do?

It listens to the testimony of the witnesses, reviews the evidence, considers the applicable laws and earlier court cases dealing with similar legal issues, and then decides the outcome. In essence, it decides what really happened in the parties' case.

The jury's decision is its "verdict." When the jury brings in its verdict, one party wins and the other loses. The winner receives a judgment.

Is a case always argued to a jury?

No. The parties can agree to argue their case just to the judge. When this happens—and it often does in complex business cases—the judge decides what actually happened and renders a decision on his or her own.

How does a jury know what legal principles to apply to a case?

After the closing arguments the judge gives the jury its "instructions," which advise the jury what laws and earlier cases to apply to the dispute between the parties.

What is a "hung jury"?

A jury is "hung" when it tries to reach a decision but can't. Since the jury is hung, no judgment is awarded, and the case must either be reargued to another jury or dropped.

Is a jury's verdict always final?

No. The losing party can ask the court—can "motion" the court—to grant a new trial. However, a judge will only grant a new trial if he or she believes that no reasonable jury could have reached the verdict that the jury returned.

DAMAGES

If the plaintiff wins, who decides how much the defendant will have to pay?

If the case is tried to a jury, the jury decides. Otherwise the judge decides. There aren't any hard and fast rules for deciding how much a plaintiff's injuries or other damages are "worth," and juries have considerable leeway in setting damage amounts, particularly in tort cases.

To calculate damages for a personal injury tort, a jury would consider evidence presented by the plaintiff's attorney regarding his or her client's medical expenses and loss of income. It might place a dollar value on both the plaintiff's pain and suffering and future employment opportunities lost due to the injury. If the damage was to property such as a car, the jury would consider the cost to repair the damage or replace the property altogether.

To determine damages in a breach of contract case, the jury would calculate the financial loss resulting from the defendant's failure to fulfill his or her side of the agreement.

APPEALING A COURT DECISION

What is an appeal? Who can appeal?

An appeal is a court review of certain issues previously decided at trial. The review is conducted by a higher court, called a court of appeals. In an appeal, the losing party—the "appellant"—claims that a mistake was made by the judge or jury during the trial, causing the appellant to lose.

Is an appeal just a repeat of the trial?

No. Courts of appeal don't take testimony or accept additional evidence—they only review the matters brought up for review. An appeals court considers the arguments of both parties on these issues, reviews the written summaries or "briefs" of their arguments, examines the applicable law, then decides to "affirm" or "reverse" the trial court's decision.

If a party loses an appeal, can he or she take the case to a still higher court?

In some cases, yes. The federal court system and most state court systems provide two levels of appeal. In federal court, the first level is the Federal Court of Appeals, and next is the United States Supreme Court. In state courts, the first level is the state court of appeals, and the second is the state supreme court. A state supreme court may refuse to hear a party's appeal, except in states (such as Wyoming) in which there is no appeals court sandwiched between its trial courts and supreme court.

The United States Supreme Court only hears select appeals, usually from the federal courts. In limited circumstances it will hear the appeal of a party who loses in a state supreme court. In Supreme Court cases the issue on appeal will involve a constitutional right or other important issue under federal law that earlier cases haven't clarified.

FOR FURTHER READING

In General

Bergman, Paul, and Sara Berman-Barrett. *Represent Yourself in Court: How to Prepare and Try a Winning Case*. 2nd ed. Berkeley: Nolo Press, 1998.

Hayes, J. Michael. *Help Your Lawyer Win Your Case*. Clearwater, FL: Sphinx Publishing, 1996.

Lovenheim, Peter. *How to Mediate Your Dispute*. Berkeley: Nolo Press, 1996.

Schwartz, Bernard. *A History of the Supreme Court*. New York: Oxford University Press, 1995.

Warda, Mark. *Simple Ways to Protect Yourself from Lawsuits*. Clearwater, FL: Sphinx Publishing, 1996.

Warner, Ralph. *Everybody's Guide to Small Claims Court*. 7th ed. Berkeley: Nolo Press, 1998.

Woodward, Bob, and Scott Armstrong. *The Brethren: Inside the Supreme Court*. New York: Avon Books, 1996.

The Jury System

Adler, Stephen J. *The Jury: Disorder in the Court.* New York: Doubleday Books, 1994.

Edah, Omatseyin Mark. *Juror: An Opportunity to Serve: An Immigrant Juror's Insight into the U.S. Jurisprudence.* Los Angeles: Milligan Books, 1998.

Opposing Viewpoints. *Does the Jury System Work?* San Diego: Greenhaven Press, 1996.

Lawyers

Azrieli, Avi. *Your Lawyer on a Short Leash.* Irvington-on-Hudson: Bridge Street Books, 1997.

Foonberg, Jay G. *Finding the Right Lawyer.* Chicago: American Bar Association, 1994.

Repa, Barbara Kate. *The American Lawyer: When and How to Use One.* Chicago: American Bar Association, 1993.

Starnes, Tanya, et al. *Mad at Your Lawyer?* Berkeley: Nolo Press, 1996.

OTHER INFORMATION SOURCES

Organizations

American Bar Association
Lawyer Referral Services
Home page: www.abanet.referral

Teen Court TV
600 Third Avenue
New York, NY 10016
Home page: www.courttv.com/teens

— 18 —

How to Find the Law

How would a young person go about finding the law for a given situation?

First, go to the public library and ask to see a set of your state's laws, also called your state "statutes." Most laws governing important day-to-day activities are in state statutes, and for that reason every public library has a complete set.

Statutes aren't hard to use. Each set has a complete topic index. The index usually cites to the statute number, not the page number. If you can't find the particular statute you're looking for, ask a reference librarian to help. Large public libraries have legal specialists on hand (sometimes called "government document specialists") to assist further.

For instance, if capital punishment is permitted in your state and you want to find out if it applies to minors as well as adults, look up "capital punishment" in the statute index. The index entry might look like this:

CAPITAL PUNISHMENT

Adults, (Statute Number)

Appeal of Sentence, (Statute Number)

Due Process Hearing for, (Statute Number)

Methods, (Statute Number)

Minors, (Statute Number)

Offenses, (Statute Number)

Next look up the statute for "Minors" and read what it says.

Follow the same process to locate a particular *city law*, or "ordinance," such as a local curfew law.

Federal laws are located the same way, but the indexes are complicated, mainly because federal law is complicated. Always ask a librarian for help locating a federal law (such as a law regulating age discrimination at the national level). Federal statutes are in the United States Code Annotated, or USCA. People often refer to it as the "Federal Code."

Aren't laws practically impossible to read?

No, although sometimes it can be rough going. The best way to understand what a law says is to read it over a number of times. Once usually isn't enough—any lawyer will tell you that. It's wise to photocopy the statute or ordinance once you've located it, then take the copy home and read it a few more times, carefully.

Isn't there an easier way to learn about the law?

Oftentimes, yes. Libraries have books on various legal topics and many are written for young people. First try the reference section of your library.

You may have noticed that each chapter of this book has a section entitled "For Further Reading" which lists recently published legal books for both young persons and adults. These books are recommended. In addition, the organizations listed under "Additional Information Sources" at the end of each chapter can be of enormous help.

How can a computer be used to learn about the law?

All state and federal laws are online, which means that anyone with access to a computer and a modem can bring up any state or federal law on a computer screen. Furthermore, organizations and businesses interested in legal matters often have online "home pages" to aid the legal researcher. See the "Additional Information Sources" section at the end of this chapter for particularly helpful Web sites.

Without question, the computer has made the law more accessible.

How do you find out what a court case says?

You may have to go to the local law library to locate a court case— such as *Miranda v. Arizona* (regarding the *Miranda* warnings) or *Roe v.*

Wade (legalizing abortion). Most larger counties have a county law library, and every law school in the country has one. To find a case, ask the law librarian to help you. You'll probably have to read it over more than once—some cases are long and complicated.

More recent court decisions are often online.

How do you find the Constitution?

Ask any librarian. The U.S. Constitution is usually printed at the back of a good dictionary. Your state constitution is usually in the first volume of your state statutes. The subject matter of state constitutions is indexed in the main statute index.

Who else can help a young person find the law?

Organizations such as those listed at the end of this chapter. If you contact the organization, it will send you information about its special areas of concern.

In addition, state and county "bar associations" usually have easy-to-read information on a variety of legal subjects. (A bar association is a professional association of lawyers.) Also, many bar associations have recorded telephone information on dozens of legal topics and good Web sites. Phone numbers of state and county bar associations are in the telephone book.

Bar associations often sponsor special programs to educate young people about the law, and often the lawyers who participate in them speak to student groups. The programs are very informative and are easy to follow, so it's important to watch for them.

Can't a young person simply call up a lawyer and inquire about a particular area of the law?

That shouldn't be your initial line of attack. Lawyers have a very hard time cutting away for phone calls from persons other than established clients. Furthermore, they are usually paid by the hour for their work, and their charges include time spent on the telephone. A lawyer would probably refer you to the library or local bar association anyway.

FOR FURTHER READING

Blackman, Josh. *How to Use the Internet for Legal Research.* New York: Find/SVP: 1996.

Elias, Stephen, and Susan Levinkind. *Legal Research: How to Find and Understand the Law.* Berkeley: Nolo Press, 1993.

Evans, James, ed. *Law on the Net.* Berkeley: Nolo Press, 1995.

Heels, Erik J., and Richard P. Klau. *Law, Law, Law on the Internet: The Best Legal Web Sites and More.* Chicago: American Bar Association, 1998.

How to Research a Legal Probem: A Guide for Non-Lawyers. Chicago: American Association of Law Libraries, 1998.

Kramer, Donald T. *Legal Rights of Children.* 2nd ed. Shepard's/McGraw-Hill, Inc., 1994.

McLeod, Don. *The Internet Guide for the Legal Researcher.* 2nd ed. Teaneck, NJ: Infosources Publishing, 1997.

OTHER INFORMATION SOURCES

Organizations

American Bar Association Center on Children and the Law
1800 M Street NW, Ste. 200
Washington, DC 20005
(202) 331–2250

American Civil Liberties Union
Children's Rights Project
125 Broad Street, 18th Floor
New York, NY 10004
(212) 549–2500
E-mail: aclu@aclu.org
Home page: www.aclu.org

Juvenile Law Center
801 Arch Street, Ste. 610
Philadelphia, PA 19107
(215) 625–0551
E-mail: HN2403@handsnet.org
Home page: www.usakids.org

National Center for Youth Law
114 Sansome Street, Ste. 900
San Francisco, CA 94104
(415) 543–3307
E-mail: info@youthlaw.org
Home page: www.youthlaw.org

Online Sources

Ask Auntie Nolo
Home page: www.nolo.com/auntie

All Law
Home page: www.alllaw.com

FindLaw
Home page: www.findlaw.com

LAWKids' Only!
Home page: wwlia.org/kidsonly

Legal Information Institute (LII)
Home page: www.law.cornell.edu

Glossary

Abandonment. Totally ignoring one's parental duties. Abandonment usually is established by actions of a parent showing an intent to both abandon a minor child and forfeit parental rights.

Abuse. Physical or emotional mistreatment of a person.

Accomplice. A person who voluntarily helps another commit or attempt to commit a crime.

Adoption. A process under state law by which a family court terminates a minor's legal rights and duties toward his or her natural parents and establishes similar rights and duties with respect to the minor's adoptive parents.

Advisory Hearing. A hearing in juvenile court at which a minor is formally charged with a delinquent act.

AFDC (Aid to Families with Dependent Children). A federal program providing financial benefits to poor persons. This program was replaced by the Personal Responsibility and Work Opportunity Reconciliation Act of 1996.

Affirm. An action of an appeals court in which the decision of a trial court is upheld.

Affirmative Action. A government or company policy to increase opportunities for women and minorities, especially with respect to employment.

Age of Majority. The age at which a young person is legally entitled to manage his or her personal affairs and enjoy the rights associated with adulthood. The age of majority is 18 in most states.

Aggravated Assault. An intentional or willful injury to another, using a weapon or other instrument.

Appeals Court. A panel of judges with the power to review and change a judgment, verdict, or other order of a trial court. Appeals courts are also called "appellate courts."

Appellant. A party seeking a review by an appeals court of a lower court's decision.

Appellee. A party opposing the review of a lower court's decision. This party will have prevailed in the lower court.

Arbitrary. A decision made by a court or jury that is not based on sound judgment. *The appeals court set aside the jury's decision because the appellate judges believed it was arbitrary.*

Armed Forces. Military, naval, and air forces, especially of a nation.

Arrest. A police action that takes away a person's freedom, usually when the person is believed to have broken the law.

Attorney. A person authorized in a particular state to perform legal services for clients. An attorney's services may include giving legal advice, drafting legal documents, and representing clients in court. Attorneys are also referred to as "lawyers."

BAC. A person's blood alcohol content.

Battered Child Syndrome. When medical exams show that a minor has been physically abused, but no obvious connection exists between the caregiver's actions and the injury. Courts often conclude that the caregiver must be the guilty party. "Sexually abused child syndrome" and "maternal deprivation syndrome" are identified in much the same manner.

Battery. Any intentional and harmful application of force to another. Examples of battery include injuring a person and giving a person medical treatment without legal permission in a nonemergency.

Beyond a Reasonable Doubt. The level of proof needed to convict a defendant in a criminal case. When this level of proof is required, the jury must be firmly convinced that the defendant is guilty of the offense as charged.

Birth Parents. A person's natural parents.

Blocking. Preventing someone, often a child, from accessing certain material online on a computer.

Breach of Contract. The failure of a contracting party to fulfill the terms of a contract.

Burden of Proof. The duty of a plaintiff (or the duty of the state in a criminal case) to prove a point or establish facts supporting his or her case. In tort actions, the plaintiff's burden of proof is to establish the case by a "preponderance of the evidence." In criminal cases, the state's burden of proof is to prove its case "beyond a reasonable doubt."

Busing. Transferring school children to a public school that they wouldn't normally attend in order to remedy a racial imbalance in the schools.

Capital Punishment. The death penalty.

Cause of Action. Specific facts giving rise to a case against a defendant.

Charter School. A quasi-independent public school that receives public money to operate.

Child Labor Law. A state or federal law limiting the type of work a minor may legally perform and establishing the number of hours a minor may legally work per week.

Child Protection Proceeding. A legal action, usually in state family court, in which a child protective agency requests court permission to protect a minor from neglect or abuse.

Child Protective Agency. A government agency possessing the legal power to protect a minor from neglect or abuse, including sexual abuse.

Civil Action. (*also* Civil Proceeding). A court case brought by a plaintiff to enforce a private legal right. Generally, civil actions include all actions which are not criminal actions. A tort action is a type of civil action.

Civil Rights. Rights of personal liberty, especially those established by certain Constitutional Amendments and certain acts of Congress.

Compensation. Money that a civil court orders a defendant to pay a plaintiff for an injury or other loss.

Complaint. A plaintiff's document, filed with a trial court, explaining the specific reason for bringing the court action.

Conflict of Interest. In a legal matter, a clash between a lawyer's interest as a servant of the court and his or her private monetary interest. When a conflict of interest arises, the lawyer usually withdraws from the case.

Conscious Objector. A person who is religiously or morally opposed to war.

Conservator. *See* Property Guardian.

Constitution. A written instrument from which a governing body derives its authority and that also describes the limits on its powers. In the U.S. the federal government is subject to the federal Constitution. State and local governments and laws are subject to both the federal Constitution and their respective state constitutions.

Contempt of Court. A serious consequence of failing to obey a court order. *Because Jane failed to produce certain important documents for the judge, he held her in contempt of court, ordering her to sit in jail until he received them.*

Contraband. A substance that is illegal to possess, produce, or sell.

Contraceptive. Any device or substance (such as birth control pills or condoms) that prevents a woman from becoming pregnant.

Contract. An agreement between two or more persons creating a legal duty to perform a certain act. For example, a contract to purchase a car is an agreement in which one person agrees to turn a car over to another in return for the second person's promise to pay for it. Once the parties have fulfilled the duties promised under the contract, it is said to be "executed."

Controlled Substance. Any illegal drug or beverage.

Corporal Punishment. Any type of punishment inflicted on a person's body.

Creation Science. A belief that the creation of the world occurred as described in the Old Testament, as opposed to finding the explanation in scientific theories of evolution.

Crime. An act committed by a person in violation of a federal, state, or local law.

Criminal Act. *See* Crime.

Criminal Action (*also* Criminal Proceeding). A court case in which an adult charged with a crime is brought to trial.

Cross-Examine. In-court questioning of a witness by a party other than the party producing the witness. The purpose of cross-examination is to test the reliability of the witness's original or "direct" testimony.

Cruel and Unusual Punishment. Punishment that is so severe, given the seriousness of the crime, that it shocks the moral sense of the community.

Curfew. A law forbidding persons (usually minors) from being on the streets at night.

Custodial Parent. The parent in charge of the care of a minor child after a divorce.

Custodian. A person who is in charge of either another person or another person's assets.

Custody. Responsibility for another person.

Damages. Money awarded by a court to a person who has sustained a loss or injury as the result of a breach of contract or a tort.

Date Rape. Forced sexual intercourse in a casual dating situation.

Debauchery. Extreme sexual immorality in light of community standards.

Decedent. A dead person.

Decedent's Estate. The property a person owns at death.

Defamatory Statement. A spoken or written statement that injures another's reputation and is untrue.

Default Judgment. A civil judgment rendered by a court to a party because the opposing party failed to appear or participate after being served with notice.

Defendant. A person against whom damages are sought in a civil action or against whom a conviction is sought in a criminal action.

Defense Attorney. An attorney who represents a civil or criminal defendant.

Delinquent. A minor who has broken a criminal law or engaged in indecent or immoral conduct. Such a person is also called a "juvenile delinquent."

Delinquent Act. An act of a minor that would have been a crime under federal, state, or local law if committed by an adult.

Desegregation Order. A court order forbidding minority status to be the basis for limiting an individual's right to hold a certain job or attend the school of his or her choice.

Designated Driver. A person who abstains from alcohol or drugs in order to drive others who don't plan to abstain.

Detention Hearing. A juvenile court hearing to determine whether a minor should be confined to a shelter or placed in foster care until a formal hearing in juvenile court takes place.

Disability. A physical or mental condition that limits a person's ability to perform at the same level as persons who do not have the condition.

Disaffirm. To back out of a contract.

Discriminate. To give rights or privileges to certain persons while denying them to others. Laws limiting the right of minors to purchase alcoholic beverages legally discriminate, but laws which discriminate in school or at work on the basis of gender, race, nationality, religion, age (over 40), or disability violate the federal Constitution.

Disposition Hearing. A hearing in juvenile court at which the judge orders a delinquent minor into treatment or disposes of the case in some other way.

Diversion. A juvenile court program keeping a delinquent minor out of court provided he or she agrees to perform certain tasks or duties.

Due Process Hearing. A type of legal hearing at which a person has a chance to present his or her side in a dispute involving personal or property rights. *See* Due Process of Law.

Due Process of Law. A course of action, usually in a legal proceeding, in which a person receives proper notice and has a chance to present his or her side in a dispute regarding legal rights. Formally defined, "due process of law" means that no person may legally be deprived of life, liberty, or property unless the matter is reviewed in a legal proceeding.

DUI. An offense committed by a person who operates a vehicle while under the influence of alcoholic beverages.

Emancipation. Acts causing parents to lose their authority over a minor child. An emancipation may be ordered by a court or be implied from conduct of either the minor or the parents.

Employee-at-Will. A person who works without an employment contract specifying why he or she can be fired or laid off.

Employment Certificate. A document issued by a school district or school superintendent giving permission to a student to hold a part-time job.

ESL (English As a Second Language). A class or course of study taken by an immigrant to learn English.

Establishment Clause. The provision in the First Amendment of the federal Constitution prohibiting the federal government or any state from aiding religion, giving a preference to a particular religion, or enforcing a religious belief.

Estate. All the property a person owns.

Exclusionary Rule. A rule of criminal law making evidence obtained in violation of the federal Constitution inadmissible against a criminal defendant in court. For example, evidence obtained in an unreasonable search is legally inadmissible and must be suppressed.

Exploit or Exploitation. To use selfishly or to take advantage, as in the crime of "child exploitation."

Fair Labor Standards Act. Federal legislation setting the minimum wage and establishing other laws relating to the workplace.

Family Court. A state court with the power to decide child abuse and neglect cases, determine paternity with respect to children born out of wedlock, and terminate parental rights.

Federal Court. United States courts (as opposed to state courts) that handle cases relating to federal law and cases between persons of different states.

Federal System. A division of power between the United States government and the governments of the 50 states. States have their own legal powers, such as the power to create a public school system. The federal government has separate powers, such as control over foreign trade. Both have powers in the areas of taxation and public health.

Felony. A crime that is more serious than a misdemeanor. Under federal law and in most states, a felony is any offense punishable by imprisonment for more than one year or death.

Fetus. An unborn child. Usually this term is used to describe an unborn child whose major body parts have begun to form.

Fifth Amendment. A Constitutional amendment providing that persons subject to the Constitution aren't required to testify against their own interests.

Financial Responsibility. A requirement that a driver must be able to arrange to pay for auto-related injuries to another person, or damages to another person's car.

FMLA (The Federal Family and Medical Leave Act). An act that permits individuals to take paternity or maternity leave without risking job loss, under certain conditions.

Food Stamps. Coupons issued by a government body to poor persons to obtain food products at grocery stores.

Formal Hearing. A juvenile court trial.

Foster Home. A private home where a minor child resides after being removed from his or her parents' home by court order.

Foster Parent. An adult person who takes a minor child into his or her home, either temporarily or permanently, after the child has been removed from the custody of his or her parents by court order.

Fourteenth Amendment. A Constitutional amendment stating that no state may enforce a law depriving U.S. citizens of life, liberty, or property without due process, and that all persons (including ethnic and racial minorities) have a right to the equal protection of the laws.

Freedom of Expression. A right set forth in the First Amendment of the federal Constitution guaranteeing the right of individuals to speak freely and openly.

Free Exercise Clause. The provision in the First Amendment of the federal Constitution prohibiting the federal government or any state government from outlawing or substantially controlling the practice of religion.

Fringe Benefit. A job-related benefit other than a wage, such as employer-provided medical insurance.

GED (Graduate Equivalency Degree). An education related degree awarded to a person who didn't complete high school; the GED substitutes for a high school graduation degree.

Gender Bias. A preference in the workplace or elsewhere based solely on an individual's sex.

Green Card. A card issued by the U.S. Immigration and Naturalization Service to immigrants, enabling them to legally live and work in the U.S.

Guardian. A person with the legal power to care for another or manage another's legal and financial affairs. Usually a guardian is appointed if a person is too young, too old, or otherwise unable to make important personal and financial decisions.

Guardianship. A relationship existing between a guardian and the person under the guardian's legal protection. In such a relationship the protected person is sometimes called the "ward."

Harassment. Excessively bothersome and inappropriate behavior of another. *Jane explained to the court how her supervisor had been sexually harassing her at the office.*

Health Insurance. A written agreement in which an insurance company promises to pay expenses associated with a certain individual's injuries, sickness, or death.

Home Schooling. Teaching and learning grade school subjects at home, subject to state guidelines, as an alternative to traditional public or private schooling.

Homicide. An act in which a person takes the life of another, either deliberately or accidentally.

Human Resources. Another term for a business's personnel department.

Impound. To seize and retain custody of the property of another. *Jo's car and its contents were impounded by the police after she was caught transporting stolen property.*

Inadmissible. Evidence that cannot be legally introduced in court to prove a party's case because it is false or unreliable, or was improperly obtained.

Indeterminate Sentencing. A sentence for a period of time determined by the agency supervising the sentenced person and not fixed by the trial court.

Initial Appearance. A person's first contact with a judge after being arrested. *Lou pled "not guilty" to violating the local curfew law at his initial appearance.*

Injury. Damage to another's person, property, individual rights, or reputation.

Insurance. A written agreement in which one party agrees to pay the other for a type of loss or damage specifically described in the insurance agreement. The party who is insured against loss or damage is the "insured," and the party who must pay in the event of loss or damage is the "insurer."

Intake. The initial processing of a case in juvenile court.

Intestacy. Dying without a will.

Joint Custody. A type of custody awarded by a divorce court in which the responsibility for the care and control of a minor child is awarded to both parents.

Judgment Proof. When a defendant doesn't have the money to pay a court judgment, making the judgment virtually worthless to the plaintiff.

Judicial Bypass. A court action in which a judge orders that parental permission for a teen to obtain an abortion isn't legally required; the judge gives permission instead.

Jury. A group of persons selected from the community who decide the facts of a case and determine the truth of a matter at trial.

Juvenile Court. A state court with the legal authority to decide cases involving delinquent, abused, or neglected minors.

Juvenile Delinquent. *See* Delinquent.

Larceny. The legal term for theft.

Lawyer. An attorney.

Legal Guardian. *See* Guardian.

Liability. A legal obligation or responsibility to do something or pay a specified amount of money. A debt is a type of liability.

Liability Insurance. Insurance that covers the cost of damage caused by the insured person to another person or another's property.

Libel. Printed material which is untrue and injures the personal or business reputation of another.

Majority. *See* Age of Majority.

Mandatory Reporter. A person such as a nurse who is legally required to report a known or suspected case of physical or sexual abuse.

Material and Substantial Disruption. A level of disruption that, in the opinion of a reasonable person, interferes with daily activities to the point that an individual cannot proceed at standard pace.

Maternal Preference. A tendency in the law to favor mother over father, particularly in child custody matters. The maternal preference may be applied when parents divorce or in cases involving children born outside marriage.

MCT (Minimum Competency Test). A test required by a state education system to ascertain how much knowledge a student has absorbed; passing an MCT might be a prerequisite to graduating from high school or passing to the next grade level.

Medicaid. A welfare program sponsored jointly by the federal and state governments providing medical care for low-income persons.

Minor. A person under the age of legal majority, which is 18 in most states.

***Miranda* Warnings**. A constitutional rule requiring that before questioning a person who is in police custody, the police must warn (a) that the person has a right to remain silent, (b) that any statement the person makes may be used against him or her, (c) that the person has a right to a lawyer; and (d) that if the person can't afford a lawyer, one will be appointed to assist him or her.

Misdemeanant. A person who commits a misdemeanor—a less serious type of crime.

Misdemeanor. A less serious offense than a felony, usually punishable by a fine of less than one year in prison. In most states misdemeanors are grouped according to their seriousness (such as Class A and Class B misdemeanors).

Necessaries. Food, drink, clothing, medical attention, and a suitable place to live.

Neglect. Negligent failure to provide care and nourishment to someone—usually to a child but also to an elderly or disabled adult.

Negligence. Failing to perform an act that a reasonable person would do, or performing an act that a reasonable person would not do.

Noncustodial Parent. One of two parents who, after a divorce, is *not* responsible for the day-to-day upbringing of their minor child.

Opinion. A written statement of a judge or appeals court setting forth the reasons for reaching a decision in a given case.

Ordinance. A law of a city government, such as a traffic or parking ordinance.

OSHA (The Federal Occupational Safety and Health Administration). The agency charged with regulating workplace conditions and assuring workplace safety.

Pain and Suffering. A type of damage in a civil tort action that compensates a plaintiff for pain and suffering endured or to be endured as the result of the tort.

Paternity Suit. A civil court action to prove that a certain person is the father of a particular child. If proof of paternity is established, the court will require the father to support the child financially.

Pension Plan. A type of fringe benefit in which the employer sets aside money for an employee to live on after retiring. Sometimes the employee is permitted to match the employer's contribution amount, either totally or partially.

Petition. A complaint filed in juvenile court that begins a case against a minor suspected of committing a delinquent act. Often a juvenile court petition is called a "formal petition."

Plaintiff. A person who brings a civil action against a defendant.

Plain View Exception. (*also* Plain View Doctrine). Important exception to the Constitutional warrant requirement for searches and seizures which permits a police officer to seize evidence of illegal activity without a search warrant if the evidence is clearly visible and the officer is already on the premises legally.

Pornography. Obscene or lewd materials in light of a community's standards of decency.

Premium. A payment made to an insurance company to obtain insurance coverage.

Preponderance of the Evidence. The level of proof needed in a civil action to obtain a judgment against a defendant. When this level of evidence is required, the evidence presented by the plaintiff at trial must have greater weight than the evidence offered by the defendant.

Prior Restraint. A law or rule preventing a statement or other First Amendment expression from ever being made.

Privileged Communication. Something spoken or written by one person to another that a legal system considers highly confidential, and therefore deems it beyond the reach of court questioning.

Probable Cause. Facts strongly suggesting that a certain person committed a crime. When probable cause exists, a police officer has a right to arrest and search the person.

Probate. A system under state law providing for the orderly distribution of a person's property after death.

Probation. A system of allowing a juvenile delinquent to avoid treatment in an institution after a juvenile court conviction.

Probation Officer. A person who works with and supervises the activities of a minor on probation.

Property Guardian. A person appointed by a family court to manage the property of an individual who is incapable of managing his or her property because of minority, old age, or a physical or mental disability.

Prosecuting Attorney. An attorney who conducts criminal prosecutions against persons charged with breaking a federal, state, or local law.

Public Law. A law passed by Congress, a state legislature, or other governmental body.

Public Policy. A moral position broadly held by a nation or community to promote its overall health, safety, and security.

Protected Class. A category of persons, such as women, racial and ethnic minorities, and disabled persons, that federal law protects from discrimination in certain circumstances.

Punitive Damages. Money awarded a plaintiff in a civil action over and above the actual damages suffered. An award of punitive damages is designed to punish the person causing the damages.

Rape. Forced sexual relations.

Reasonable Doubt. The amount of doubt justifying the dismissal of a criminal case or juvenile court action. To convict a person, his or her guilt must be established in both adult and juvenile court "beyond a reasonable doubt."

Reasonable Person. A person who exercises ordinary or reasonable prudence.

Reasonable Suspicion (of criminal activity). An amount of suspicion needed to arrest a minor. Reasonable suspicion is less suspicion than probable cause; it is also the amount of suspicion needed by a police officer to "stop-and-frisk" a person on the street. "Reasonable suspicion" and "reasonable cause" are synonymous.

Recidivist. A repeat offender.

Recklessness. Paying no attention to the fact that an act could seriously endanger the safety or life of another.

Remand. A court order returning an appealed case to the trial court for further action.

Reverse (a court decision). An action of an appeals court in which the decision of a trial court is revoked. *The appeals court reversed the trial court's decision to convict a man of intentional homicide after deciding that the trial court refused to admit evidence regarding the man's lack of intent.*

Reverse Discrimination. Unfair discrimination against a nonprotected class.

Revocation Hearing. A juvenile court hearing held to decide whether a juvenile delinquent's probation should be set aside.

Search and Seizure. Law enforcement activities that are highly regulated by the Constitution and public laws.

Search Incident to an Arrest. A personal search that a police officer may legally make at the time of arrest. No search warrant is necessary to make a search incident to an arrest.

Search Warrant. A written order, issued by a judge or other court employee (such as a magistrate), authorizing the search of a person or place in order to secure evidence of a crime.

Segregation. A policy, often applied forcibly, requiring the separation of a racial or other group from the rest of society.

Selective Service. The division of government that administers matters relating to both required and voluntary military service.

Sexually Transmitted Disease (STD). A type of disease passed from one person to another during sexual activity.

Sibling. A brother or sister.

Slander. Making false oral statements about another that result in damage to the person's reputation.

Social Security. A national program in which payments are paid to a former worker or his or her family to replace a modest portion of earnings lost by the worker as a result of retirement, death, or disability.

State Action. Action taken by the federal government, a state or local government, or any division of such government bodies.

State Court. A court system established under the laws of a state to hear civil and criminal cases arising under that state's laws.

State Supreme Court. The highest appeals court in a state court system.

Statutory Rape. A crime occurring when a person above a certain age has sexual relations with a minor, regardless of whether the minor may have consented.

Stop-and-Frisk Search. A patdown of a person's clothing by a police officer to check for weapons.

Subpoena. An order issued by a court commanding a particular person to appear at a certain time and place to give testimony.

Subrogate. A procedure by an insurance company to recover money previously paid out pursuant to the terms of its insurance policy. *Bill's insurance company subrogated against Bob's insurer after it paid money to Bill's doctor for accident-related injuries caused by Bob.*

Suppression of Evidence. A court order forbidding the use of certain evidence to obtain a conviction because the police obtained the evidence illegally.

Supreme Court. The highest court in the United States; the Court to which certain state supreme court cases and all federal appeals court cases may be appealed.

Symbolic Speech. Unspoken expression of an idea, such as an insignia or armband.

Taking. Losing a valuable personal or property right under a particular law or regulation. In the United States, such "takings" cannot occur without due process of law.

Taxes. Money legally required to be paid to a government entity.

Teen/teenager. A person between 13 and 19, and generally under the age of majority.

Termination Proceeding. A court case that seeks to break the legal bonds between parent and child.

Terry Stop. An encounter by a police officer with an individual that occurs when the officer has "reasonable suspicion" but not full probable cause to believe the individual has committed a crime.

Testimony. Information given by a witness in court in response to a question or judge's order.

Tort. An act caused by a person's lack of care that causes emotional injury or property damage. In tort actions in civil court, plaintiffs recover "compensation" or "damages" from defendants for injuries or losses resulting from their torts.

Unconstitutional. A law or action that violates either the federal Constitution or a state constitution.

United States Supreme Court. *See* Supreme Court.

Vagrancy. Loitering in a public place without a means of support and with the intention of begging or committing an immoral act such as prostitution.

Verdict. A decision of a jury in a trial.

Viable. Being able to exist or survive independently. This term is often applied to describe an unborn child that is able to live outside the mother's womb.

Visa. A legal document or a mark in a passport indicating that the visa holder may legally enter or stay in a particular country.

Visitation Right. The legally enforceable right of a noncustodial parent or relative to see his or her minor child.

Void for Vagueness. A term describing a law that is too loosely drafted to be enforced fairly.

Waiver. Intentional surrender of a legal right or legal privilege. *The man waived his right to remain silent after receiving the* Miranda *warnings and then confessed to the robbery.*

Ward. A person who is being cared for by a guardian appointed by a court.

Warrant. A written order issued by a judge or other court employee (such as a magistrate) authorizing an arrest or search.

Welfare. Money received by a poor person from a government entity for his or her modest needs.

Welfare Reform Act. The shorthand name for the Personal Responsibility and Work Opportunity Reconciliation Act of 1996.

Workers' Compensation. A program under state law that pays employees or their dependents for employment-related accidents and diseases regardless of who is at fault for the accident or disease.

Index

About the Author

KATHLEEN A. HEMPELMAN is an attorney in Phoenix, AZ. She is the author of *Teen Legal Rights: A Guide for the '90s* (Greenwood Press, 1994).